100 THINGS HOOSIERS FANS SHOULD KNOW & DO BEFORE THEY DIE

Stan Sutton

TRIUMPH BOOKS

Library of Congress Cataloging-in-Publication Data

Sutton, Stan.
100 things Hoosiers fans should know & do before they die / Stan Sutton.
p. cm.
Includes bibliographical references.
ISBN 978-1-60078-731-7
1. Indiana University, Bloomington—Basketball—History. 2. Indiana University, Bloomington—Miscellanea. 3. Indiana Hoosiers (Basketball team)—History. 4. Indiana Hoosiers (Basketball team)—Miscellanea. I. Title. II. Title: One hundred things Hoosiers fans should know and do before they die.
GV885.43.I53S87 2012
796.323'6309772255—dc23

2012028754

This book is available in quantity at special discounts for your group or organization. For further information, contact:

Triumph Books LLC
814 North Franklin Street
Chicago, Illinois 60610
(312) 337–0747
Fax (312) 280–5470
www.triumphbooks.com

Printed in U.S.A.
ISBN: 978-1-60078-731-7
Design by Patricia Frey
Photos courtesy of AP Images unless otherwise indicated

To my supporting cast:
Judy, Greg, Shari, Jill, Aeden, and Avery

Contents

Acknowledgments

Any nonfiction book is truly a team effort. Even if someone like myself has followed Indiana University basketball for a lifetime, his memories are tainted by time and human failings. Sources, both human and recorded, are essential to producing a detailed document.

Members of the Indiana media relations office have been my friends and confidants for almost three decades, especially since 1984 when I was assigned to cover the Hoosiers for The *Courier-Journal* in Louisville, Kentucky. Beginning with Kit Klingelhoffer and continuing through Jeff Fanter, Pete Rhoda, and J.D. Campbell, my dealings with media relations directors have been professional and enjoyable. Their willingness to provide photographs, vintage box scores, and a variety of information has been critical to this project.

The working relationships are so numerous it is impossible to thank them all. But over the years help always came from Eric Ruden, Brian Teter, Gregg Elkin, Scott Strassmeier, Susan Zaltsberg, Todd Starowitz, Jeff Keag, Nathan Wiechers, Melanie Schneider, Shelli Washel, John Decker, Garrett Ewald, Jay Jameson, Mike Sobb, Matt Brady, Gavin and Christy Lang, and Kristen Smith.

Special thanks goes to everyone at Triumph Books and Associate Editor Karen O'Brien for keeping a watchful eye on this project.

Assistant athletic director Chuck Crabb was a wealth of information as were a number of former IU players who granted interviews. Several years of transcribing interviews with IU coaches provided helpful background material. Assistance over the years from former Indiana coaches, especially Bob Knight and Mike Davis, helped make this book possible.

This book really was launched in 1956 when I began a journalism career while in high school. Help from older peers greased the skids toward an enjoyable writing career. Stan Koester, John D. Scott, Norman Thurston, Bill Holtel, Larry Lee, and Bob Marshall are gone now, but what they taught is remembered.

Saving the best for last, this book was inspired by Judy, my wife of 44 years. Also by Greg and Shari, who I honestly believe are better writers than their father but who wisely chose more honorable careers.

Introduction

My early recollections of Indiana University basketball are vivid, a lot clearer than the radio broadcast of the national championship game on March 18, 1953.

I had been given permission to spend the night with my eighth-grade classmate, Lynn Gardner, which was special in winter because his basketball goal was inside his barn. It didn't matter that all shots had to be from the left side of the basket because the right side was blocked off by farm implements.

We lived 40 miles from Indianapolis, which was barely within range of the broadcast. I'm not certain if the game was on television because neither of us owned a TV, and radio static was a staple of life.

Waves of static were present throughout the game, clearing up just long enough to learn the score or hear brief mentions of Indiana stars Don Schlundt and Bob Leonard. March Madness had a different meaning then.

With 27 seconds remaining, the reception cleared enough to learn of Leonard's game-winning free throw. By the next season my dad had purchased a television set, and many IU games were on Channel 4. IU basketball ranked right alongside *I Love Lucy* in neighborhood discussions.

I would have killed to have seen the Hurryin' Hoosiers in person, and sometimes when I'm sitting in Assembly Hall, an appreciation of how that dream eventually came true looms large. As a sportswriter, first in Louisville and then in Bloomington, I watched almost every Indiana game between 1984 and 2006, when I retired.

Covering the Hoosiers enabled me to go to Hawaii four times and Alaska once. IU also was my ticket to such places as San Francisco, Miami, New York, Chapel Hill, Buffalo, Hartford,

Albuquerque, Denver, Orlando, Washington, and Winston-Salem. There were more trips than I care to recall to Iowa City, Champaign, Ann Arbor, and East Lansing, some of them coming in 25-below-zero weather or eight inches of snow.

Thanks, Hoosiers. All of it was fun.

This is my fourth book about Indiana basketball, and it was done with a bit of hesitation. I co-authored two books with former Hoosiers John Laskowski and Landon Turner, which were enjoyable assignments. A third book was under contract five years ago, but the publishing house went bankrupt before its release.

Several months ago an editor from Triumph Books contacted me about this book. It was to be titled *100 Things Hoosiers Fans Should Know & Do Before They Die* and would require 70,000 to 80,000 words. I choked a bit over that because nothing looks more overwhelming than 70,000 words when you have only a few hundred of them in mind.

There also was another consideration. Since retirement I had developed Parkinson's Disease, which over four years hasn't prevented me from living a fairly normal life. However, it has made my cursive writing almost illegible and my typing good for about an error per word. While convinced I could still compose words, I had to convince myself that I could still type them.

The positive side of writing the book was renewing acquaintances with fellow friends among the Hoosiers: former players, publicists, coaches, trainers, and managers. As my Triumph editor, Noah Amstadter, had predicted, I already had a memory bank that was waiting to be tapped and a collection of notes and quotes that had been sitting around unused. Many of those came from the book that didn't get published, so not all of the effort put into that work was wasted.

I also reminded myself of a wealth of things from yesteryear, including the night we tried to listen to an NCAA title game on the radio.

1 The Hoosiers Are a Perfect 32–0

From November 29 in St. Louis until March 29 in Philadelphia, the 1975–76 Indiana Hoosiers were unblemished, unbeaten, and unfazed. Over the course of four months and 32 games they reached a level of perfection that no one has equaled in the 36 years since.

There were unbeaten teams before them but none since. Each season hence, Indiana fans have watched another university open with 10—or maybe even 15—straight victories only to know that somewhere before or during March Madness, that team was almost certain to fall.

There are multiple reasons why Indiana's perfect season may not be matched again.

For one thing, the season is longer. By November 29, the date the 1976 Hoosiers launched the season, the 2012 IU team had played six games and one exhibition contest. Since '76, major college powers are more likely to play in an early-season tournament, sometimes meeting a couple of teams that could contend for the national title. One may argue that the Maui Invitational or preseason National Invitation Tournament (NIT) have the second strongest field of the year, trailing only the NCAA.

Another factor might be intersectional battles in the middle of the conference season, something such as North Carolina vs. Michigan State as a national television showpiece. These games offer great exposure but can detract from the conference games at hand.

Finally, the 1976 Hoosiers enjoyed a slightly shorter road to the title, playing five opponents that were all ranked in the top 20. The current winner must play at least six games and often is shipped across the country to increase parity in the field. The only break IU received in that area was to play its first game in South Bend, prior to two in Baton Rouge and two in Philadelphia.

Other teams received breaks no longer available through rule changes. Kentucky won the 1958 NCAA without leaving its home state. UCLA's string of national titles was easier because it always played in the West Regional, which was deemed weaker at the time.

The building blocks that led the Hoosiers into college basketball's throne room began with the hiring of West Point coach Bob Knight in 1971. The once-proud Hurryin' Hoosiers of Branch McCracken had become an average team while archrival Purdue was enjoying more success. The Boilermakers recruited three straight Indiana Mr. Basketballs between 1964 and '66, landing Denny Brady, Billy Keller, and Rick Mount. Mount had led Purdue to the national championship game in 1969 and Purdue had a new playing facility, Mackey Arena, while the Hoosiers were still playing in a building largely used for track and field.

Knight, who became head coach at West Point at age 24, wasn't timid about making changes. He switched the team's nickname from Hurryin' Hoosiers to Hoosiers then replaced McCracken's hurry-up offense with a slower-paced one.

Both changes struck a nerve with some of the old-time IU fans who liked both the name and game of McCracken's teams.

The cupboard wasn't bare when Knight arrived; the roster included Steve Downing, Joby Wright, John Ritter, and Bootsie White but was missing George McGinnis who turned pro after his sophomore season. In short order Knight supplemented them by adding Steve Green, John Laskowski, Quinn Buckner, Bobby Wilkerson, Kent Benson, and Jim Crews.

Indiana went to the NIT in Knight's first season then rallied to overcome Minnesota and win the Big Ten in 1973. He then reached the Final Four while starting two freshmen guards, Buckner and Crews, and building around Downing, a first-round draft choice.

Coach Bobby Knight (left) and players Scott May (center) and Quinn Buckner (right) hold the trophy after winning the NCAA Basketball Championship in Philadelphia on Monday, March 29, 1976. (AP Photo)

McCracken won two national championships, but his 1964 team lost 15 games despite having three future NBA players, Dick and Tom Van Arsdale and Jon McGlocklin. McCracken retired after the 1965 season and was replaced by assistant Lou Watson, a star for IU in the late 1940s and early '50s.

Watson won a Big Ten championship in 1967, but the Hoosiers finished with three losing seasons in the next four years. Watson missed the 1970 season because of cancer surgery on his back, and aide Jerry Oliver stepped in as acting head coach.

When IU set out to hire a new coach in 1971, they were determined to hire a disciplinarian. The man they came up with was the alpha wolf of disciplinarians—Knight.

Knight was 30 years old, and as one of his early players said, "He wasn't about to mess this up."

Joby Wright recalled being called into Knight's office. "I went in and I had my Afro and my blue jeans. I was going to show this guy. He's never seen no tough guy like me," Wright said. "And the first time I met him he read me the riot act. Coach went off, 'You're going to go to class! You have to toe the line!' Then he put his nose against my nose and said, 'Did you hear me?'"

There was nothing cheap about Indiana's 32–0 slate. The Hoosiers opened with a 20-point victory over defending champion UCLA in what can best be described as a grudge match. The Bruins won the title in 1975 that surely would have belonged to Indiana had not star forward Scott May broken his arm late in the season. That set the stage for a stunning 92–90 loss to Kentucky in the regional final—a loss most IU fans believe was a direct result of May's injury.

The preconference schedule in 1975–76 featured four ranked opponents, including No. 2 UCLA. At times the perfect season appeared in peril, including back-to-back narrow victories in December when IU edged eighth-ranked Notre Dame 63–60 in Bloomington and 14th-ranked Kentucky in overtime at Louisville's Freedom Hall. St. John's—ranked No. 17—fell to IU 76–69 three days after Christmas.

The difficulty of IU's schedule is reflected in the fact that the Hoosiers' non-conference opponents won more than three-fourths of their other games.

Although Indiana had gone unbeaten within the Big Ten in 1975, the '76 campaign loomed as more of a problem. Coach Johnny Orr's Michigan team posed perhaps the biggest challenge, but IU managed an 80–74 win in Ann Arbor against the No. 19 Wolverines. The February rematch in Bloomington would be a bigger threat with Indiana rallying from near defeat to win in overtime. Only Kent Benson's tip-in at the end of regulation saved Indiana's bacon.

Purdue was always a threat to the Hoosiers, but IU won by four in Bloomington and by three in West Lafayette.

The Hoosiers' closest game in the NCAA Tournament was a 74–69 victory over No. 6 Alabama. UCLA, now ranked fifth nationally and anxious for revenge for the 20-point loss in November, went down 65–51 in the semifinal of the Final Four. That left Michigan, a team even more anxious to avenge two regular-season defeats by IU.

The lightning-fast Wolverines led by six at halftime, boosted by an early-game injury that sidelined Bobby Wilkerson for the night. But the Hoosiers rebounded for 57 points in the second half and won going away 86–68. May led the Hoosiers with 26 points, and Benson had 25.

2 Smart's Shot Bails Out Title

For the past 25 years it has been known simply as The Shot. Any 15-year-old kid could have made it. It was the kind of shot where one goes to the left of the basket, tells himself this is for the national championship, and launches a 16' jumper that finds nothing but net. The kid jumps up and down in mock celebration and imagines the roar of 65,000 people surrounding him.

The only difference is that Keith Smart lived the real dream. Destiny, or perhaps it was the Syracuse defense against Steve Alford, put him in the right spot at the right time He really didn't have time to think, but his play over the preceding 12 minutes suggested the moment belonged to him.

Swish!

It was the most important shot in IU history, a play that gave the Hoosiers a 74–73 victory and their fifth national championship. For Smart it brought lasting fame, lifting him from a moderate role on a great team to fame that will last well into the twenty-first century.

The play can still be seen on YouTube, where one version has more than 150,000 hits. Syracuse freshman Derrick Coleman, who had 19 rebounds in the game, barely hit the front rim on a free throw with 26 seconds to play. Indiana's Daryl Thomas rebounded and gave the ball to Joe Hillman as Alford headed up court on the right side with defender Sherman Douglas guarding him tightly.

After crossing the center line, Hillman passed to Smart on his right then got the ball back as Smart crossed over to the left side of the court. Keith dribbled toward the baseline, but orange jerseys surrounded him so he dropped the ball off to Thomas, who was perhaps 8' from the basket with no openings. As Smart headed closer to the baseline Thomas returned the basketball to him, and the 6'2" junior launched his jump shot with six seconds remaining.

Indiana was a point behind as Syracuse's Howard Triche tried to defend against Smart, but the shot was perfect and the stunned Syracuse players didn't call a timeout until one second remained. The Orange tried a long pass, but Smart, who scored 17 points in the second half, intercepted.

Had Douglas not stuck so tightly to Alford, the hero's role might have fallen on Steve's shoulders. An Olympic starter three years earlier, Alford was playing the final year of a fantastic career and had scored 33 points in the semifinal game and 23 so far in the Championship Game. His name was synonymous with "one shining moment."

Yet, when Smart's shot penetrated the Superdome net, Alford was standing helplessly under the basket, looking for a possible rebound.

"On the final play Daryl Thomas made an incredible decision not to force up a shot," Smart recalled years later. "After the pass to Daryl, I moved to another area of the floor. Our post players understood that when I moved they would pass the ball back to my new location. Howard Triche ran back to where I originally was, and I was able to get the shot off because it allowed me enough space to get off a shot.

"I wasn't thinking about pressure, I was just playing. I wasn't thinking about what I had to do or the situation. If I had been thinking about the time, or what I had to do, or the situation in the game, I probably wouldn't have taken the shot. I was just focused on playing, and that was what was available."

Smart had been removed from the game with about 12 minutes left after making a bad pass to Thomas that went out of bounds. While sitting Smart received constant encouragement from coaches Joby Wright, Royce Waltman, and Ron Felling, and when he returned to the floor Smart was ready to play.

"I wanted to make sure I didn't do the same thing that got me out of the game," Smart said.

Shortly after his return, Keith made a play to score and was fouled.

The game featured 13 ties and 19 lead changes, and with 13 minutes left Syracuse led 52–44 while Smart rode the bench with only six points. He returned at 12:04 and displayed a hot hand, scoring seven quick points and assisting on four others. His layup, on a feed from Alford, tied the game.

The addition of two junior college transfers, Smart and center Dean Garrett, provided the impetus for Indiana to shake off the effects of two previous seasons in which it had lost 22 games. The Hoosiers had failed to make the NCAA Tournament in 1985 and were upset in the first round by Cleveland State in '86.

But with Smart and Garrett, and returning starters Alford, Thomas, and Rick Calloway, Indiana won 30-of-34 games in 1987 and tied Purdue for the Big Ten championship. Entering the tournament IU was ranked second in the United Press International poll behind UNLV, and third in the Associated Press rankings behind UNLV and North Carolina. Purdue and Iowa were also among the top seven teams, indicating the strength of the Big Ten.

Smart's arrival in Bloomington was unpredictable because Knight had shied away from junior college players. Smart, however, had needed the stop at Garden State Community College in Kansas to attract a scholarship.

"I got cut from the 11th grade team that won the state championship that year," the native of Baton Rouge, Louisiana, told Ryan Yamamoto of Sacramento's Channel 10. "The next year I broke my wrist in the third game into my senior season, and that was it for high school."

When Bob Knight finally saw him, Keith was wearing a gold chain and a weird haircut, which would be enough to ruin most chances of going to Indiana. His hair had a part all the way around his head with an arrow engraved in the back.

"I thought I was history," Keith said. "We had this game where we were playing against one of our rivals, and all of our players decided to cut our hair. We had a little outlet mall behind the campus that sold inexpensive gold chains. That's when Mr. T and *The A-Team* was a big thing, so we bought some of those real cheap chains. I didn't know Knight was coming to the game that night, and when I walked to the locker room I saw him sitting there. I had my hair and my gold chain and I thought, 'Oh, my!'"

Permanent use of the three-point shot began that season, and UNLV was one of the most effective with it. In the preseason National Invitation Tournament title game in New York the Rebels had fallen 20 points behind Western Kentucky only to use the three-pointer to pull out a victory. It was one of the early signs that no lead was safe with the new rule.

Although Knight had reservations about the three-point shot, he also had one of the best outside shooters in the country in Alford. IU's only loss in its first 15 games was a four-pointer at Vanderbilt. Iowa beat the Hoosiers in Iowa City, but they didn't lose again until late in the season against Purdue and Illinois. Syracuse was IU's seventh straight victim.

The tournament opened with Indiana beating Fairfield and Auburn in Indianapolis, and beating Duke in Cincinnati. The team reached the Final Four by rallying for a one-point win over LSU and then outshooting UNLV 97–93 in the semifinal in New Orleans.

Smart was drafted by the Golden State Warriors and played nine seasons in the Continental Basketball Association where he averaged 10.3 points through 297 games. He later coached the Fort Wayne Fury of the CBA for five seasons and guided that team to its first back-to-back winning seasons. During his first season (1997–98) he led the Fury to a franchise record 31 victories.

Smart also played in the Philippines, China, France, and South America.

In 2011, Keith was named head coach of the Sacramento Kings while marking more than two decades as a professional player or coach.

3 Knight's Firing Angers Thousands

It was a September morn that would have put a blush in Neil Diamond's voice, a Sunday that dawned with autumn on the horizon and joy in the hearts of most Hoosiers. It would end amid a sea of protests and delusion circling the Indiana basketball program.

Bob Knight had been fired. The General was relieved much like MacArthur, for much the same reason and with similar pubic reaction. There were no words to describe what happened the afternoon of September 10, 2000. Surreal isn't strong enough.

There had been rumors for months that Knight's 29-year reign as IU coach was in jeopardy. The bulkhead surrounding the Hall of Fame coach began crumbling when a video was mailed to the Cable News Network showing Knight's hand planted on the neck of former player Neil Reed during a practice. The word "choke" was used in most newscasts, the words "improper" and "unconscionable" in more conservative reports. Among his many followers, the action was described as it always had been before.

"It's just Bobby being Bobby," many said.

John Meunier, a reporter for *The Herald-Times* in Bloomington, had been expecting a call for some time and it came in mid-morning that Sunday from editor Bob Zaltsberg, who had been alerted that the firing was forthcoming by Knight's best friend, former *H-T* sports editor Bob Hammel. Meunier prepared for his biggest assignment.

"Until it became clear that the university was going to fire him, I thought they'd figure out a way not to fire him because they would be afraid of the consequences," Meunier said. "Up until the moment it happened, I thought they'd figure out a way not to have to do that."

IU president Myles Brand made the decision backed by the trustees, and the reaction was immediate. Brand's office was blanketed by thousands of email messages, and some 75 phone calls were directed at the president's number. A school official said many messages were threatening or profane. Several IU players said they might transfer to other schools.

The final domino in Knight's firing was but a popgun on the heels of heavier salvos of controversy involving the coach. Three days before the firing, IU student Kent Harvey was entering Assembly Hall when Knight appeared in the doorway. Harvey was chastised by the coach for simply addressing him as "Knight," which touched off its own controversy. Harvey, whose stepfather, Mark Shaw, had been critical of Knight on his Bloomington radio show, was hanged in effigy.

Brand came close to firing Knight in the spring, but the coach talked him into keeping his job. Instead, the president put Knight on a "zero tolerance" policy—or probationary period—that was designed to avoid any further controversies. Knight's public reaction to the policy during the summer months led to Brand's decision to terminate him.

At the press conference Brand listed reasons behind his decision, citing a series of "uncivil, defiant, and unacceptable" acts by Knight. He said these acts included failure to report to athletic director Clarence Doninger despite orders from Brand to do so.

Knight had publicly declared himself the "athletic director for basketball," and he and Doninger had been at odds for some time. After a tough loss in which Doninger tried to console him, the coach reportedly came close to blows with the athletic director.

"I don't remember much about the press conference, but I remember Clarence Doninger leaning against the wall, smiling like the cat that had eaten the canary. You could tell that he was enjoying himself that day," Meunier said.

Coinciding with the zero-tolerance announcement was a $30,000 fine imposed by the university and a three-game suspension. In September, Brand further said Knight had made "angry and inflammatory remarks" in private and in public about university officials and the trustees.

Meunier said he had been assigned to cover a boosters meeting earlier that summer at a Bloomington restaurant and that Knight "got up and the first three or four minutes were spent making fun of the board of trustees."

"I don't think he insulted Brand directly, but it was all barbs," the reporter said.

Brand said at the press conference that Knight refused to attend Varsity Club meetings in Bloomington, Indianapolis, and Chicago, and Knight "verbally abused a high-ranking female university official" in the presence of others.

Knight was on a fishing trip that weekend, which Brand termed "gross insubordination" after requesting that he stay in town. The coach returned late Sunday and was welcomed by more than 2,000 people outside Assembly Hall. Police in riot gear had faced a crowd that was surrounding Brand's home on campus.

The Assembly Hall parking lot featured a large number of television trucks for days. Media members close to the program had dozens of requests for television and radio interviews, and CNN set up shop in *The Herald-Times* offices.

Several members of the basketball team admitted to feeling a great loss and considered transferring. Forward Jarrad Odle said he had experienced almost every emotion and said, "It's going to be tough to work through this."

Two days later when assistant Mike Davis was named interim coach, most of the team remained intact.

"We love him. We put our lives on the line for him," Odle said. "We support him. Us 12 guys were in Coach Knight's pocket.

He had us, and we had him. We were more than happy to play for him."

Three days after the firing the coach and his wife, Karen, appeared before a student rally on campus. Knight thanked the students for their support and enthusiasm and urged the group not to blame Kent Harvey, saying, "The kid is not responsible for me not being the coach any longer."

A dozen years after the fact Knight still hasn't publicly returned to Indiana University, or attended one of IU's games as an analyst for ESPN. Knight returned after a one-year hiatus to coach Texas Tech for almost seven seasons before retiring from coaching. He was voted into the Indiana Athletics Hall of Fame in 2009 but decided not to return for the induction, claiming he didn't want to detract from the others being honored.

4 1981 Hoosiers Turned Season Around

Basketball teams are the most obvious of airport travelers. Often dressed in school colors, usually listening to music via earplugs, college players draw more attention than hot blondes in short skirts.

In December 1980, two basketball teams ran into each other in the Kansas City airport. North Carolina was returning from Los Angeles where the Tar Heels had been trounced by Minnesota. Indiana was coming home after losing two of three games in the Rainbow Classic in Hawaii. Coaches Dean Smith of Carolina and Bob Knight met while awaiting their flights and compared their problems.

Years later Knight recalled the conversation, saying, "We were standing there talking about what we were trying to do and how we were trying to play, and neither one of us was doing real well at that point."

Probably to the surprise of both coaches, their teams would meet three months later for the national championship with Indiana winning 63–50.

It's hard to be unhappy after a trip to Honolulu, but the Hoosiers' visit had been a disaster. They defeated Rutgers 55–50 to run their season record to 7–3 and then lost to Clemson 58–57 on a last-second shot. Already beaten on the mainland by Kentucky, Notre Dame, and North Carolina (by nine points), the Hoosiers closed the Hawaii visit by losing to Pan American.

Dispositions were surly during the visit for different reasons. Center Ray Tolbert recalled the team staying 40 miles from the arena, which required a boring bus ride. Steve Risley had a serious battle with Montezuma's Revenge, but most of the Hoosiers were more worried about Knight's revenge.

"True colors came out on that trip," said Mike LaFave, who later would transfer to Ball State.

Five years earlier Indiana became the last team to win the NCAA championship undefeated. The 1981 team lost nine times, yet you will find IU fans who believe that team was as good as the 1976 team at the end of the season. In its five tournament games, IU beat Maryland by 35 points, Alabama–Birmingham by 15, St. Joseph's by 32, LSU by 18, and North Carolina by 13.

LSU was ranked No. 4 in the country, the Tar Heels No. 6.

Although Indiana struggled early in the Big Ten season, losing to Michigan, Purdue, and Iowa (twice), the Hoosiers won their final 10 and had an average victory margin of 22.6 points in the tournament. Although Isiah Thomas was the unquestioned star of the team, the turn-around play of junior forward Landon Turner is considered the main reason for the reversal.

The 6'10" Turner had been an enigma to Knight through his first 2½ years in Bloomington. The former Indianapolis Tech star was inconsistent on the court, in the classroom, and in life. Knight responded by making him run at dawn, by benching him, and by throwing countless verbal assaults upon him. Still, Turner's play failed to reach Knight's expectations.

Former IU assistant coach Jim Crews was selected to make sure Turner carried out Knight's discipline. Crews later recalled being assigned to make Landon run at 7:00 each morning.

"Well, the first day it's ten 'til seven and, boom, the phone rings. 'Coach, I've got some extra work I've got to do academically,' he said.

"'Landon, I'll see you in 10 minutes.'

"The next day it's, 'I've got a headache.' I mean, it's ten 'til seven every time.

"'Landon, I'll see you in 10 minutes.'

"The third day it was probably his great, great grandmother had passed away in China or some place. I said, 'Landon, I'll see you at seven.'

"The fourth day the phone rings at ten 'til seven and I thought, 'Here we go again,' and he said, 'I'll see you in ten minutes.'"

"I was immature. I didn't prioritize things like I should have," Turner admitted. "I knew I was supposed to be studying, but I'd rather be with a young lady or something. There were things that took my mind away from what I was supposed to be doing. And when I wasn't doing good with the books, it seemed like I wasn't doing good on the court, either."

Turner's attitude reversal improved not only Indiana's offense but its defense. Knight discovered Landon could defend smaller people on the perimeter, which Tolbert also did well. That allowed Ted Kitchel, a bull-in-a-china-shop type of defender, to guard opponents down low.

Turner said the Hoosiers entered the NCAA Tournament full of confidence built up over five straight victories since a February 19 loss at Iowa in which he came off the bench and defended Kevin

Boyle so well that he excited Coach's doghouse. Indiana closed the regular season by defeating Minnesota, Ohio State, Michigan, Illinois, and Michigan State by an average margin of 13 points.

The tournament field in 1981 included 48 teams, and IU was seeded third in the Mideast Region behind DePaul and Kentucky. Other No. 1 seeds were LSU in the Midwest, Oregon State in the West, and Virginia in the East. IU earned a first-round bye and would play the winner of Maryland vs. Tennessee–Chatanooga in Dayton, Ohio.

IU's previously unbeaten 1975 team had been upset in Dayton by Kentucky, probably preventing the Hoosiers from winning back-to-back national titles while unbeaten.

Maryland was a difficult opening game and was led by 6'6" forward Albert King, 6'8" center Charles "Buck" Williams, and 6'7" forward Ernest Graham, all of whom averaged more than 14 points per game. Much like Indiana, the Terrapins' record was deceiving at 21–9, but their talent was among the best in the country.

IU assistant coach Gerry Gimelstob thought Maryland lacked the patience to defend the Hoosiers if they were deliberate on offense.

"They were just not going to have the defensive intensity to stay with us, even though they were scary athletically," Gimelstob said. "We knew they wouldn't dig in defensively against us, and if we just had some patience on offense our guards would annihilate their guards."

The Maryland game tipped off at 3:50 PM, which would have been unlikely timing in today's television-dominated tournament. Before the teams took the court, top-seeded DePaul had lost to St. Joseph's, which may have inspired the Hoosiers and definitely excited the IU fans having a late-afternoon drink at Bloomington watering holes.

Tolbert had five dunks in the game, and the Hoosiers' outburst marked one of their best showings ever. Tolbert and Turner

Louisiana State's Howard Carter (No. 32 at right) tries to steal the ball from Indiana's Landon Turner (32) at the NCAA semifinals in Philadelphia on Saturday, March 28, 1981. (AP Photo)

combined to hit 19-of-26 field-goal attempts, while Isiah Thomas missed only 2-of-11 shots as IU shot 65.1 percent.

Indiana was successful doing all the little things, including drawing three charging fouls in the first six minutes. Indiana didn't have a turnover for 16 minutes and built a 50–34 halftime lead on 22-of-30 shooting.

Both Turner and Kitchel believed Maryland wasn't prepared for Indiana, noting during pregame warm-ups that Coach Lefty Driesell was pointing out the IU players. Turner said he doubted if Driesell even knew the numbers of IU's players. "We were a lot more prepared. We knew their numbers. Man, we *had* their numbers," Turner said.

IU knew a victory in Dayton would return them to friendly Assembly Hall, where they beat UAB and St. Joseph's to earn a trip to the Final Four.

The field for the Final Four in Philadelphia was a classic one, featuring Dale Brown's LSU Tigers against IU and including Atlantic Coast Conference strong boys Virginia and North Carolina. Louisiana State was 31–3 and featured Rudy Macklin and Greg Cook. LSU's season had included a 17-game winning streak within the Southeastern Conference.

Indiana's shooting was off in the first half, and the Hoosiers missed their last 10 attempts of the period, but a defense that held the Tigers scoreless through 11 straight possessions helped IU to a 67–49 victory. Turner's 20 points led the way.

As brilliantly as he had played during two seasons, it was the final game against North Carolina that solidified Isiah Thomas' legacy as a college player. The Tar Heels led 16–8 about eight minutes into the game, and Kitchel was in foul trouble. Knight eventually replaced him with Jim Thomas, who became a key to the game by guarding North Carolina star Al Wood. After a 39-point outburst against Virginia, Wood scored only one basket against

Thomas in the final 9:56 of the first half. Randy Wittman's jumper at the buzzer gave IU a 27–26 halftime lead.

Isiah got a couple of steals early in the second half that turned the game in IU's favor. Wittman hit from outside, and North Carolina never got closer than five points thereafter. Jim Thomas had eight assists in the championship game and made the all-tournament team despite getting just one basket in the Final Four.

Isiah Thomas went on to score almost 19,000 points in a Hall of Fame career in the NBA. He later coached the Indiana Pacers and New York Knicks and was head coach at Florida International through the 2011–12 season.

IU teammate Chuck Franz was amazed by Isiah's peripheral vision.

"It seemed like his eyes were set forward a little bit. He wasn't the quickest player on that team even; Tony Brown was quicker, but the toughest kid on that team was Isiah. He wasn't going to stop short of an NCAA championship once he got going."

5 Any Seats Available?

The morning of February 23 was a harbinger of warmer days to come, a time often marked by lingering snow, but in 1985 the day was blessed with the kind of moderate temperatures that send college students into the outdoors wearing shorts. Baseball's spring training was already under way in the South, but in Southern Indiana, basketball was still king. Archrivals Purdue and Indiana would meet that afternoon in a renewal of their longtime heated rivalry.

As with the students, Coach Bob Knight was looking forward to spring and ditched his usual plaid sport coat and loose tie in favor of a white-striped golf shirt. Later he would cite his clothing choice as one reason for one of college basketball's most unique occurrences, an incident perhaps more famous than any of Knight's 902 coaching victories.

Five minutes into the game, Knight protested a foul called against Indiana's Marty Simmons, and 58 seconds later the Hoosiers' Daryl Thomas was whistled for a foul as the Boilermakers inbounded the basketball. That led to a technical foul against the IU coach.

As Purdue's Steve Reid stepped to the foul line, Knight reached back and took a firm hold on his chair, a red vinyl seat like those found in a factory lunch room. Reaching back to gain momentum, the coach threw the chair across the foul lane in front of Reid, and it slid into a group of photographers at the end of the court.

That marked his second technical, which called for his ejection from the game, but the volatile Indiana mentor wasn't done yet. After Knight's third technical, IU athletic director Ralph Floyd was summoned to the floor, and Knight subsequently left the floor to a roar of approval from his partisan fans.

With Purdue leading 11–6, Reid was awarded six free throws and made three of them, helping the Boilermakers to a 72–63 victory.

The capacity crowd, never laid back anyway, became even louder as the game progressed. A couple of fans raced from their higher seats to courtside while protesting subsequent calls. There was some concern among security people that things might get out of hand and lead to a melee.

Knight had nothing to say after the game, but later he said the fact that he was wearing only a knit shirt contributed to his actions. He claimed he would have thrown his coat had he been wearing one, but not having a coat he settled for the chair.

The action led to a longstanding series of wisecracks, such as, "Did you hear about Bob Knight buying a furniture store? Buy a sofa, and he'll throw in the chair."

Purdue coach Gene Keady, who cared only about the final outcome, tried to sway journalists into downplaying Knight's tirade and giving his team credit instead. Keady said the big news that day was the Purdue victory.

No one agreed, and history barely mentions the winning team.

The Big Ten's director of officials was at the game and was verbally confronted by the coach's wife, Nancy, after the game, according to a conference official.

"I was shocked. That's about as simple as I can put it," Reid said. "I've never seen anything like this happen before."

Neither had Indiana officials, who a short time later changed the bench seating to a heavier, more sturdy chair. These were attached to each other at the base to ensure they remained in place.

After the ejection IU president John Ryan, vice president Ed Williams, and Floyd followed the coach into the locker room where Ryan said Knight was in tears, "remorseful, even contrite."

"He said he was terribly sorry, and he hoped this didn't bring problems to the university. That impressed me. He was genuinely sorry," Ryan said.

Indiana's players apparently were less stunned by their coach's actions. Guard Delray Brooks, who later transferred to Providence and was part of a Final Four team, remarked, "Basically, it wasn't a shock to us. I guess it is bad, it was during the game, you know. But we didn't all go woooo because how many times have we seen him throw something. It wasn't a big deal."

IU officials at first felt they should discipline the coach and Knight reportedly said he would accept that, but he later changed his mind and Floyd allowed Big Ten commissioner Wayne Duke to take action. Duke, who would have preferred that Indiana dole out the punishment, ended up handing down a one-game suspension.

Knight later issued an apology of sorts through IU that read, "While I have been very concerned of the way some things have been handled in the Big Ten, in particular the officiating, which has really frustrated me the past couple of years, I do not think my action in the Purdue game was in any way necessary or appropriate. No one realizes that more than I do."

Said Keady, "I think that technical fired us up, and we wanted to beat them by 30 points. It was probably won or lost right there."

Knight's emotions undoubtedly were frayed long before the Purdue game. The Hoosiers' record was a modest 14–9, which included a 6–7 record in the Big Ten entering the game. Coming on top of Knight's successful direction of the U.S. Olympic team to the 1984 Gold Medal, the Hoosiers were a mystery to their coach all season. They recorded eight straight victories during the non-conference season and opened Big Ten play with a 25-point victory at Michigan.

Then Indiana dropped five of its next seven games and finished the regular season by losing six of its last seven games.

The preseason had seen Knight take away the scholarship of forward Mike Giomi, who later transferred to North Carolina State, and saw forward Winston Morgan's playing time diminish from vast to minimal. IU finished the campaign with a 19–14 record, improved when the Hoosiers won four National Invitation Tournament games before losing to Reggie Miller and UCLA in the final.

6 Five Points from Going Undefeated

With a little bit of luck, Indiana's 1953 NCAA champions could have been unbeaten, just as its 1976 counterparts were at 32–0. Branch McCracken's '53 squad went 23–3, and the team's losses were by a total of five points.

The Hurryin' Hoosiers lost their second game of the season at Notre Dame 71–70, and then they lost at Kansas State 82–80 in the next game. Both losses came on last-second shots.

IU then won its next 17 before another loss on the road at Minnesota 65–63. True to their nickname, the Hurryin' Hoosiers ran up 113 points in a 35-point victory over Purdue. The following season, with the same starting five, IU went 20–4 with losses at Oregon State and Northwestern, a home loss to Iowa, and an NCAA defeat at the hands of Notre Dame in Iowa City.

Indiana's lineup included two All-Americans, Don Schlundt and Bob Leonard; a prolific defender in Dick Farley, who went on to the NBA; a solid rebounder in Charlie Kraak; and swift guard Burke Scott. In 1953, Schlundt and Scott were sophomores, while the others were juniors.

Leonard's free throw with 27 seconds left gave IU a 69–68 victory over Kansas in the title game. One of the Jayhawks reserves was Dean Smith, later a Hall of Fame coach at North Carolina. Schlundt's 30 points led IU, and B.J. Born led Kansas with 26 while making only eight of his 27 shots.

Schlundt, who died in 1985, averaged 25.4 points in 1953 and made 80 percent of his free throws. He averaged 27 points over six career games in the tournament.

Leonard said McCracken was not only a coach but a father figure. "A coach is your father away from home, and the way it is today, a lot of kids don't even know who their dad is," he said.

Surrogate father or not, Leonard claims McCracken was a tough coach. "Everybody talks about Bobby [Knight] being tough. Well, let me tell you one thing, you let the Big Bear get mad at you.... He was an All-American in football, too, just a wonderful man," Leonard said. "He simplified the game, but with the full-court press, we dreaded practices. We'd press all the way up the floor, guys knocking the hell out of each other."

Hurryin' Hoosiers Weren't Always Fastest

Branch McCracken's Indiana teams were known as the Hurryin' Hoosiers, a fast-breaking band of players who ran up the score even in close games. However, Indiana led the Big Ten in scoring only six times during McCracken's two terms as the IU headmaster.

Conference statistics only date back to 1939, the year the NCAA Tournament was launched. IU averaged a modest 42.3 points in 12 conference games that season. Indiana increased that by one point during its national championship season the following year.

The pace had stepped up substantially by the time Indiana won its second NCAA title in 1953. Don Schlundt and Company averaged 80.7 points per game during 18 league games that year, but for the 1954 season the Hurryin' Hoosiers finished second to Ohio State's 77.7 points per game.

IU didn't lead Big Ten scoring again until 1958 when it averaged 83.6 PPG. McCracken's team was also tops in 1962 at 86.7 and in '63 at 90.4. The highest scoring Big Ten team ever was Iowa with 102.9 in 1970.

Illinois led the conference in scoring 10 times during the McCracken years, including eight times between 1948 and 1957. Defenses have taken over since 1999, with the top scoring team falling into the '70s.

McCracken's teams led the league in scoring defense only twice, in 1941 and 1951. During Bob Knight's 29-year reign, the Hoosiers led the Big Ten in scoring defense seven times.

Playing road games in the 1950s was arguably tougher than it is today because most of the Big Ten schools had small gymnasiums where the students sat right against the floor. In fact, the late IU publicist Tom Miller recalled IU's Charlie Meyer having a lighted cigarette pushed against his leg while he was taking the ball out of bounds at Illinois' Huff Gym.

"Illinois was like Notre Dame, where they sat the band behind the visitors' bench. Branch would call time out, and they'd strike up that 'Notre Dame Victory March' and you couldn't hear yourself think," Leonard recalled.

Indiana's 1953 team opened the tournament in Chicago needing four wins to take it all.

"We played DePaul in the first game and beat them by a couple in a really tight ballgame," Leonard said. "Notre Dame beats Pennsylvania, and the next night in the rematch—Schlundt just killed them. Don had 41 and we ended up beating them by 13 and we headed to Kansas City for the Final Four.

"I remember coming back from Kansas City. We had to fly into Indianapolis and take a bus to Bloomington. By the time we got to the south end of Martinsville, the highway was lined with cars all the way to Bloomington. When we hit town, ol' Bloomington was wild. It was a great thing, one of the thrills of my life."

Unlike Schlundt, who chose to enter the insurance business and bypass the NBA, Leonard went on to play for the Minneapolis Lakers.

"In 1960 Bob Short bought the Lakers for about 10 cents on the dollar and moved them to Los Angeles. I was on the first Los Angeles Lakers team where Jerry West was a rookie with Elgin Baylor. We had a pretty good ballclub," said Leonard, who played seven years in the NBA.

Leonard was named coach of the Baltimore Bullets shortly after that team was moved from Chicago. He was in private business when asked if he was interested in coaching the Indiana team in the American Basketball Association. He laughed when told that the new league would have a three-point shot and play with a red, white, and blue basketball. Leonard was hired as a consultant with the Pacers and the next year was asked to coach.

Under Leonard the Pacers won three ABA championships and when his coaching days ended, he became a popular color commentator on the Pacers' broadcasts.

7 Hoosiers Adjust to New Coach

Sometimes the success of Indiana athletics is adjusted by what is going on in West Lafayette, Indiana. If Purdue's teams are struggling, it sometimes occurs when the Hoosiers are doing well. Bill Mallory's triumphs with the Indiana football team came when the Boilermakers were in a down cycle.

Indiana basketball was a national power in the early and mid-1950s, while Purdue had hit the skids. When the Hurryin' Hoosiers won the national title in 1953, the Boilermakers finished last in the Big Ten. When IU topped the national polls in 1954, Purdue was again the bottom feeder in the conference.

However, by the late 1960s the Boilermakers were threatening to become the most dominant of the pair. Between 1964 and '66, Purdue had successfully recruited three straight Mr. Basketballs from in-state: Denny Brady of Lafayette Jefferson, Billy Keller of Indianapolis Washington, and Rick Mount of Lebanon. The Boilermakers climbed to third place in the Big Ten in 1968, while IU dropped to ninth. Led by Mount and Keller, Purdue reached the national title game in 1969 and won the Big Ten by four games. Indiana finished last and repeated that finish in 1970.

Branch McCracken had retired in 1965 and Lou Watson succeeded him, winning a Big Ten title in 1967 but missing the 1970 season after back surgery. Assistant Jerry Oliver took over the team in 1970 as IU went 7–17, and a coaching change was imminent.

The word around town was that Indiana wanted to hire a disciplinarian to replace Watson, who had resigned. The man they hired was the motherload of disciplinarians.

Knight was hired in April 1971, three years after he accepted the job at Wisconsin and then pulled out. The new coach had a new arena, Assembly Hall, but he would soon lose leading scorer George McGinnis to the pros. His discipline would be a shock to most players, including Dave Shepherd, who was booted from practice for throwing a behind-the-back pass during free-throw practice.

The acceptance of the new coach was slow to come, especially when McCracken's fast-breaking style was ditched in favor of a slower offense. As part of that package, Knight changed the team's nickname from Hurryin' Hoosiers to simply Hoosiers. Fans who loved both the nickname and the fast pace were offended—or angry in many instances.

If Knight was a culture shock for the fans, he was more of one for the reporters who covered the team. He quickly had a fallout with Bob Owens, sports editor of *The Courier-Tribune* in Bloomington. Owens, who previously worked for papers in Chicago and Miami, had been close with most of the IU coaches and occasionally entertained them at his home. He and Knight did not become drinking buddies.

Owens sent one of his young reporters, J.D. Lewis, to cover the Hoosiers, and Lewis and Knight hit it off only until Lewis wrote a column mocking the new coach's alleged temper. The column

IU Plays Same Team Consecutively

Because of the excessive cost and difficulty in making cross-country trips, Indiana played Oregon State on successive nights in December 1953. The Hurryin' Hoosiers beat the host Beavers 76–72 on November 21, the sixth straight victory for the defending NCAA champions. The next night No. 12 Oregon State turned the tables with a convincing 67–51 victory that was Indiana's only defeat in its first 16 games.

The two games marked a battle between IU's All-American center, Don Schlundt, and Oregon State's 7'3" Wade "Swede" Halbrook. Halbrook was considered the tallest player in basketball at the time and later played two seasons for the Syracuse Nationals of the NBA.

may have been cute to everyone but Knight, who roasted the writer verbally.

Knight's first team at Indiana, built from Lou Watson holdovers, had a 17–8 record and went to the National Invitation Tournament, where it lost to Princeton. IU won eight of its first nine, lost five straight at midseason, and closed the regular season with a 9–1 spurt. Knight's recruiting, which included Steve Green and John Laskowski in his first class, paid immediate results. His second IU team reached the Final Four with two freshmen, Quinn Buckner and Jim Crews, starting at guard.

By that time, Indiana fans didn't care about Knight's style of play or the team's nickname. Almost three decades later, the fans roar when his picture appears as part of a promotion on the Assembly Hall scoreboard.

8 Loss to Kentucky Bitter End to '75 Season

Most players and fans who were involved with both the 1975 and '76 Hoosiers believe the team with the best record probably wasn't the best of the two teams.

The 1976 team is the last college team to go unbeaten through the regular season and NCAA Tournament, but its predecessor won its first 31 games before being upset by Kentucky 92–90 in a classic struggle in Dayton, Ohio.

Both teams went 18–0 in the Big Ten, and Scott May, Kent Benson, Quinn Buckner, and Bobby Wilkerson started both years. The '75 team also had Steve Green, one of the better shooting forwards in school history, and John Laskowski, who became famous as the team's sixth man. Laz not only could have started for almost every team in the country but could have started for the Hoosiers, except that Coach Bob Knight thought he was better served with Laskowski in reserve.

May broke his wrist one month to the day before the Kentucky game, and while he started against the Wildcats, Knight quickly realized Scott wasn't ready for such physical action. As he had done late in the season, the coach inserted Laskowski at guard and moved the agile 6'7" Wilkerson to forward.

Wilkerson and Buckner were probably the best defensive guards in college basketball, and a certain amount of chemistry was lost for the Hoosiers.

Indiana had not lost a game since after the 1974 season, when it dropped a playoff with Michigan for the Big Ten title. At stake against Kentucky was a berth in the Final Four.

Kentucky had finished the regular season strongly to earn a tie for the Southeastern Conference title. The Wildcats also came with strong memories of a 98–74 thrashing in Bloomington on December 7 in which Knight had slapped Kentucky coach Joe B. Hall on the back of the head during a sideline talk.

Kentucky won the game in Dayton by forcing IU into 20 turnovers and staring down the nation's No. 1-ranked team. The underdogs gained an edge when Kevin Grevey and Rick Robey scored six straight points and IU was looking at a 89–81 deficit with 5:32 to play.

Indiana's Benson, a sophomore, kept IU in the game with 33 points and 23 rebounds. Kentucky guard Mike Flynn, a product of Jeffersonville, Indiana, scored 22 for the Wildcats.

The heated rivalry was still smoldering from the Knight-Hall confrontation in December. Entering that game Knight and Hall were purported to be good friends, but the relationship soured after the slapping incident. Indiana won by 24 points but had led by 34 and with the game winding down, Knight ventured toward the Kentucky bench to rail at officials.

Kent Benson (54) of Indiana takes the rebound away from Rick Robey (53) of Kentucky as the two teams fight for the NCAA Mid-East Regional championship at Dayton Arena on March 22, 1975. (AP Photo/Charles Knoblock)

"He was yelling at the officials from in front of my bench, in front of me," Hall said. "And, as he turned to go back to the bench, I said, 'Way to go, Bob, give 'em hell,' good naturedly because this was a friend of mine.

"And he turned and broke down, almost like an attack position, and he screamed at me, 'Don't ever talk to me during a game! Why don't you coach your own [bleeping] team!'"

Hall said he told Knight that he didn't mean anything by the comment. "And I turned to walk away, and he popped me with an open hand at the back of the neck. Pretty strongly," Hall said.

Knight retorted that he didn't mean anything by that either, insisting he meant it as an affectionate pat. However, Kentucky assistant coach Lynn Nance, a recently retired FBI agent, jumped into Knight's path and the two snarled at each other with Nance calling Knight an SOB.

Not surprisingly, Knight was reluctant to discuss the incident at the postgame press conference. Dave Kindred of *The Courier-Journal*, who had a decent relationship with the coach, asked, "What happened between you and Coach Hall?"

Knight tightened up, saying, "We're here to talk about basketball. Any basketball questions?

Basketball questions were forthcoming, before Kindred against asked, "Now could you tell us what happened with you and Coach Hall?"

"I said basketball questions. Any basketball questions?" Knight said.

Kindred stayed with his topic. "Coach, 17,500 people saw you hit the Kentucky coach at midcourt with the game going on in front of you. What happened?"

Later, the coach explained to Kindred that he often slapped players on the back of the head. The reporter wrote a column saying Knight had been condescending when Knight approached him on press row.

"How do I get myself into these things?" Knight asked.

9 A New Sheriff in Town

Branch McCracken had a theory: if his players ran faster and shot more often, they would win more basketball games. Under the "Big Sheriff," Indiana's teams would win 364 and lose only 174.

Until McCracken became coach in 1939, Indiana's basketball team lacked a real nickname. Most of the time it was simply called the Crimsons, and after Mac arrived it was often called the Mac men. But because of Branch's fast-breaking style of play, they became known as the Hurryin' Hoosiers. The nickname was beloved around the state, and when new coach Bob Knight opted for simply Hoosiers in 1972, a lot of longtime fans were offended.

In the early years, IU went through coaches like a kid goes through M&Ms. McCracken was the twentieth coach in 39 years, and he would serve two terms on the bench, from 1939–43 and, following four years as a lieutenant in the U.S. Army, from 1947–65. The Hurryin' Hoosiers won NCAA championships in each of those periods (1940 and 1953).

McCracken's teams would also win four Big Ten championships, and four of his teams would post at least 20 victories, a figure not achieved before his arrival.

Like UCLA coaching icon John Wooden, McCracken was a native of Monrovia, Indiana, a small town just southwest of Indianapolis in Morgan County. Monrovia was also the home of another coaching legend, Ward "Piggy" Lambert, who won 371 games as head coach at Purdue.

Wooden earned his first fame as a player at nearby Martinsville, where the Artesians won three state championships and went on to become an All-American guard at Purdue.

According to Tom Miller, the late IU publicist, McCracken was offered the coaching job at UCLA. Not interested himself, Branch recommended that the West Coast school contact Wooden, who went on to win 10 national championships with the Bruins.

"Branch told me they had talked to him and he had recommended Johnny Wooden because they were kids together at Monrovia," Miller said. "At that time John was over at Indiana State. Wooden went out there, and the rest in history."

Indiana returned all five starters from the 1953 NCAA championship team, but the Hurryin' Hoosiers were ousted by Notre

Dame in the first round of the 1954 tournament. Vintage Hoosiers believe a bad officiating call cost them the game.

Trailing by a point, IU was victimized by a charging foul against All-American guard Bob Leonard in the waning seconds of the game. To this day Leonard believes the foul should have been against the Fighting Irish's Dick Rosenthal.

"We win that game and we win our back-to-back national titles," Leonard said 50 years later. "We had the rest of the tournament field covered."

Indiana's lineup in 1953–54 also included Don Schlundt, Dick Farley, Charlie Kraak, and Burke Scott. Reserves included Phil Byers, Paul Poff, Dick White, and 7' Lou Scott.

The 6'4", 200-pound McCracken won three letters for Indiana coach Everett Dean, playing every position and leading the Hoosiers in scoring each season. Branch became head coach at Ball State in 1930 and stayed eight years before leaving to coach IU. He was only 31 when he won his first NCAA title.

The court in Assembly Hall is named after the Hall of Fame coach, who died in 1970. The 1954 team won the Big Ten with a 12–2 record and was favored to win the 16-team NCAA Tournament.

10 The Night Dan Brought Michael Down

"He said, 'Dakich, you've got Jordan.'"

Bob Knight issued that challenge on March 22, 1984, in Atlanta, Georgia, as his Indiana Hoosiers prepared to take on top-ranked North Carolina in the NCAA's Sweet Sixteen. Dan Dakich, who claims his vertical leap was about 2', would try to defend Michael "Air" Jordan, seemingly a mismatch of majestic proportions.

John Feinstein's *Season on the Brink* characterized Dakich as "the prototype slow white kid...a non-athlete who knew lots about playing the game."

As it turned out, Jordan was overmatched. Like Superman, Jordan may have been able to leap tall buildings in a single bound, but Dakich brought him down to earth in IU's 72–68 victory.

Jordan, who would be playing his final college game, scored 13 points, but during a 13-minute stretch of the second half, failed to score. Michael made only 6-of-14 shots and retrieved only one rebound.

"Guys will tell me, 'The only thing you ever did was guard Michael Jordan.' I wasn't an All-American. I wasn't a draft choice. I didn't play in the NBA. It's all kind of crazy," Dakich admitted. "I still get fan mail. I went to a cookout and someone said, 'Hey, how about Jordan?' It's amazing. You could be remembered for a lot of things, but being remembered as the guy who stopped Michael Jordan ain't bad."

Before the team meal 3½ hours before tipoff, Dakich wasn't even sure if he would start. After the meal Knight paced the floor and, one-by-one, went over the North Carolina starters and revealed who would guard them. He assigned defenders to Kenny Smith, Matt Doherty, Brad Daugherty, and Sam Perkins, and Dakich still wasn't sure he would start.

Then Knight told the junior forward his fate.

"He got this sick look on his face. It was like how far Indiana basketball has fallen, like it should be, 'Isiah, you've got Jordan,' or, 'Wilkerson, you've got Jordan.' But it was, 'Dakich, you've got Jordan,'" Dan recalled.

Dakich has told how he went back to his room and threw up, although he didn't tell his coach at the time he was battling the flu. After fouling out with four minutes to play, he sat on the bench, put a towel over his head and a bucket under his face, and vomited again.

Jordan was a two-time All-American whose shot with 17 seconds left against Georgetown had given the Tar Heels the 1982 NCAA championship. In 1984, he averaged 19.6 points and carried a 24.5 average over his prior 11 games, during which he had shot 58 percent.

Shortly after the game began, Dakich wondered if the prophets of doom might have been right. Jordan scored two baskets against him in the first minute, and Dan was alarmed.

"I swear to God, I ran down the court at the Omni and noticed this scoreboard on the façade. I'm running down the left side of the court and I look up and thought, 'There's 39 minutes to go. He's going to score 160. Oh, shit!'"

Knight's help defense called for the other Hoosiers to help out against Jordan, but the coach's instructions to Dakich were clear. He wanted Dan to keep Michael off the backboards, especially the offensive board.

The IU forward said Jordan played totally within the North Carolina offense, making no attempt to set up for outside jump shots or drive from the outside against his defender.

The game was a classic matchup between two eventual Hall of Fame coaches. North Carolina had two losses, while the Hoosiers' young team had eight. Indiana was led offensively by freshmen Steve Alford and Marty Simmons. Junior Stew Robinson might have started in place of Dakich had he not sprained his foot in the previous game against Richmond.

Alford, who would be a starter on the U.S. Olympic team later that summer, played like a senior with 27 points. The future All-American made 9-of-13 shots and 9-of-10 free throws, even collecting six rebounds. Uwe Blab made 5-of-7 shots and scored 16 points. Jordan's statistical line included one rebound, one assist, one steal, four turnovers, and five fouls.

Kenny Smith scored on a drive with 13 seconds remaining to cut IU's lead to 70–68, but Alford coolly inbounded the basketball to Robinson near midcourt and he passed it forward to Mike Giomi. The 6'9" forward appeared headed for a driving layup when Doherty fouled him, leading to Giomi's two game-clinching foul shots.

The Hoosiers nearly gave away the game by missing 11 free throws. Simmons missed three straight one-on-one attempts within a 38-second stretch.

While coaching at Bowling Green, Dakich was included in a list of the 50 sexiest men in college basketball, as picked by collegeinsider.com. He appears embarrassed at its mention. "How dumb is that?" he said. "I've got two things going for me. I'm one of the 50 sexiest men, and I stopped Jordan. I know my wife doesn't believe that."

11 A Cold Day in July

No Indiana basketball player ever looked more foreboding in an airport than Landon Turner before July 25, 1981. He was 6'10", something around 250 pounds, and his outgoing personality was as infectious as Santa Claus in a toy store.

Landon Turner loved life, not just until the morning his 1975 Ford LTD overturned on an Indiana highway but well past that date. Through the struggles of rehabilitation, past the moment when he realized he couldn't move from the shoulders down, overcoming the realization that he would have been a first-round pick in the NBA Draft, Turner persevered.

More than three decades later, Turner still can't walk, but that doesn't mean he doesn't expect to someday. He has faced life nose to nose, just as he did the night in 1981 when IU blew out North Carolina to win the school's fourth NCAA championship.

Turner really didn't want to go to Kings Island, the amusement park north of Cincinnati, on that July day. He offered a line of excuses to his friends who wanted to go, so Landon arose before 6:00 AM on that July 25, gassed up his LTD, and picked up his girlfriend and two others. At about 8:45 AM Turner's car slipped off Indiana 46 between Columbus and Greensburg. There were some nasty curves (since redone) along the two-lane road, and Turner's car got off the edge of the payment on one of them.

He corrected his steering, but the car veered back across the asphalt and struck an abutment. It overturned, and it was five days before Landon remembered anything.

"We weren't wearing seat belts, and besides, back in those days the belts only went around the waist," Landon recalled. "I don't know if that would have helped because the car came to a stop upside down. If we'd been strapped in, we'd have been hanging upside down, and I don't know if that would have caused a problem."

Meanwhile, a state, yea a nation, took Landon to its bosom. There were prayers, cards, letters, contributions, and anything else his fans thought might help. No one assisted more than Coach Bob Knight, who rushed home from a fishing trip to Idaho to be with Turner. Led by the coach, well-wishers contributed heavily to pay Landon's medical expenses. Turner's Bible-believing parents, Rita and Adell, stood by his side constantly.

"At first I could move my fingers only a little, but that eventually improved, and I consider that to be a tremendous blessing," Landon said. "I'm now able to move my hands and arms. I'm a big person, and I'm the kind of guy who likes to be independent and do things on my own. It would have been real tough to have had to depend on someone to wash me all the time, brush my teeth, put on my clothes, and drive me around."

Turner can operate a car with special hand controls.

Four months before the crash, Turner's play, both offensively and defensively, was the catalyst behind a national championship. Late in the 1981 season the light had clicked on in Landon's mind, and his once-inconsistent play was converted to a total effort. Previously, there was a doghouse in Bloomington with Landon's name on it.

Turner's conversion was so complete that a team that had lost nine games before mid-February won its final 10, including five lopsided victories in the tournament.

Had Turner not been hurt and had Isiah Thomas not turned professional early, IU probably would have had a strong chance to repeat as national champions in 1982. Many believe Turner would have been a first-round pick in the 1982 NBA Draft, maybe even the No. 1 pick overall. In a kind gesture by the Boston Celtics, Landon was drafted anyway late in the draft.

Behind Knight's prodding, Turner earned an IU diploma in 1984. He later worked at Indiana University–Purdue University Indianapolis as coordinator of minority affairs. While there he began giving motivational speeches and worked to assist young people with debilitating injuries. The U.S. Basketball Writers Association named him its Most Courageous Athlete of the Year in 1989 and flew him to Seattle for the Final Four.

12 Jimmy Rayl...the Splendid Splinter

With apologies to the folks who gave us the movie *Hoosiers*, Jimmy Chitwood couldn't come close to Jimmy Rayl as a shooter. Rayl, from Kokomo and Indiana University, was the type of stereotyped marksman that made the state famous. A skinny kid with a fade-away jump shot accurate up to 30', Rayl twice had 56-point games as a Hoosier, eight points more than any other IU player has scored.

Jimmy's career, which ended in 1963, occurred before the three-point shot became part of the game. One can only imagine how many points he would have scored otherwise because Rayl's range was basically from Bedford to Bloomington.

Jimmy was probably more famous for his exploits in high school than in college. In the late 1950s when Rayl set all kinds of scoring records, Kokomo played in the North Central Conference, the state's toughest at that time and one that included Muncie Central, Lafayette Jeff, Marion, New Castle, and Logansport, among others. Rayl led Kokomo, a nationally noted program that reportedly was the basis of John R. Tunis' *Yea Wildcats*, to the state finals in 1959.

Playing against future IU teammate Tom Bolyard in the Fort Wayne Semistate, Rayl scored 41 points to beat Fort Wayne South's defending state champions. Rayl had entered the state tournament averaging 40 points during his final 10 regular season games.

Rayl's coach at Kokomo, Joe Platt, was an Indiana graduate and considering that IU's run-and-shoot style perfectly suited Rayl's game, there was no doubt he would enroll at Bloomington.

Freshmen weren't allowed to play on the varsity team in those days, so Rayl anxiously waited for his sophomore season, which turned out to be a major disappointment. That was a shock, considering he had scored 25 against a veteran varsity team as a freshman. For whatever reasons, Coach Branch McCracken played Jimmy sparingly as a sophomore, and he averaged only four points per game.

Irritated as he was, Rayl didn't waste the rest of his college career, averaging 29.8 points per game as a junior and 25.3 as a senior.

Neither of his 56-point outbursts, which came against Minnesota and Michigan State, probably is as famous as the night he scored 49 for Kokomo in New Castle's tiny gym. New Castle's Ray Pavy, a future IU teammate, outscored Rayl that night 51–49 in one of Indiana's most storied high school games.

Jimmy was simply an unabashed shooter—with no style points. He made shots falling out of bounds in the corners. He stopped 10' from the foul circle on fast breaks and popped home jump shots. There are differences of opinion regarding whether he could have played for another IU coach who came along a decade later.

Bolyard emphasized there is no way Jimmy could have played for Bob Knight.

"Jimmy couldn't have played for Knight. Jimmy was lucky to play for McCracken, personality-wise" Bolyard said. "Knight? No way! If Rayl had taken those 30- to 40-footers, Knight would have had his ass on the bench, and Jimmy would have been in his car headed back to Kokomo."

"I couldn't have played for him," Rayl admitted. "I just don't like people like that. I'm opinionated, but I try to treat people nice. There's no question he's a good coach, but he didn't have to be like he was. He didn't do anything to me; he treated me pretty nice, really."

Knight is a strong proponent of the straight-up jump shot, a shot that former Hoosier John Laskowski frequently defended on IU telecasts.

"I was the luckiest guy in the world playing for Joe Platt in high school, who was a McCracken man, and then I had Branch. They wanted you to shoot it. These coaches today act like you're stealing money if you shoot too many shots."

"I get tired of Laskowski saying you have to get squared up. I never had a squared-up shot in my life," Rayl said.

Knowing Laz's theory was based on Knight's teaching, Rayl continued, "The guy teaching that wasn't worth a shit as a player. If I had had to wait for squared-up shots, I'd probably have shot about five shots in my career."

Rayl's 56 is Third Best in Big Ten

Jimmy Rayl had a pair of 56-point games for Indiana, but in the list of all-time big games by Big Ten players, Jimmy's performances rank third and fourth. Purdue has the first two spots with Rick Mount's 61 points against Iowa in 1970 and Dave Schellhase's 57 against Minnesota in 1966.

There have been three games when someone scored 53 points, and two of those were by Mount in 1970. Dave Downey of Illinois had a 53-point game at Indiana in 1963.

All of the above games occurred before the three-point field goal was implemented.

Mount had 27 field goals in a game against Iowa in 1970, and Rayl's 23 in his 56-point effort against Michigan State are tied with Schellhase's 23 against Michigan in 1966.

Rayl claims he once hit 532 straight free throws in a church gym in Kokomo, taking two at a time and rotating with other players at the line. He was a perfect fit for the racehorse game favored by McCracken.

"It's more fun to watch. I'm not saying that's the best way to win games because there are going to be nights when you're not hitting," Jimmy said. "The way Bob Knight does it is probably the best way to win games, but I know the fans sure enjoyed our play."

Rayl's most famous game as a Hoosier was on January 27, 1962, when IU beat Minnesota 105–104. In Bloomington's old Seventeenth Street Fieldhouse, Indiana entered the contest averaging a nation's best 87.6 points per game. However, the Hoosiers were giving up 85 points a game.

Minnesota had won 104–100 some 19 days earlier in Minneapolis. IU was seeking revenge but was also coming off final examinations and hadn't played in 14 days. Rayl, whose 79 points as a sophomore would be only 23 more than he scored that day, was especially ready.

The Golden Gophers had a losing conference record but had beaten Purdue and Iowa before losing three straight. Rayl recalled hitting a shot that put the Bloomington game into overtime.

Minnesota had two foul shots, which Tom McGrann converted, leaving IU trailing 104–103 in overtime. Rayl told teammate Jerry Bass that if McGrann made the free throws to call a timeout because McCracken probably would want to set something up.

"Jerry got the ball as it came out of the net, stepped out of bounds, and threw me the ball. I started down the floor as fast as I could and crossed the 10-second line. By then I figured there had to be two or three seconds left, and the last thing I wanted to do was take it farther and have the buzzer go off without me taking a shot. That was in the back of my mind.

"I took maybe three or four more steps across the 10-second line and shot. I don't know how long it was, but it had to be 30'to 35'. I was way out there, and it hit the bottom of the net. The place went crazy. The next year's schedule had a picture of me being carried off the court."

Rayl hit 20 of his 39 shots in that game.

Rayl's winning basket officially came with two seconds remaining. His 56 points broke the school record of 47, set and later equaled by Don Schlundt. Rayl's 39 field-goal attempts broke Bob Leonard's record of 35, and his 20 field goals tied a Big Ten mark set by Michigan's John Tidwell.

The previous Big Ten one-game scoring record was 52, set the previous season by Purdue's Terry Dischinger.

Entering the game Rayl was averaging 26 points per game and carried a 30-point average for his two conference games. At game's end his Big Ten average had grown to 38.7 and his season mark to 29.3.

Rayl scored Indiana's last four baskets in regulation and had eight of IU's 12 points in overtime. The Hoosiers never led until Jimmy made a 15' shot with 1:37 remaining in overtime. Minnesota's Tom McGrann had 37 points.

A year later, Rayl equaled the 56 points in a 113–94 win over Michigan State. He scored 32 points in the first half, calling that the finest half he ever played.

"Branch took me out with three and one-half minutes left. The crowd booed like crazy," Rayl recalled.

Rayl has lived in Kokomo all of his life. He played two seasons for the Indiana Pacers when the American Basketball Association was formed in 1967.

13 Although Criticized, Hall Helps IU Win

One television announcer called IU's Assembly Hall the "Carnegie Hall of college basketball arenas," but thousands of fans stuck in bad seats call it a "joke."

The basketball hall of the Hoosiers is most often called an architectural nightmare, but it has also provided a major home-court advantage for Indiana teams because it holds and reverberates loud crowd noises. It has 17,456 seats, most of which are chair seats built on a steep incline on both sides of the playing floor. There are bleacher seats surrounding the court on both sides and larger 20-row areas of bleachers at the ends.

The corner areas are basically wasted areas since walls fill areas that would be seats in some arenas. However, the most condemned seating involves the giant balconies on both sides of the floor, which were built at a steep incline. Seats at the top of the balconies are probably farther from the court than any seats in the Big Ten.

Some people afraid of high places avoid sitting in the balconies, and others don't want to climb the steep aisles for fear of falling. Some have health situations that preclude such climbing, and it is not unusual for students to watch the game on television when their season tickets place them in the balcony.

From the beginning, a few balcony views were obstructed by railings. A giant scoreboard installed above center court in 2005 isn't visible to some lower-tier fans because the balcony blocks their view.

Philip N. Eskew Jr., a member of the IU Board of Trustees and chairman of the facilities committee, said Assembly Hall will be replaced sometime in the future.

"We'll have to build a new Assembly Hall. It's really a matter of getting that lead gift," he said. "We will build a new arena south of where it is, between Assembly Hall and Seventeenth Street. That's already in the master plan."

Eskew said the ideal plan would be to tear down the present building and rebuild a new one on its tracks, but that would require the Hoosiers to play somewhere else for about two seasons. The closest facility that would fill IU's needs would be in Indianapolis.

"But," Eskew continued, "you can't go two years without a stadium."

Since tax dollars can't be used, Eskew said a donation of about $40 to $50 million would be needed. "The rest we would get from ticket franchises, suites, and things like that. We would like to have 16,000 to 17,000 seats, about the same size we have now, but more in line with what Missouri has. Just a nice bowl.

"You just can't have that balcony. It's just ludicrous the way that thing was built," Eskew said.

"The original design for Assembly Hall had 25,000 seats, all on one level in eight different positions: your parallel sides, your ends, and then the corners—much like a large football stadium," said Chuck Crabb, assistant athletic director for facilities. "But it was felt that some of those seats would never be sold, so they redesigned Assembly Hall and elected to add a balcony."

Crabb said architects could only go so wide with the type of roof they could construct, which meant all of the seats would be built at a very steep pitch.

"You get a great view from the main level seats, but the balcony is 16 rows above the main level," Crabb said. "The view you have tends to flatten out the flight of the ball; you really have no perception of the arch of the shot. The steep pitch on the steps makes it very uncomfortable for people to walk. You are also at the top of the building, and with the ventilation it gets a bit warm up there."

Crabb said that, as with many college arenas, the most undesirable seats end up being assigned to the students. IU students often stayed home and watched the game on television when their tickets were upstairs. Student packages often had their seats downstairs for some games and in the balcony for others.

"For Tom Crean's first three years, [athletic director] Fred Glass saw this as an opportunity. We could see $5 tickets for balcony seats," Crabb said. "A lot of fans really enjoyed that. We told them up front, 'You're in the balcony. You won't be able to move down to the lower seats. This is what you bought.'"

Ground was broken for Assembly Hall in 1970, and the arena was opened on December 1, 1971. In 2007, the trustees approved the demolition of Assembly Hall and construction of a new arena "when appropriate." The trustees decided against renovating the Hall, which would have cost an estimated $115 million in favor of a new building with an estimated outlay of $130 million.

The opening of Assemby Hall coincided with Bob Knight's arrival as Indiana coach in 1971. The Hoosiers have profited from the home court, where they have posted winning streaks of 50 and 35 games.

Assembly Hall has been the site of NCAA Tournament games on three occasions, including 1981 when the Hoosiers won two games en route to the national championship. The Hall also played host to sub-regional games in 1977 and '79. In 1972, the building was the site of games between the Indiana Pacers and New York Nets during the American Basketball Association championship series.

The original floor, which was replaced in the mid-1990s, was dismantled and used for the 1978 Final Four played in St. Louis. Kentucky beat Duke in the final even as a large map of Indiana covered the center circle.

The first game played in the Hall saw Indiana defeat Ball State 84–77 on December 1, 1971. Over four decades the arena featured such performers as Bob Hope, Petula Clark, Elton John, Elvis Presley, and the Rolling Stones. Such dignitaries as Bill and Hillary Clinton, Barack Obama, and Bill Gates have spoken there.

14 Schlundt Set Standard for Big Men

Don Schlundt was the kingpin of Indiana's 1953 national championship team, and at 6'10" he was the first real big man to play for IU. Almost 60 years later, he may still be the best big man Indiana has ever had.

In the early 1950s, when Schlundt migrated to IU from South Bend, Indiana, college players of his size were still a bit of a novelty. Paul Ebert, Ohio State's outstanding center, was a modest 6'4". Among members of *Sport* magazine's 1955 preseason All-America team, Schlundt was 3" taller than anyone else on the first three teams.

Although he led the Big Ten in scoring three straight seasons, Schlundt may have been underrated by today's standards because he bypassed a career in the NBA. In those days the NBA was less prestigious than it is now, and Schlundt was a simple man who preferred to be at home every night in lieu of the fast-paced and not always lucrative life of a professional basketball player.

Indiana teammate Bob Leonard, who enjoyed a long career as an NBA player and coach, dismisses any thoughts that Schlundt wouldn't have been a great professional player.

"Don could shoot the ball. If Don had chosen to play in the NBA, he wouldn't have had a problem at all," said Leonard, pointing out that Schlundt held his own against Hall of Famer Bob Pettit and Johnny Kerr, a longtime NBA player. "He should be in the Hall of Fame. He was making more money in the insurance business than he could make playing professional basketball," Leonard said.

Schlundt averaged 25.4 points per game in 1953 and shot 80 percent at the foul line, where he was a frequent visitor. The Hurryin' Hoosiers went 23–3 in '53 and 20–4 the next season when they were upset by Notre Dame in the NCAA Tournament.

Schlundt was a three-time All-American who twice scored 47 points in a game and set Big Ten records with 1,207 Big Ten points and 2,192 overall. He once made 25 free throws in one game and hit 77 percent of his foul chances in four seasons. Known as the Gentle Giant, he averaged 23.3 points for his career with a season best of 27.1.

It was 32 years before Steve Alford beat his school scoring record, and Schlundt still trails only Calbert Cheaney and Alford among IU's all-time scorers. Schlundt was a prolific foul shooter, making 77 percent of his 1,076 career attempts. That's almost twice as many as Cheaney attempted and almost 500 more than Alford shot.

Schlundt was outstanding at running the court during an era when the Hurryin' Hoosiers had one of the best fast breaks in America. He possessed a soft arching hook that was deadly from up to 10', and he had a quick drop step that allowed him to get easy layups. When opponents defended with two or three players, Schlundt could go into the corners and make soft one-handed shots of up to 20'.

Schlundt died of cancer at age 52.

15 A Great IU Team Not Allowed to Dance

When Indiana fans reminisce about the greatest IU teams of all time, they start with the five teams that won the national title. After that they may mention the Calbert Cheaney teams of the early 1990s or, if they have a vintage memory, the 1960 Hurryin' Hoosiers.

No less an authority than Bob Knight once said that the 1960 IU team may have been the best team never to play in an NCAA Tournament. That squad went 20–4, beat that season's NCAA champions by 16 points, ended its season with 12 straight victories, and watched on television as rival Ohio State captured the NCAA title.

Those Hoosiers were victimized by a rule that allowed only one Big Ten team to play in the postseason.

Indiana may have been a better team than the Buckeyes, who featured a sophomore crew led by Jerry Lucas, John Havlicek, and Knight, a reserve forward. There was also senior Joe Roberts and underclassmen Larry Siegfried, Mel Nowell, and Richie Hoyt on a team that would lose in the national title game each of the next two years.

Indiana, built around 6'11" junior Walt Bellamy, also had Frank Radovich, Bob Wilkinson, Herbie Lee, Charley Hall, Gary

Long, Leroy Johnson, and Jerry Bass. Branch McCracken's team was tall, deep, and fast—so were the Buckeyes, coached by Fred Taylor.

On January 9 the teams met in Columbus for a classic match in St. John Arena. Ohio State won 96–95 in a game that still wrinkles the foreheads of Hoosiers who remember it. A couple of critical turnovers in the waning moments doomed IU's hopes.

Earlier in the season Indiana had opened with eight wins in nine games, the loss coming at Missouri 79–76 on December 7. The Hurryin' Hoosiers followed that with seven non-conference wins over such teams as Kansas State, Detroit, Notre Dame, Maryland, and Louisville.

However, IU opened Big Ten play with losses to Purdue at home and Northwestern on the road going into the Ohio State game. After the heartbreaking loss in St. John Arena, IU never lost

Famous Parents of IU Players

Two sons of former professional standouts played basketball for the Hoosiers. Patrick Ewing Jr., son of the Hall of Fame center, played his freshman and sophomore seasons at Indiana before transferring to Georgetown, his father's alma mater.

Jeremiah Rivers, son of Boston Celtics coach Doc Rivers, went the other direction by transferring from Georgetown in 2009–10 to play his last two seasons for Indiana.

Current Indiana guard Jordan Hulls is a grandson of John Hulls, who was an assistant coach under Bob Knight in the early 1970s.

IU forward Will Sheehey is the nephew of Tom Sheehey, a standout player at the University of Virginia in the early 1970s. Will's father, Mike, played at Syracuse and St. Bonaventure.

Of course, IU coach Tom Crean has a couple of famous relatives. John Harbaugh, Crean's brother-in-law, is head coach of the Baltimore Ravens in the NFL, and John's brother, Jim, coaches the San Francisco 49ers.

again. When the Buckeyes came to Bloomington on February 29, they were steamrolled 99–83.

Ohio State finished 13–1 in the Big Ten, two games ahead of the runner-up Hoosiers, then went on to beat Western Kentucky and Georgia Tech to reach the Final Four in San Francisco. The Bucks were champions after wins there against New York University and California 75–55. No opponent came within 17 points of Ohio State in the tournament.

Lucas led the Buckeyes that season with averages of 26.3 points and 16.4 rebounds. Knight contributed 3.7 points per game.

The final Associated Press basketball poll in 1960 had Cincinnati, led by Oscar Robertson, ranked first with California, OSU, Bradley, and West Virginia rounding out the top five. Indiana was seventh and was 10th in the United Press International poll.

Bellamy led Indiana scoring in 1960 with a 22.4 average, and IU had three other players in double figures. Despite Bellamy's presence the following season, the Hurryin' Hoosiers dropped nine games, including a pair to No. 1 Ohio State.

Bellamy was a member of the 1960 U.S. Olympic team that won the gold medal in Rome, and then went on to a 14-year career in the NBA. He was the first pick in the league's 1961 draft, and he was Rookie of the Year in '62. Bellamy ended his professional career with 20,941 points and 14,241 rebounds. He was voted into the Naismith Memorial Basketball Hall of Fame in 1993.

16 Edwards Just Beats the Clock

Jay Edwards came to Indiana with the reputation of a superior marksman, certainly the best since Steve Alford if not Annie Oakley. Edwards and IU teammate Lyndon Jones led Marion High to three state championships (1985, '86, '87) while running up a record of 85–4 under Coach Bill Green. Edwards and Jones came to Indiana as co-Mr. Basketballs and were expected to make up the nucleus of the team for the next four years.

Jones was a playmaker, defender, and dependable scorer, but his running mate was the kind of shooter his home state had long produced. Edwards' 6'4" frame gave him a squared-up foundation to bomb away from long distance.

In addition, Edwards had no fear as a gunner, although he seldom took a bad shot. He stepped into IU's lineup as a freshman in 1987–88, one year after Alford took the Hoosiers to their fifth national title, and was named Big Ten Freshman of the Year while living up to his nickname of "Silk" for his smooth style.

Edwards wasn't the prototypical Knight disciple off the court. To some degree, he considered class attendance optional and sometimes thought parking meters were a nuisance. He was a reluctant interview to reporters who sometimes asked questions for five minutes and received no usable answers.

Edwards will long be remembered for one shot, a three-pointer that beat Michigan 76–75 on February 19, 1989, in Bloomington. More than two decades later, arguments persist about whether Jay's jumper from the top of the lane beat the time clock. Film seems to confirm that the shot should have counted, but the margin is so tight that opinions differ.

Edwards finished that game with 23 points, and three other Hoosiers scored in double figures—Jones 15, Joe Hillman 13, and Eric Anderson 10. The Wolverines, who would win the NCAA Championship six weeks later, were led by Rumeal Robinson's 24 points.

Indiana won the Big Ten title, but conference foes Michigan and Illinois made it to the Final Four while the Hoosiers lost to Seton Hall in the Sweet Sixteen. Edwards' foul difficulties proved critical to IU's hopes in the Seton Hall loss.

The victory over the visiting Wolverines came 32 days after the Hoosiers beat Michigan in Ann Arbor 71–70. Edwards led all scorers in that game with 28 as Indiana shot 57 percent from the field. Michigan was coached by Bill Frieder, who before the NCAA Tournament would accept a job at Arizona State. Athletic Director Bo Schembechler then named assistant Steve Fisher to coach the team in the tournament. "Michigan will be coached by a Michigan man," Schembechler said.

That Wolverines team not only had Robinson, whose free throws would clinch the national title, but Glen Rice, Loy Vaught, Terry Mills, and Sean Higgins. Michigan entered the Bloomington game as the national leader in shooting. Frontcourt aces Vaught and Mills combined to make 14 of their 21 shots.

Indiana's game plan was to drive to the bucket in an attempt to get to the foul line. Knight hoped Jones' driving might get Robinson in foul trouble. The lead seesawed throughout the game as IU took a 16–15 lead only to see the visitors score seven straight. Indiana answered with six straight of its own and ended the first half with a mini-spurt that followed Rice's third personal foul.

Still, IU's 42–37 lead didn't please Knight who rued several missed layups and off-center free throws. "In the first half we may have played as well as we can play," he said.

Stopping the fleet Robinson was a key point for the Hoosiers. Said Knight, "We told our kids at the half that Robinson last year against us here really took it to us—I think he scored the first 11 points of the second half [in IU's 72–60 loss]. And he damn near did the same thing this year."

This time Robinson had four driving layups in the first five minutes of the second half, and the final one put Michigan ahead 50–49.

"We weren't talking on who was going to pick him up," IU senior Hillman said. "The one time he just blew by me; the other three times we had two guys back and we got confused who was going to pick him up."

The lead then changed hands nine times before a three-pointer by Edwards tied the game at 60. The Hoosiers moved ahead by four points with five minutes to play but missed four straight shots.

Rice, an All-American whose shooting skills were comparable to Edwards, made only 2-of-10 shots for seven points, but the visitors still managed a four-point lead with 1:08 to play.

With 54 seconds left, Edwards cut the margin to two with a pair of foul shots, setting the stage for Jay's buzzer beater. Knight, wearing his traditional red sweater, jumped off the bench with unusual enthusiasm when Edwards scored.

17 Slim Bill from Shelbyville

There are numerous reasons to recall the accomplishments of the late IU All-American Bill Garrett.

While he wasn't the first African American to appear in a Big Ten game, he was the first to make a significant contribution to his team. Garrett, who played three years at IU ending in 1951, led the Hoosiers every year in scoring and rebounding and, at the time, held the school's career scoring record with 792 points. Although only 6'2", Garrett played center and outshone many players who were several inches taller. Most notably, he overcame 6'9" Clyde Lovellette in the championship game of the 1947 Indiana state tournament.

Lovellette went on to become an All-American at Kansas and enjoyed an 11-year career in the NBA. His Terre Haute Garfield team was undefeated when Garrett's Shelbyville squad beat it for the coveted state title.

"Here was Lovellette, 6'9", big and burly, and Garrett was 6'2" and very slightly built, and Garrett just ate him up. Just ate him up," the late IU publicist Tom Miller once recalled.

That Shelbyville team apparently made history of another sort, much as Garrett did by becoming Indiana's first black player. Tom Graham, co-author of the book, *Getting Open: The Unknown Story of Bill Garrett and the Integration of College Basketball,* did exhaustive research and believes Shelbyville was the first team (high school, college, or professional) to feature three African American starters. Emerson Johnson and Marshall Murray were the others.

While Shelbyville coach Frank Barnes may have been receptive to playing his best players, regardless of race, many college coaches followed a harder line in the 1940s. A year before Garrett became Indiana's Mr. Basketball, Anderson High won the state title with a star center known as Jumping Johnny Wilson. IU coach Branch McCracken was reluctant to recruit Wilson and even told an Anderson audience that he didn't know if Wilson was good enough to make the IU team.

Wilson enrolled at Anderson College, where he became a star, and he later played for the Harlem Globetrotters.

When Garrett left high school, he had a short list of supporters who put pressure on McCracken to take the Shelbyville star. Those included IU president Herman B. Wells, Shelbyville insurance man Nate Kaufman, and Faburn DeFrantz, executive director of the

Indianapolis Senate Avenue YMCA. McCracken knew bad publicity would erupt if Garrett was boycotted and he agreed to play him if Bill could make the team.

Wells was interested in bringing down racial barriers across the Bloomington campus, and athletic director Zora Clevenger had concerns that a black Hoosier might create scheduling difficulties. Eventually, the decision came down to McCracken.

Upon leaving IU, Garrett was selected in the second round of the NBA Draft. He was only the third black player drafted by an NBA team, but he couldn't play professionally until he served his military obligation. Garrett spent two years in the U.S. Army, but when his time was up, the Celtics had no spot for him, so he joined the Globetrotters. Bill later was assistant dean for student services at Indiana University–Purdue University Indianapolis.

Following his days with the Trotters Garrett returned to Indiana as a coach at Crispus Attucks High in Indianapolis. That school had enjoyed success as the prep home of Oscar Robertson, who led the Tigers to state titles in 1955 and '56. Garrett took a less talented team to another state championship in 1959.

His late IU teammate, Bill Tosheff, recalled Garrett as a quiet guy known as "Bones" to his friends. In Tosheff's words, Bill was "quietly lethal."

"He wouldn't say too much, but boy could he fly. He worked as a center in the system, but we were always in transition, the Hurryin' Hoosiers. I would say, 'If they score on us, you take off.' He was a low-hurdles champion, and I'd throw a football pass to him and he'd score in about three seconds," Tosheff said before his death in 2011.

During Garrett's three seasons at IU, the Hurryin' Hoosiers were 50–16, including a 19–3 record in his final season. Garrett was extremely well liked by teammates, and the high school gym in Shelbyville was named in his honor. However, Tosheff frequently joked about how Bill didn't like air travel.

A former military pilot, Tosheff was allowed to take over the controls of the team's DC–3 on a trip to Manhattan, Kansas. The former airman took advantage of the opportunity to do a few uneven maneuvers.

"McCracken about had a hemorrhage. I looked back and Garrett had a blanket over his head," Tosheff said later. "McCracken kidded him, saying, 'Don't worry, Bill. We're not going to crash unless your time is up.'"

"I'm just worried about when the pilot's time is up," Garrett countered.

In 1974, one day after he and wife, Betty, marked their 32nd wedding anniversary, Bill went to an Indianapolis discount store to get a replacement for a broken window. As he stood in a checkout line, Garrett collapsed. He died three days later from heart failure. He was 45 years old.

18 Tournament Was Different in 1940

It's hard to imagine a March when there was no madness, yet until 1939 there was no one shining moment—no Sweet Sixteen or Elite Eight, or even a Final Four.

Indiana, of course, became the second winner of the NCAA Tournament in 1940, marking the first of five IU championships. But in those days nobody worried about their fate on Selection Sunday.

In fact, the NCAA Tournament almost didn't get off the ground because no governing bodies were interested in determining a champion through a tournament. The NCAA actually had this rich extravaganza dropped in its lap by the National Association of Basketball Coaches (NABC).

In 1938, a group of New York sportswriters staged the first major college tournament—the NIT—in New York City. Many coaches in the NABC believed any national tournament should be sponsored by a collegiate organization and not by writers.

The first national championship was held in 1939 under the auspices of the NABC. The field consisted of eight teams, one selected from each district, and Oregon won the inaugural event by beating Ohio State 46–33 in the final. Harold Olsen, a former Wisconsin player and Ohio State coach, is given much of the credit for setting up a national tournament. His team happened to lose the first title game.

Total attendance in 1939 was only 15,025, less than a fourth of what a national title game now attracts. The event also produced a $2,531 deficit, and because the coaches' group was short on funds, it asked the NCAA to take over the tournament.

The NCAA boxing tournament, now long since abandoned, was held in Madison, Wisconsin, in 1939 and drew big crowds. The University of Wisconsin turned over $18,000 from that event to the NCAA, which in turn put the money into boxing instead of basketball.

By that time World War II was on the horizon, and a number of major universities failed to field teams for at least one season. The war led to numerous college players leaving school to help in the war effort. Some of the better known were Alex Groza of Kentucky, Vince Boryla of Notre Dame, Arnie Ferrin of Utah, and Andy Phillips of Illinois.

Indiana's Ernie Andres was a member of the 1939 All-America team; and the national Premo Power Poll rated Indiana sixth, trailing Long Island University, Bradley, Loyola of Chicago, Oregon, and St. John's. Kentucky was ninth and Ohio State tenth.

The 1939 national championship game was played in Northwestern's McGaw Hall, now known as Welsh-Ryan Arena.

Indiana was not among the top 10 schools in winning percentage during the 1930s, but archrival Purdue was at No. 6. LIU, Kentucky, St. John's, and Kansas topped the list.

IU (20–3, 9–3 Big Ten) finished second to Purdue in the 1940 conference race, but the Bloomington team topped that year's Premo Power Poll. Indiana was trailed by USC, Colorado, Duquesne, Oklahoma State, and Purdue.

The 1940 season broke ground that would lead to major changes in the next seven decades. The first televised basketball game was on February 28, 1940, when WXBS showed Pittsburgh versus Fordham and New York University versus Georgetown from Madison Square Garden.

Seton Hall, led by future NBA star Bob Davies, won all 19 of its games in 1940 but didn't participate in either the NCAA or NIT.

Indiana won its first NCAA Tournament in only three games. Branch McCracken's team beat Springfield (Massachusetts) 48–24 in Indianapolis, and a day later it overcame Duquesne 39–30. That enabled Indiana to go to Kansas City the following week where it defeated Kansas 60–42 for the NCAA championship before a crowd of 10,000. The all-tournament team included IU's Jay McCreary, Bill Menke, and Marvin Huffman, who was the Most Valuable Player.

The only game all season in which Huffman reached double-figure scoring was the title game, when he equaled McCreary's 12 points. Huffman was IU's only senior starter and was the younger brother of Vern Huffman, a consensus All-American four years earlier.

McCreary had been a star at Frankfort High School, which in 1936 was considered to be the strongest team the state had produced. He later became a successful high school coach at Muncie (Indiana) Central before coaching LSU for eight seasons. His

Muncie team was the victim of Bobby Plump's game-winning shot for Milan in 1954.

IU's only regular-season losses came on the road, at Minnesota, Northwestern, and Ohio State. Indiana beat Purdue twice, which was instrumental in IU being added to the tournament field instead of the Boilermakers. All three members of the national selection committee, including Butler coach Tony Hinkle, opted for the Hoosiers to be included.

Although McCracken's fast-breaking teams later would be dubbed the Hurryin' Hoosiers, in 1940 they were mostly known as the Crimsons or Macmen. As an indication of the time, they were neither tall nor especially talented marksmen. The tallest player was 6'4" Andy Zimmer, and in 1939 four IU players shot less than 20 percent for the season.

This was not a time when players stayed on campus all summer and worked on their basketball skills. Before the 1940 season, Zimmer had worked on a farm, and Chester Francis had raised chickens. Everett Hoffman was a grocery story clerk, and Clarence Ooley worked as a bellhop. Harold Zimmer was a bodyguard, and Edward Newby drove a truck. Clifford Wiehoff and Don Huckleberry were factory workers, and Thomas Motter worked in a brewery.

19 IU Got Off to Rough Beginning

Indiana University basketball officially began on February 8, 1901, with a 20–17 loss to Butler at its Irvington campus in Indianapolis. A box score lacking most information included in today's boxes said Ernest Strange led Indiana with nine points, including all seven of IU's free throws.

Years later, Butler University moved its campus from the East Central Irvington location to Fairview Park off 46th Street on the city's north side. Once relocated, Butler built its historic Butler Fieldhouse, which was later renamed Hinkle Fieldhouse, and it remains in use today.

Three weeks later IU played Butler again in Bloomington and lost 24–20. That game was played in the original Assembly Hall, a newly constructed gymnasium that measured 135' x 67' and had seating for about 1,500. Featuring a bell tower on the roof, Assembly Hall had two balconies on each side of the playing floor as well as one at the west end. The court was also the site of the Indiana high school tournament's inaugural final game in which Crawfordsville defeated Lebanon 24–17 in 1911.

The original Assembly Hall, located directly east of Owen Hall, was used for various student activities, including athletics, until 1917 and was demolished in 1938.

After the two losses to Butler, Indiana traveled to Purdue on March 1 and lost 20–15. Coached by James H. Horne, IU then posted its first victory on March 8 at home against Wabash 26–17. A team picture revealed that Horne had a handlebar mustache and parted his dark hair in the middle. The players wore crimson jerseys, white shorts that came to the knees, and long socks with horizontal stripes.

Indiana finished its 1–4 season with a second loss at Purdue 23–19. Indiana had three coaches in its first three seasons with Phelps Darby coaching in 1902 and Willis Koval taking over in 1903. IU went 4–4 in its second season when it split two games with Butler and beat Indiana State twice. In 1903, Indiana posted an 8–4 record and defeated such opponents as Crawfordsville Business College 23–10, and Indianapolis Shortridge High School 23–18. For the third straight year, Purdue beat IU twice.

IU wasn't finished playing high school teams. It walloped Salem High 60–18 in 1904 and met a number of YMCA teams in the early years. Opponents included the Indianapolis YMCA (a 32–19 loss) and the Rayen Athletic Club and Buhl Athletic Club in 1905 when Zora Clevenger was coach. In 1906 and '07 IU had multiple games against YMCA teams from New Albany and Hartford City.

Indiana didn't become a national power in the early part of the twentieth century. IU had only five winning seasons in its first 16 years of fielding a team and went through 13 coaches in the process. IU lost its first nine games and 22 of its first 25 against Purdue. It dropped 14 of its first 18 meetings with Illinois and 10 of its first 11 against Minnesota.

20 Watch IU and See a Crean Pep Talk

One resemblance between Tom Crean and Bob Knight is that both are familiar with the microphone at Assembly Hall. Knight often grabbed the mic from public address announcer Chuck Crabb and admonished IU students for what he thought was conduct unbecoming an IU fan. Often, his language was salty.

Before every home game Crean addresses the Hoosier fans in a more positive light. His pep talk is filmed and recorded for playing over the JumboTron minutes before tip-off. Its intent is to raise the crowd's noise level to a fever pitch with the hope it will inspire the players.

In Crean's opinion, the crowd's enthusiasm has paid dividends numerous times, especially in victories over No. 1 Kentucky and

Head Coach Tom Crean talks to the crowd after the Hoosiers defeated Michigan 71-65 in a game in Bloomington, Indiana, on Thursday, December 31, 2009. (AP Photo/Darron Cummings)

No. 2 Ohio State. His waving to the crowd before and after games has become traditional.

For years, the pregame festivities was mostly limited to rendering the fight song a few times and whatever excitement the cheerleaders and pompon girls could produce. But when IU added its giant scoreboard, it paved the way for videos that are part Sports Classics and part History Channel. About the only thing missing is boxing orator Michael Buffer yelling, “Let’s get ready to rumble.”

Flickering film clips show IU teams of the 1950s and work the highlights into the days of Kent Benson and Calbert Cheaney before showing more modern Hoosiers. There are quick looks at Branch McCracken and Bob Knight, the latter always bringing forth a loud roar. Visiting coaches who are smart keep their players off the court during these lovefests.

Crean’s pep talks to his players can’t be more animated than those to the fans. That, along with improved play during the 2011–12 season, has resulted in a decibel level unseen for several years.

Crean, a native of Mount Pleasant, Michigan, was hired by IU in 2008 after the Hoosiers had gone through four full-time head coaches in nine years. He came with a mission—to clean up the mess left by Kelvin Sampson and to reinstall the winning program popularized by Knight.

Crean’s reputation as a good coach and a good man preceded him. Although he had been an assistant at four schools, his only head job was at Marquette. While he was at the Milwaukee school, he established a reputation as a strong recruiter, especially when he brought in Dwyane Wade and reached the 2003 Final Four.

Crean’s term at IU started with a roster of one senior, five true freshmen, and six walk-ons, which set the stage for the worst record in school history (6–25). Indiana won 10 games the next season and 12 the year after that, but the Hoosiers’ recruiting paid bigger dividends in 2012 when freshman Cody Zeller picked IU over North Carolina and Butler.

Crean is almost as well known for his family connections as for his coaching. He is married to Joani Harbaugh whose brothers, John and Jim, are both head coaches in the National Football League.

21 Dean: A Winner at Two Schools

Today's quick quiz—which IU basketball coach besides Branch McCracken and Bob Knight won an NCAA championship?

We all know McCracken's teams won national titles in 1940 and 1953, and Knight's Hoosiers were champs in '76, '81, and '87. That accounts for the five big red banners hanging at the south end of Assembly Hall.

But Everett Dean, perhaps the first great Indiana coach, also won an NCAA crown. It came after he had left Indiana and was coaching Stanford in 1942.

Dean was born in 1898 in Livonia, Indiana, a town of just more than a hundred residents near Salem. He started three seasons as a player at Indiana and was an All-American center in 1921. IU had a 15–6 record that season under Coach George Lewis. The Hoosiers played a unique schedule with wins over Armour Institute, Indiana Dental, Evansville YMCA, and Indiana Normal.

IU won 11 of its first 12 games, the loss coming at the hands of Merchants Heat and Light. Indiana also had good luck against programs that would hold up over the years, beating Ohio State and Northwestern twice and Michigan, Minnesota, and Louisville once.

In his three seasons as a player, Dean played for three different coaches: Lewis, Dana Evans, and Ewald Stiehm.

After graduating from IU, Dean coached basketball and baseball for three seasons at Carleton College in Minnesota. He had resounding success, winning 46 games and losing only four.

Dean then returned to IU in 1924 as baseball and basketball coach and remained through the 1937–38 season. His basketball team posted a 162–93 record and tied for three Western Conference (now Big Ten) championships. His baseball team was even more successful, winning four conference championships.

Before his death IU player William Silberstein described Dean in glowing terms often used by others, including Bob Knight.

"He was one of the finest gentlemen you'd ever want to meet," Silberstein said. "Everett Dean was a clean-cut, good-looking man about 6'1" who had a full head of sandy hair. He married the daughter of a banker in Salem. He was very articulate and never flamboyant. I never saw him jump off the bench or argue with a referee."

Silberstein said Dean put him in a game against Vanderbilt, and he followed with three straight baskets. "Coach took me out. He said, 'Look, I really don't want to run up a score here. The coach is a good friend of mine,'" Silberstein recalled. "He had that kind of gentleman-like attitude. Very, very much a gentleman. I think everybody respected and loved him."

In 1938 Dean left Indiana and went to Stanford where he also coached two sports. His basketball team beat Dartmouth 53–38 to win the NCAA championship in 1942. Only eight teams were in the tournament, and Stanford defeated Rice and Colorado to reach the final.

Stanford (28–4) was led by forward Jim Pollard, who would become a professional star playing alongside George Mikan with the Minneapolis Lakers. Pollard was considered one of the first players to effectively use the jump shot. However, Pollard had to sit out the championship game with the flu after scoring 26 of Stanford's 53 points against Rice.

In 1953 Dean became the only coach to win a basketball game in the tournament and a baseball game in the College World Series. He coached basketball through the 1951 season and retired as baseball coach after the 1955 season. His basketball record at IU was 162–93, and he won conference titles in 1926, 1928, and 1936. His Stanford teams had an overall record of 167–120.

Dean died on October 26, 1993, at age 95. He was living with his daughter in Caldwell, Idaho, at the time.

22 Cheaney Still Part of IU Basketball

A Louisville sportswriter who selected the top 25 high school players of 1989 was about to sit down to dinner when the telephone rang. The caller, a man who scouted hardwood talent as a business, was emphatic about his point.

"You've got Cheaney too high," he said. "Way too high!"

Calbert Cheaney, who had missed part of his senior season at Evansville Harrison High because of injury, had been picked on the third team. That was higher than almost any of the basketball "gurus," including the caller, had placed him.

As it turned out, the sportswriter rated Cheaney too low. The left-handed sharpshooter became the National Player of the Year in 1993 at Indiana University.

When Bob Knight brought in his newest recruits after the 1989 season, there was doubt about which of the seven newcomers would prove to be the best. Among the group was Indiana's Mr. Basketball, Pat Graham, and Ohio's celebrated standout, Lawrence

Calbert Cheaney drives around Xavier's Tyrice Walker in the 1993 NCAA Midwest Regional Round 2 game in the Indianapolis Hoosier Dome. Indiana advanced to the Round of 16 with a 73–70 win behind Cheaney's 23 points. (AP Photo)

Funderburke. There also was Greg Graham, Chris Reynolds, Chris Lawson, Todd Leary, and Cheaney. In addition, redshirt freshman Matt Nover was about to make his debut.

Funderburke lasted only six games before leaving school, turning up at Ohio State and eventually achieving NBA status. Lawson transferred to Vanderbilt where he enjoyed some success. Greg Graham went on to a brief NBA career, and Pat Graham overcame injuries to have a solid career. Reynolds became a catalyst on IU's 1992 Final Four team, and Leary's trio of three-pointers almost lifted Indiana to a Final Four upset of Duke.

The 6'7" Cheaney was the best of the group, rising to become the Big Ten's all-time leading scorer and spending 13 years in the NBA.

Cheaney's return to Bloomington was one of the most popular moves made by current coach Tom Crean who added Calbert to his staff before the 2010–11 season as director of basketball operations.

As a player Cheaney was quiet, yet he didn't back down from adversity. The product of a Christian home, he brought strong ideals to IU and continued them after leaving. Calbert donated a new gymnasium to his church in Evansville during his early years in the NBA.

Indiana was fortunate to recruit Cheaney because Evansville coach Jim Crews, a former Hoosier, seemingly had him locked up for the Purple Aces. "Coach Crews was working me to death. I played for an AAU team down in Evansville, and we played in Coach Crews' camp," Cheaney said. "He was kind of wearing me out a little bit, recruiting me hard. I almost went there, but I didn't want to stay at home. At the same time I wanted to stay close, and Indiana was just perfect for me."

"The only people who knew he was any good were his high school coach and me," Crews recalled.

Is the State Fruit a Sour Grape?

There was nothing politically correct about former Minnesota Governor Arne Carlson's stand against Big Ten officiating in 1993. Following a 61–57 loss by his Golden Gophers to Indiana, Carlson was so dismayed that he wrote a letter to Big Ten supervisor of officials, Rich Falk.

"I was saddened to watch the Minnesota-Indiana game and see the referee take away a victory from Minnesota," the governor's letter began. "I have never written a letter like this, I must confess. I am still outraged. It was not a question of an occasionally bad call here and there, which all basketball fans can expect. It had the earmarks of a deliberate plan to simply take the game away from Minnesota. In all the years that I have been watching basketball, I can honestly say that I have never seen worse refereeing.

"Indiana was physically strong and extremely aggressive, yet they were rarely called and almost never in the second half. On the other hand, every time Minnesota applied pressure, the whistle blew."

The first game in which Bob Knight witnessed Cheaney he had a mediocre game. "We played Jasper, and they just drubbed us something terrible," said Dennis Bays, Harrison's athletic director at the time. "We got beat something like 82–47, and Calbert put up about 15 or 16 shots and hit about three or four."

"It was a nightmare," said former Harrison coach Jerrill Vandeventer, who said that after the game that Knight "didn't have any interest in staying around afterward."

Vandeventer said Calbert's mother was a great influence on him, and she insisted that her son not make any early commitment to Evansville. "I lived in constant fear of her, as Calbert did," Vandeventer said while Cheaney was at IU, "but she did an excellent job with him."

Although Knight's early impressions of Cheaney weren't that strong, IU assistant coach Ron Felling had taken a liking to Cheaney and insisted his boss take another look.

Cheaney wasn't recruited as hard as he would have been had he not missed some games as a senior because of a broken foot.

Chris Reynolds, Calbert's roommate, said it took a while for even his teammates to realize how good Cheaney was. "He didn't get a lot of publicity that a lot of other guys got, but he worked so hard," Reynolds said. "When we came in, we had a lot of guys who were Parade All-Americans or McDonald's All-Americans. I hadn't really heard of Calbert. I think my name was ahead of Calbert's on the All-American list in high school.

"We played pickup games, and Calbert just seemed to hit all his shots."

Cheaney said his eventual progress surprised even himself. "When I came in as a freshman, I just wanted to contribute and play hard and play my heart out," he said. "I never had any aspirations to all of this. It's surprising to me."

Cheaney became the Big Ten's all-time leading scorer on March 4, 1993, when he scored 35 points against Northwestern in Assembly Hall. Cheaney was the Big Ten's MVP as a senior and the U.S. Basketball Writers Association College Player of the Year. He scored 30 or more points 13 times, and his teams won 105 games in four years, including a 46–8 record in the Big Ten.

After Cheaney set the conference scoring record, Knight was asked the secret of his success.

"He can do a little bit of everything. He can shoot the ball to begin with. He can shoot it from outside. You've got to guard him, but he's quick enough to get past you, and then he can play the post. He just, I think, does everything better than anybody else does right now," the coach answered.

Calbert went to the Washington Bullets as the sixth overall pick in the 1993 NBA Draft. He retired in 2006 after playing his third season with the Golden State Warriors, and he also played with Boston, Denver, and Utah. Calbert spent two seasons working in the Warriors' front office, and in 2010–11 he served as an assistant coach on the Warriors under another former IU star, Keith Smart.

23 Steve Alford—The Perfect Hoosier

Steve Alford always looked too perfect to be true.

First of all, there was the hair. Never out of place. Steve would have been the guy who could have stolen Barbie from Ken. He could have taken a ride in Barbie's Corvette convertible and never needed a comb.

His jump shot was mechanical, always in balance, and always on line. After making it he would run down court with perfect posture. If there ever was a player who didn't sweat, surely it was Steve Alford.

Yet this perfect model of a basketball player really didn't look like an athlete. His vertical leap was modest at best. He didn't appear to be that fast afoot, and he had this coach who kept yelling at him—apparently, Bob Knight didn't think he was perfect.

Often called "Stevie Wonder," Alford was largely overlooked by many of the national recruiting gurus when he came out of Chrysler High in New Castle, Indiana. Most of them rated James Blackmon of Marion, Indiana, at a higher level, probably because Blackmon was the prototypical high-wire type of the modern era.

Yet Alford upstaged Blackmon and almost everyone else as a collegian, leading IU to the 1987 NCAA Championship. This former gym rat scored 2,438 points during his four years as a starter and trails only Calbert Cheaney (2,613) among Indiana's all-time scorers.

Steve Alford dribbles past UNLV's Jarvis Basnight as the Hoosiers won 97-93 in NCAA semi-final play on March 30, 1987, in New Orleans. Alford was Indiana's high scorer with 33 points. (AP Photo / Susan Ragan)

Arriving just in time for the three-point shot, Alford made 53 percent of his 202 three-point attempts. That's the best career percentage in Big Ten history, far outdistancing former Hoosier Jay Edwards who is second at 48.1 percent.

Above all else, Alford was a winner. The son of a coach, he had the savvy, grit, and intelligence to shine at the most opportune moments. Plus he always looked cool doing it, as he did in nailing a long jump shot at the end of the first half against Syracuse. Alford barely broke stride after the basket while heading for the Superdome's locker room.

After averaging 37.7 points per game as a high school senior, Alford averaged 15.5 as a freshman at IU. He shot 59 percent from the field and 91 percent at the foul line, and he scored 27 as the Hoosiers upset No. 1 North Carolina in the Sweet Sixteen. The following summer he not only made the Olympic team but started on it.

As an Olympian he averaged 10 points per game, was second on the team in assists, and shot .644 from the field.

Obviously, Alford was an icon in Indiana by the time the 1987 NBA Draft rolled around, and most fans expected the Indiana Pacers would draft Steve.

Instead they went with UCLA star Reggie Miller, and his pro career far exceeded Alford's. Steve was picked by the Dallas Mavericks and played four years professionally before going into coaching.

Alford's first coaching job was at Manchester College in Indiana. Hired by the Division III program in 1991 his teams posted a 78–29 record in his four seasons there. The Spartans dropped their first eight games under Steve's leadership and lost 16-of-20 games that season. The next year Manchester was 20–8, and in his final year the team went 31–1 and reached the national championship game before losing.

Alford's second coaching job was at Southwest Missouri State where in a three-year period the Bears won 78 and lost 48. In 1999 Southwest Missouri reached the NCAA's Sweet Sixteen before falling to Duke.

Iowa hired Alford in 1999, and the Hawkeyes beat defending national champion Connecticut in Steve's first game there. After one losing season, Iowa went 23–12 in the regular season and upset Indiana to win the Big Ten Tournament. The Hawkeyes won only five Big Ten games in 2002 but again stunned Indiana in the semifinal round of the conference tournament. Former Hoosier Luke Recker beat IU with a late bucket, but Iowa lost the title game to Ohio State.

After the 2007 season, Alford resigned at Iowa and took the job at New Mexico where he won at least 22 games in each of their first four seasons. He is a member of both the IU and the Manchester Halls of Fame.

24 Davis Became Coach by Default

Mike Davis woke up one morning and was the Indiana University basketball coach. Just like that.

Davis didn't come to IU expecting to be the head coach. He joined Bob Knight's staff in 1997, hoping to learn from IU's Hall of Fame coach, build his reputation, and eventually land a head coaching job in the South. The latter part was important because Davis was more Dixon than Mason. His comfort zone was in Birmingham, not Bloomington. His roots grew out of cotton fields, not corn fields.

Then one Sunday afternoon, IU president Myles Brand fired Knight, and Davis got the job by default. The staff of assistants consisted of Pat Knight, who burned his bridges by standing up for his dad, John Treloar, and Davis.

Treloar had been a head coach in the Continental Basketball Association, and Davis' lone experience as a head coach was in Venezuela. Someone foolishly suggested the two assistants become co-coaches, but Treloar quickly squashed that idea. It was too late to go outside for a new coach.

Mike, I guess the job is yours.

Succeeding a legend may be the hardest job in sports, especially when the legend fails to support you. Davis admitted he really wasn't an authority on the motion offense that Knight had run for 29 years. Once plagued by stuttering, he didn't especially enjoy speaking in public. Raised in a Christian home, he was honest to a fault.

Davis' problems arrived immediately when several of his players threatened to leave school. Many IU fans soured on his offense, which was the same one run by many professional teams. Some of his critics offered a variety of reasons for disliking him, including such folly as, "His fingernails are too long," "He whines too much," and, "He's too religious." Unspoken, but probably a factor in some criticism, was the fact that he was IU's first African American head coach.

Davis was raised in the small Alabama town of Fayette. He was the youngest of four children raised in a two-bedroom house of which he admitted to being ashamed. "I used to play football and basketball and baseball, and I'd have coaches bring me home," Davis said. "I would always point to the house next door, which was my grandparents' home, and they'd drop me off there and I'd walk back to my house."

Davis was three days shy of his 40th birthday when he was named interim head coach. His first job was cutting grass as a boy in Fayette, and he played basketball on dirt and grass in those days. There wasn't a paved court available until Mike was in the

Vaden Moved on from IU

Robert Vaden played two seasons for the Hoosiers before joining his IU coach, Mike Davis, when Davis was hired at Alabama–Birmingham. Vaden finished his college career with more than 2,000 points.

Vaden, from Indianapolis, started every game as a Hoosier, and as a sophomore he averaged 13.5 points per game and 5.5 rebounds while leading the team in assists. He made 12 consecutive three-point attempts over a stretch of three games.

As a junior at Alabama–Birmingham, Vaden averaged 21 points per game and made the All-Conference USA first team. His 142 three-point baskets ranked second nationally. He also had 41 points in a game against Texas–El Paso.

Vaden was drafted by the Charlotte Bobcats of the NBA and was traded to Oklahoma City shortly thereafter. He played in the NBA Summer League and wound up playing in Italy.

ninth grade. Still, he was good enough to be named Alabama's Mr. Basketball and earned a scholarship to the University of Alabama where he was a defensive standout and a second-round pick of the Milwaukee Bucks.

The Bucks released Davis a week before the season opener, and he went overseas to play. Mike said he was overwhelmed while with the Bucks.

"I was nervous. When I went into camp, I didn't really play well. I was never relaxed the whole time I was there," he said.

Davis became an assistant at Miles College, then at Alabama, and in 1997 he got an interview with Knight. "I come up and met him at Marsh. He was there having lunch. He was with a couple of friends, and we never even talked about the job," Davis said. "I didn't say much. I was real quiet the whole time. I told my wife when the weekend was over, 'Well, I didn't get the job.'"

Davis began his days at IU with aspirations of bringing nationally ranked players to Bloomington. He had established a solid reputation as a recruiter under Knight, and he went after some of the nation's top players, many in the South. Many thought Davis should have hit the in-state schools harder.

Still, the new coach guided his team to a 21–13 record in his first season, and in his second the Hoosiers unpredictably reached the national title game, beating No. 1 Duke along the way. When IU beat Kent State to reach the Final Four, Davis went into the stands to present the game ball to Myles Brand.

At a press conference preceding the next game against Oklahoma, Davis admitted that he'd love to coach in the NBA some day. Indiana fans, who view their coach as obligated to spend at least two decades in Bloomington, perceived that as a lack of loyalty, and somewhere along the line a "Fire Mike Davis" website was founded.

Indiana had lost center Kirk Haston to the NBA after Davis' first season, and the next year All-American Jared Jeffries left school early. Most of Davis' recruits failed to reach his vast expectations and criticism increased. Bolstered by an 8–0 start, the Hoosiers went 21–13 in 2003 but split even in the Big Ten where they lost five straight in midseason. During the next two seasons they went 29–29 and missed out on the NCAA Tournament.

Davis coached one more year, won 19 games, and resigned. He was eventually hired as head coach at Alabama–Birmingham. One of his best players, Robert Vaden, transferred with him.

Looking back, Davis admits he wasn't ready for the Indiana task, especially considering that Knight wasn't supportive of him getting the job. He had modest success at UAB but was dismissed in March 2012. Athletic Director Brian Mackin said the team's record was only one of the reasons for the dismissal and cited waning fan support and a lack of postseason success.

UAB had four consecutive 20-win seasons under Davis but fell to 15–16 in his final season.

25 Three Guards Were Key in 1989

Fans can debate which season represented Bob Knight's best coaching job, but it would be hard to find a better example of coaching excellence than the 1988–89 season.

For starters, Indiana was coming off one of its most perplexing years. The 1987–88 campaign was more frustrating than successful when, despite keeping three starters from a national championship team, the '88 squad had a modest 19–10 record that included a first-round loss in the NCAA Tournament. At the end of that season, forward Rick Calloway left the program and Knight threatened to do so, talking with New Mexico about the job there.

Indiana began the 1989 campaign without Calloway, Keith Smart, Dean Garrett, and Steve Eyl, but Knight still had sophomores Jay Edwards and Lyndon Jones and seniors Joe Hillman and Todd Jadlow. His reserves included Magnus Pelskowski, Chuckie White, Brian Sloan, Kreigh Smith, Mark Robinson, and Mike D'Aloisio, and he added newcomers Eric Anderson and Jamal Meeks. The coach elected to redshirt freshman Matt Nover.

The Hoosiers opened the season with uneventful victories over Illinois State and Stanford before going to New York for the semifinals of the preseason NIT.

The two games in Madison Square Garden were disasters for the defense-conscious Hoosiers. Syracuse, still smarting from Keith Smart's famous jump shot in 1987, buried IU 102–78. The Orange took a 54–30 halftime lead and didn't let up.

Knight started Robinson and Sloan at forward, Jadlow at center, and Hillman and Edwards at guard. Two nights later, in a 106–92 loss to North Carolina, he would go with Anderson and White at forward while starting Jadlow at center and Hillman and Jones at guard. Edwards came off the bench to score 31 points and Jadlow had 27, but the rest of the team made only 13-of-53 shots.

Never before had a Knight team yielded more than 100 points in successive games. Then, after a win in Oxford, Ohio, over Miami, the Hoosiers played Louisville in Indianapolis and were beaten 101–79. Louisville, nicknamed the Doctors of Dunk, scored more than 50 points in each half and repeatedly dunked over the Hoosiers.

Rick Bozich of the *Louisville Courier-Journal*, playing off a controversial "If rape is inevitable, relax and enjoy it" remark by Knight, wrote, "If dunking is inevitable, relax and enjoy it."

"After the Louisville game, Coach Knight came to me and said we were going back to the three guards," Hillman recalled. "'Do you want that?' he said, and I said, 'Yeah, I do.' It meant I didn't have to handle the ball. It definitely was easier for me because I didn't have to play point guard. I could run around and shoot it."

Hillman had averaged more than 40 points per game as a high school player in Glendale, California.

Indiana then lost to Notre Dame, giving up 84 points, but Knight started a lineup that included three guards: Edwards, Jones, and Hillman. The secret ingredient was Hillman, a 6'2" Californian with a grit level than equaled his coach. Hillman successfully guarded taller forwards all season, went to the backboards oblivious of his shorter size, and provided leadership on the court. If a teammate was dogging it on the court, he heard about it from Hillman. By season's end, Knight was talking about Hillman's leadership being at the same level as Quinn Buckner's.

Indiana won 13 straight after the loss to Notre Dame and won eight more in a row after losing at Illinois. The Hoosiers won 21-of-22 during that stretch, including a big victory at Purdue.

The switch to a three-guard lineup allowed Jones and Edwards, who had been co-Mr. Basketballs at Marion High, to play together. Anderson and Jadlow represented the frontcourt.

Hillman frequently had to guard much taller players, including Michigan All-American Glen Rice. "The guy who gave me the biggest problem was Nick Anderson [of Illinois]," Hillman said. "I guarded Roy Marble, Jerry Francis of Ohio State, Willie Burton at Minnesota, Steve Smith at Michigan State, and Danny Jones of Wisconsin. I was overmatched, but it sure made it a lot easier for me at the offensive end because those guys had to guard me, too.

"Glen Rice was actually fairly easy because he was a catch-and-shoot guy that you could fight and make him put the ball on the floor," Hillman said.

Indiana won the Big Ten with a 15–3 record and went 27–8 overall. IU was a second seed in the NCAA Tournament—a notch below rival Illinois—and defeated George Mason and UTEP to reach the Sweet Sixteen. Then Seton Hall ousted the Hoosiers 78–65 and went on to the championship game before losing to Michigan. Two teams that had trailed Indiana in the Big Ten standings, Illinois and Michigan, reached the Final Four.

26 Kentucky Wanted Kent Big Time

Every redheaded center to play at Indiana in the past 35 years has been compared with Kent Benson, but it was a comparison not even Uwe Blab could live up to—let alone Chris Lawson.

At 6'11" and 245 pounds, Benson was one of the most sought after players in the country when he came out of Chrysler High in New Castle, Indiana, in 1973. Bob Knight's recent arrival as IU basketball coach found him in need of a center to replace Steve

Downing from the Final Four team of '73, and Benson was the perfect fit to play alongside Quinn Buckner, Scott May, Bobby Wilkerson, and Steve Green. If the Hoosiers were to win their third NCAA Championship—which they would do in '76—Benson would have to be an integral part of the team.

However, about a hundred miles south of Bloomington, another school had a similar goal, and Benson was the focal point of its intentions. Kentucky, which had won four national titles under Adolph Rupp, believed Benson could lead Joe B. Hall's troops to the throne room again. And when the University of Kentucky recruits a player, it has been known to pull out all the stops.

Benson recalls his trip to Lexington as resembling nothing short of a presidential visit. He was escorted to the Lexington airport via private jet, and some 4,000 UK fans greeted him there. He recalls the governor being present along with a band and cheerleaders. Kent was taken to an elite dinner with a big crowd and had breakfast at Claiborne Farm, where Triple Crown winner Secretariat stood at stud following his outstanding racing career.

The recruit was also taken to Keeneland Race Course, where he said one person tried to hand him cash for what he was told was a winning mutuel.

"I didn't bet," Benson told him.

"He said, 'That's okay. We bet it for you,'" said Benson, who refused the money.

Sensing that the young recruit had to be impressed, Hall reportedly tried to convince Kent that playing for the Wildcats would be a logical step to playing in the NBA. Benson said he responded with the brash remark, "If I come to Kentucky, that would mean I'd have to take a cut in pay in order to try pro, and I don't think I'm willing to do that."

"His mouth flapped open, and he didn't know what to say. That's kind of the way I ended it," Benson said.

The New Castle product said it was less formal at Indiana, where he was taken to a fast-food restaurant and slept on an old mattress on the floor of the Fiji house.

"I fell in love with the place," he said.

According to teammate John Laskowski, Benson underwent a period of adjustment with the Hoosiers. "We needed to have a center, so Coach was really on him to get going from Day 1," Laz said, "But Bennie really took it hard. He couldn't understand why he was being picked on. I remember seeing him in the locker room after practice and he said, 'Laz, I'm going to quit the team. I'm going to get in the car and drive back to New Castle. I just can't handle this.'"

Benson eventually adjusted very well, scoring 1,740 points in four seasons and helping the Hoosiers go 63–1 during his sophomore and junior seasons. In the single loss—to Kentucky in the 1975 NCAA regional—Benson had 33 points and 23 rebounds.

Benson spent 11 seasons in the NBA after being the top pick in the 1977 draft. Perhaps his most famous moment as a pro came in his debut with the Milwaukee Bucks during which he crossed paths with Kareem Abdul-Jabbar of the Los Angeles Lakers.

Benson recalled scoring the game's first basket against Abdul-Jabbar and then getting nailed in the chest with a strong elbow from the Lakers' star.

"We jostled for position, and at that point in time I gave him an elbow, not a malicious elbow but as if to say, 'You're not going to elbow me. If you can dish it out, you're going to take it.' It was not an intent to hurt him in any way but a statement. I was watching the ball come up the floor, and he had dropped back about 10' or so and took a running start and sucker punched me in the temple. It didn't knock me out, but it knocked me silly."

27 Look Out for the First Step

What do Cleveland State, Richmond, California, Missouri, Boston College, Colorado, Pepperdine, and Kent State have in common? They all embarrassed the Hoosiers by beating them in the first round of the NCAA Tournament between 1986 and 2001.

That 16-year period was hardly a disaster for IU, considering that it won the NCAA championship in '87, reached the Final Four in 1992, and won four Big Ten championships in the interim. But IU's eight first-round losses were to lower-rated teams on seven occasions.

The Hoosiers were a No. 3 seed in 1986 when they went to Syracuse, New York, and fell to 14th-seeded Cleveland State 83–79. The Ohio team, coached by Kevin Mackey, came in with a 24–3 record as a member of the Association of Mid-Continent Universities (AMC–8). Mackey joked that the conference reminded him of a motor oil.

Some might say Mackey outcoached IU's Hall of Fame coach Bob Knight. Perhaps not, but his team certainly outplayed the Hoosiers. Cleveland State's full-court press took Indiana out of its game, and IU was not only beaten but embarrassed.

Perhaps the loss sharpened the Hoosiers' senses for the 1987 tournament, where they won their fifth national championship. But when a disappointing '88 season ended, the Hoosiers again were embarrassed in an eastern city, losing to Richmond 72–69 in Hartford, Connecticut. IU had been a No. 3 seed against Cleveland State, one notch lower against the underdog Spiders.

Indiana bounced back from its tournament upset to win the conference title in 1989 and entered the NCAA Tournament as a

No. 2 seed. IU lost in the Sweet Sixteen to Seton Hall but again went out in the opening round of the 1990 shootout. California, seeded ninth to Indiana's eighth, posted a 65–63 victory in Hartford.

IU owned a 44–36 lead with just more than 14 minutes to play, but California scored 10 answered points.

Indiana was a freshmen-laden team against Cal, but those freshmen included future All-American Calbert Cheaney and classmates Greg and Pat Graham and Chris Reynolds. The Golden Bears roster included Brian Hendrick, son of former major league outfielder George Hendrick.

California was playing in the NCAA Tournament for the first time in 30 years, dating back to its Final Four appearance in 1960. The Bears lost the '60 title game to Ohio State, which had a reserve named Bob Knight.

Cheaney and his mates, who included Damon Bailey as a freshman in '91, reached the Sweet Sixteen each of the next four years. That included a Final Four advancement in '92 and an Elite Eight run in '93 when Alan Henderson's injury contributed to a loss to Kansas. However, with the Cheaney-Bailey group gone, Indiana fell back into its first-round doldrums in 1995.

Missouri, a No. 8 seed, ousted the No. 9 Hoosiers 65–60 in Boise, Idaho. Indiana appeared to lack its usual enthusiasm, leading IU's Steve Hart to remark, "Our heart was missing.... We must have been in another land." As was the case in some other first-round defeats, Indiana's best player, Alan Henderson, had a subpar game.

"I just wasn't finishing plays all night long," Henderson said. "I'm very disappointed—such a sad way to end my Indiana career."

Henderson missed seven of his nine shots in the first half, but forward Brian Evans had a hot night and scored 19 of his 25 points before intermission. With Evans cooling off, Missouri opened the second half with a 12–2 spurt.

The major news of the night wasn't Missouri's win but Bob Knight's outburst against press conference moderator Rance Pugmire, who had been told the IU coach was skipping the news interviews. Knight did appear before reporters and immediately tore into the University of Idaho official.

> Knight: You've only got two people that are going to tell you I'm not going to be here. One is our SID (sports information director), and the other is me. Who the hell told you I wasn't going to be here? I'd like to know. Do you have any idea who it was?
>
> Pugmire: Yes, I do, Coach.
>
> Knight: Who?
>
> Pugmire: I'll point him out to you in a while.
>
> Knight: They were from Indiana, right?
>
> Pugmire: No, they're not from…
>
> Knight: No, weren't from Indiana, and you didn't get anybody from Indiana, did you?
>
> Pugmire: Could we please handle…
>
> Knight: No, I'll handle this the way I want to handle it now that I am here. You [bleep] it up to begin with. Now just sit there or leave. I don't give a [bleep] what you do.

The NCAA fined the coach $30,000 for his outburst. Missouri lost to UCLA in the regional final when guard Tyus Edney drove the length of the court for a buzzer-beating layup.

Indiana's tournament debut in 1996 was against Boston College in Orlando, Florida, where IU lost 64–51. IU had been seeded sixth to the Eagles' 11th, but Boston College solidified the win by scoring the last 10 points of the game.

As with Henderson in Boise, Brian Evans struggled with his shooting while making only 2-of-14 and being held to seven points. Evans was the Big Ten Player of the Year. Meanwhile, the Eagles' bulky Danya Abrams burned the Hoosiers with 22 points and 17 rebounds.

Opening-game tournament losses had become routine for the Hoosiers, and their seed in 1997 was one spot higher than Colorado. Nonetheless, the Buffaloes pounded IU from the start and won 80–62 at Winston-Salem, North Carolina. In many ways it was IU's most devastating tournament loss as Colorado, led by Chauncey Billups' 25 points, dominated every facet of the game. The Buffs took a 12–3 lead at the start, and Billups ended the half with 20 points. IU made only 35 percent of its shots and was an equal-opportunity team in turnovers as 10 different Hoosiers committed at least one.

According to reports, Knight walked several miles from the Wake Forest campus to his hotel following the game.

Bob Knight's final game as IU coach was another first-round loss at the hands of Pepperdine 77–57 in Buffalo, New York. At the time the rumble over the coach's alleged "choking" of Neil Reed was very much in the news.

At a press conference the day before the game, Knight defended himself and his program while citing his graduation rates and contributions to worthwhile agencies. Knight took the opportunity to note that the players had unanimously voted Reed off the team, and he insinuated that another player, Richard Mandeville, was laughed at by his teammates because of his poor work ethic.

With Knight gone, replacement Mike Davis coached Indiana to a 21–12 regular-season record in 2000–01. That earned IU a No. 4 seed in the West Regional at San Diego. However, No. 13 Kent State of the Mid-American Conference pinned a 77–73 loss on the Hoosiers.

Foul trouble contributed to IU's problems as Tom Coverdale fouled out, Dane Fife was saddled with four personals, and Jared Jeffries sat out several minutes with foul troubles. Kirk Haston, who had been injured early in the Pepperdine game a year earlier, led IU with 29 points.

Indiana rebounded the next season with an unexpected trip to the tournament's championship game, beating No. 1 Duke and Kent State to make the Final Four.

28 IU Broke Ground with Telecasts

The popularity of Indiana basketball escalated in the early 1950s, not only because the Hurryin' Hoosiers (as they were known at the time) were good but because a new communication medium showed fans in Central Indiana just *how* good they were.

To a large degree college basketball's popularity has paralleled the rise of television over the past 60 years, and the epicenter of that merger occurred around the IU basketball program. Indiana games first appeared on television in 1951–52, one season before Branch McCracken's IU team won its second NCAA championship. The NCAA had made it possible for member schools to negotiate with media for television rights, and IU games began appearing on Channel 10 in Bloomington.

Most vintage fans recall the Hurryin' Hoosiers playing on Channel 4, another Bloomington station. WTTV had traded rights with a Terre Haute station, which enabled WTTV–4 to build a new tower near Trafalgar, Indiana. That tower still stands in southern Johnson County, and WTTV–4 is still on the air. In fact, Channel 4 was the home of Indiana basketball for years before cable television giants began buying the rights for college basketball.

The original broadcasters for IU were Paul Lennon, a retired advertising executive, and Bob Cook, a well-known personality around campus. The telecasts were primitive by today's standards, obviously not offering any replays and being shown only in black

Radio Reaches Across Indiana

The Indiana University Radio Network reaches all parts of the state via 32 local affiliates covering the state from Evansville to Michigan City. The network is owned by Learfield Communications of Jefferson City, Missouri.

The patriarch of the IU Network is Don Fischer who works as an independent contractor and has been the Voice of the Hoosiers for 39 years.

Fischer, whose golden voice and sports knowledge has been an earmark of Indiana sports, has been named Indiana Sportscaster of the Year 24 times by two organizations, the National Sportscasters and Sportswriters Association (20 times) and the Indiana Sportswriters and Sportscasters Association (four times). The later group inducted him into its Hall of Fame in 2004.

Fischer has been at the microphone for more than 1,500 IU football and basketball games, which include eight bowl games, four NCAA Tournament championship games, and two NIT final games.

For the past two seasons Fischer has worked with Royce Waltman, a former head coach at DePauw and Indianapolis and a onetime assistant to Bob Knight at IU. Waltman won more than 100 games at all three of these colleges.

Rounding out the broadcasting team is Joe Smith, who has been on Bloomington radio stations for 42 years. He has handled pregame, halftime, and postgame duties since 1983. Smith is a member of the Indiana Sportscasters and Sportswriters Hall of Fame and was the state's Sportscaster of the Year in 1998.

and white. Even then, the picture often had the familiar snowy interference of that day, but most IU fans didn't mind because Don Schlundt, Bob Leonard, and the other players looked great in any dimension.

The original television tower was on Walnut Street in downtown Bloomington and, in Lennon's estimation, the telecasts traveled about 35 miles. Lennon gave a speech to a group in Columbus, barely 35 miles from the WTTV tower, and was reminded of the limitations by a man in the audience. "He said

WTTV reminded him of his wife, and I said, 'How's that?' And he said, 'Hard to get and once you do, it isn't very good.'"

Chesty, a Terre Haute potato chip company, was the sole sponsor of the telecasts and found the exposure to be a bonanza. Fans still remember Lennon holding up a bag of Chestys before the games and saying, "I've got my ticket. Have you got yours?"

The telecasts were so popular that Chesty Foods, which made the chips, couldn't keep an ample supply in stock. George Johnson founded the Chesty Company after World War II and it sponsored Indiana games for about eight years.

"Chesty went bananas. They couldn't handle the stores. They ran out of potatoes in a couple of weeks and had to go to other states to buy potatoes out of other people's potato bins," Lennon said.

29 Santa Comes Early for Watford

Christmas was approaching, but the sports world was being dominated by Grinches when Christian Watford made the biggest shot of his life on December 10, 2011. As far as IU fans were concerned, all that is good had suddenly arrived for their basketball program.

For some four years IU basketball had lived in disgrace, and the program had become unranked, uninvited, and unwanted in many circles. The Hoosiers, of all people, had become the doormats of the Big Ten, a team that had lost eight straight to Wisconsin and six straight to Ohio State. IU had dropped six of its previous seven to Northwestern, Michigan State, and Penn State and five of its last six to Iowa. Butler, the mid-major neighbor, had reached the NCAA Tournament's final game twice, while IU hadn't even won a Big Ten Tournament game since 2006.

Furthermore, the holiday season was approaching with bad news all over talk radio. Penn State and Syracuse were embroiled in stories about sex scandals. The National League's Most Valuable Player, Ryan Braun, had tested positive for illegal drugs. Two hours from Bloomington, on the same night Indiana upset No. 1 Kentucky 73–72 on Watford's last-second three-pointer, the universities of Cincinnati and Xavier were engaged in an ugly on-court brawl.

But among all of the aforementioned depressing things, Watford's jump shot brought some civility to the sports world. Kentucky, which retools almost annually with new McDonald's All-Americans, supposedly had a huge edge in talent over the unbeaten, but at that time, unproven Hoosiers.

What the Hoosiers had was heart. They played the Wildcats even for 39 minutes, 55 seconds and then beat them during the final five seconds.

Watford's jumper, on an assist from Verdell Jones III, brought a full complement of IU students surging onto the court in a scene similar to the one when Kirk Haston's three-pointer beat top-ranked Michigan State in 2001. It marked Indiana's first win over a No. 1 team since it beat Duke in the 2002 NCAA Tournament. It also gave the Hoosiers a 9–0 record for the first time in 22 years.

At one time it would have been just another nail-biter in a fiercely competitive series between teams that had combined for 12 NCAA championships. However, the Wildcats had dominated the series during the past two decades, winning 14 times in 17 meetings. Many Indiana fans consider Kentucky to be an even bigger rival than Purdue, so their celebration was multi-faceted.

Watford's jumper made believers out of skeptics who had watched the IU program struggle since Kelvin Sampson's recruiting scandal five years earlier. The win put the stamp of approval on a team that had built its 8–0 season record with wins over such teams as Stony Brook, Savannah State, and Gardner-Webb.

Christian Watford (2) celebrates with teammates (from left) Will Sheehey, Verdell Jones III, and Victor Oladipo after Indiana defeated Kentucky 73–72 in a game on Saturday, December 10, 2011, in Bloomington, Indiana. Watford hit a three-pointer at the buzzer to seal the victory.
(AP Photo/Darron Cummings)

Kentucky's Terrence Jones, a preseason All-American, aided Indiana's cause by scoring only four points; and Kentucky's failure to foul in the final five seconds, when it had two fouls to give, was a critical mistake. IU also got a tremendous lift from its 17,472 fans who provided a significant home-court advantage. They supported the Hoosiers as IU built a 30–22 lead late in the first half and remained vigilant as UK's Anthony Davis missed the first of a one-and-one with 19 seconds left.

Indiana turned over the basketball, which led to Doron Lamb making one of two foul shots with 5.6 seconds to play. Jones rushed the ball up the left side of the court and, upon hearing Watford yell his nickname, fed the ball back to the 6'9" junior for the winning hoop.

30 Bailey, a Legend in the Eighth Grade

Damon Bailey has been called a smaller version of Larry Bird because he wasn't particularly fast, nor could he jump especially high. His critics were usually from out of state, or at least from West Lafayette. He's the leading scorer in Indiana high school history, and he became a legendary figure in junior high school.

Damon—and that's all you have to say to identify him around Indiana—reached iconic proportions long before putting on an IU uniform. As a collegian, a sign outside his hometown of Heltonville claimed him as the town's own.

Bailey was so popular that Heltonville and neighboring Bedford revolved around him. When a student teacher asked how long her boss had been in Bedford, the veteran teacher said she had moved there when Bailey was in grade school.

"Good grief, they're on Damon Time down here," the aspiring teacher told her friends.

From the day IU coach Bob Knight scouted him in the eighth grade until the day he left IU, Bailey was a major newsmaker. He was the principal reason that more than 40,000 fans turned out to see a high school game. He scored 3,134 points in four years at

Damon Bailey (22) listens to Coach Bobby Knight during Indiana's loss to Kansas in NCAA Southeast Regional action in Charlotte, North Carolina, on Thursday, March 22, 1991. Bailey had 20 points, but Kansas beat Indiana 83–65 to eliminate the Hoosiers from the NCAA Tournament.
(AP Photo/Chuck Burton)

Bedford North Lawrence and was the first to make first-team All-State four times. He led his small-town team to a 99–11 record and a state championship.

When he got to IU he was Big Ten Freshman of the Year and scored 32 points in a game at Ohio State. For four years there were constant rumors that Bailey was going to transfer away from IU, but he persevered. Simply put, Damon was a guy who loved basketball and small-town life. When his friends looked for entertainment in Bloomington they often found that Bailey had gone home to Heltonville instead. He admitted that was his favorite place.

Fame first touched Bailey in the eighth grade when author John Feinstein accompanied Knight and other IU coaches to scout

Bailey's junior high team. Knight proclaimed him better than any guard IU had at the time and Feinstein wrote about the trip in his best-selling book, *Season on the Brink*.

Bailey was to be the final ingredient on an IU team that already had Calbert Cheaney, Alan Henderson, Matt Nover, and Greg and Pat Graham. Although a four-year starter and All–Big Ten performer, Bailey was constantly under Knight's microscope.

Knight addressed Bailey's career as it wound down. "Was he a combination of Jack Armstrong, Superman, King Kong, Magic Johnson, Larry Bird? Was he a little of all those things, or was he an 18-year-old who wanted to come to Indiana and play basketball and play for a coach who wanted him to be all those things, I guess, all the time?"

Knight said Bailey could play every position, which he sometimes did. "Maybe nobody who ever played in the Big Ten was in first place as much as Damon Bailey was," the coach continued.

Damon was the 44th overall pick by the Indiana Pacers in the 1994 NBA Draft. He was cut early in his second season after one year on the team's injured list. He continued his career in the Continental Basketball Association before starting a series of basketball camps for children. He coached his high school team for a short time and established ownership in Hawkins Bailey Warehouse in Bedford.

31 Archie Dees Walked Among Giants

The 1950s marked a golden era for college basketball, a period that produced Wilt Chamberlain, Bill Russell, Oscar Robertson, Elgin Baylor, and Jerry West. The 1959 Newspaper Enterprise

Association's All-America team included Chamberlain, Robertson, Baylor, and Guy Rodgers.

The fifth member of that team was Archie Dees of Indiana.

Time has left shadows across the accomplishment of Dees, a 6'8" center who was the Big Ten's leading scorer in 1957 and '58. Although freshmen couldn't play in those days, Dees is still the No. 14 scorer in IU history despite playing only 68 games. The leading scorer, Calbert Cheaney, played in 132 games.

Dees, who preceded Walt Bellamy and followed Don Schlundt as Indiana's center, had 56 double-doubles in his three-year career. A two-time All-American, Dees averaged 25 points as Indiana tied for the 1957 Big Ten championship, then he increased that to 25.5 as the Hurryin' Hoosiers captured the '58 title outright. Indiana lost six of its first seven games in 1958 but went 10–4 in the conference to make the NCAA Tournament.

Because the varsity didn't practice against the freshmen, Dees and Schlundt played against each other only once—in the popular Varsity-Freshmen game before the season. Dees said the freshmen were winning when most of them were called to the bench. Other freshmen included a pair of talented Chicagoans, Charlie Brown and Paxton "Sugar" Lumpkin. Neither finished their careers at IU, but Brown played at Seattle with Baylor as a teammate.

"Bellamy was a freshman when I was a senior, and he was a little awkward," Dees said. "He damn near killed me in the Freshman-Varsity game when I made the mistake of giving him a fake underneath the basket. He was really raw, but he got a lot better."

Dees' family moved to Grayville, Illinois, when he was in the eighth grade. Originally from Mississippi, the Dees family moved to Mt. Carmel where Archie had two great seasons.

His high school coach was Roy Gatewood, a former player at Illinois, and Illini coach Harry Combs assumed Archie would enroll at Champaign.

"I never considered going to Illinois. Harry Combs was the coach, and they took me in this room and more or less said, 'You're from Illinois, and you ought to come to Illinois.' Well, hell, I wasn't from Illinois. I was from Mississippi. That turned me off," Dees said.

Dees first decided to go to Northwestern but changed his mind partly because many Indiana games were telecast and the snowy black-and-white signal reached Mt. Carmel along the Indiana border. Fans there got on the IU bandwagon.

"I fit right in with IU's fast-breaking style, although at the time I didn't know that. I didn't dream that I would want to be on a fast-breaking team, but I could run. I played against a lot of guys who were bigger and stronger than me, but they couldn't run like I could. Guys would say 'slow down' but there wasn't any slowing down with that team."

Dees became the second selection in the 1958 NBA Draft, going to the Cincinnati Royals and finishing a four-year career with the St. Louis Hawks. Archie doesn't feel the NBA was a good fit for him because he was smaller than many centers and didn't consider himself a great ball-handler as a forward.

"One of the really lousy things of my life was the NBA," said Dees, who played four years in the league but has received no pension and is bitter about it. "They had a five-year qualification for a pension, and I played four years. I got hurt right at the end of my fourth year. I had surgery and tried to go back but just couldn't play."

Dees remained in Bloomington as an insurance representative following his playing days.

Some of Dees' better games came against Wilt Chamberlain, who he described as "real arrogant."

"Walter Dukes was our center, and Walter fouled out of about every game he played. If he didn't foul out he killed people and Wilt hated Dukes," Dees said. "Walter would beat him up, and when I came in the game Wilt knew as long as I scored I'd stay in the game. I had probably my best games against him because I'd just go out in the corner and shoot it. As long as I didn't embarrass him, he didn't bother me."

Dees said the 7'1" Wilt was capable of leaping up and catching Archie's jump shot as it was being launched.

Dees said he and Chamberlain were waiting for a train once when Archie deeply alienated Wilt with a remark. "I said, 'You know, Wilt, I'm not having too much success in the NBA. I'm really a center trying to play forward, and I can't handle the ball well enough, but if I could get me a contract to shoot your free throws...,' Boy, he just blew up. He didn't like that stuff at all because he didn't want anybody telling him he couldn't make free throws, but he couldn't."

32 Bob and Bob Make a Great Team

The friendship between Bob Knight and Bob Hammel has exceeded 40 years in duration. It's an association that at first appears to make no sense but upon further thought makes all the sense in the world. Knight reportedly dislikes sportswriters, and the now-retired Hammel covered Indiana basketball for the *Daily Herald-Telephone* (later renamed *The Herald-Times*) for most of Knight's career in Bloomington.

Knight was a top-notch athlete, a fact that his senior years cannot disguise. Hammel, bald and bespectacled, is of a similar age and girth, but whatever athleticism he enjoyed as a youth has dissipated with time. Somehow during the mid-1970s, the men formed a bond that is among the strongest in sports.

Much of Hammel's travel while covering the Hoosiers was done on the Indiana team bus or plane, and he usually used the same hotels as the players. He ate many of his meals with Knight, usually was available as a companion when Knight wanted to take a walk on game days, and often had lengthy postgame visits with the coach before starting to write his game story.

Although it might seem strange that Knight gravitated to Hammel as a best friend, he enjoyed somewhat similar relationships with other writers. Billy Reed and Dave Kindred of *The Courier-Journal*, Sid Hartman of *The Star-Tribune* in Minneapolis, and a few others forged friendships with the coach, but most were tenuous.

Reed supported Knight for many years, usually choosing to write about the coach's good points and letting others write about the controversies. Kindred gained Knight's confidence in the early years but didn't directly cover Indiana thereafter. Hartman was so pro-Knight that when Mike Davis succeeded the deposed coach at IU, Hartman alienated other writers by repeatedly talking about what a horrible job Davis was doing.

One thing Knight and Hammel have in common is intelligence. Both men have IQ's that resemble good bowling scores, and both are thorough in preparing for their jobs. Hammel is a walking encyclopedia when it comes to sports, as well as many other subjects. Ask him who hit the winning free throws against Michigan 25 years ago, and he'll answer immediately. He's wrong so infrequently that you're almost wasting your time to check his answer.

A fellow writer once told Bob he hadn't made a mistake since 1978, and that was when he thought he had made one but really hadn't.

A product of the pre-Internet days, Hammel seemingly never threw away a note or failed to know where a certain fact was stored. One of his successors at *The Herald-Times* found Hammel's footprints all over the building. It's not surprising that Knight always referred to *The H-T* as "Hammel's paper."

During a remodeling phase at the paper, the new sports editor decided to clean out a five-drawer file cabinet that included hundreds of Bob's leftover notes and pamphlets. There were handwritten notes from 25 years earlier that surely had no importance anymore. In the building's basement, in a chilly room mostly used for storing old newspapers, the retired Hammel had set up a desk and a room-length wall of books and notes that he couldn't bring himself to throw away.

On another occasion a *Herald-Times* reporter, tired of seeing file cabinets full of old notes and programs that seemingly had no current purpose, started heaving armloads of Hammel's old files into the recycling bin. That night sports editor John Harrell decided the master's resources were sacred and reloaded all of them back into the file cabinet.

In a way, Hammel was like a prize fighter who had retired and then decided he still wanted to hang around. After quitting as sports editor he wrote two books, one of them about Knight, and then he agreed to be managing editor of the Sunday newspaper. That appointment proved to be complex and highly controversial among other reporters.

When Hammel retired as sports editor, Knight had a ceremony after the final game of the 1996 season during which he presented the writer with keys to a new car. Actually, the keys already belonged to Hammel because the coach had asked Hammel to pick out a car before Knight purchased it for him. The vehicle turned out to be a new Ford Taurus that Hammel drove for almost a decade.

Why was this complex? Because there probably isn't another situation in the country where a newspaper would allow a reporter to accept a new car from a source. As with many publications, *The H-T* has a written code of standards that, among other things, preclude a reporter from becoming too close to his sources. Other writers were told they could be removed from their beats if such a thing occurred.

The Herald-Times wasn't about to discharge Bob Hammel, who had been the paper's most visible asset for more than three decades. Besides, when he accepted the car he didn't realize he would be returning to the staff. Yet, not until 2006 did Hammel's byline disappear from *The H-T.*

Hammel was still managing editor of *HoosierTimes* (the name of the Sunday edition at the time) when Knight was fired on September 10, 2000. One would have thought *The Herald-Times* would have access to information sought by the rest of the nation's media, but instead of joining the reporting effort, Hammel caught a flight to Maine to meet the coach and offer sympathy. It was 48 hours later before Hammel wrote anything about the firing.

Gary McCann succeeded Hammel as sports editor in 1996. McCann was a North Carolina native with objective ideas and reporting talent who enjoyed a decent relationship with the coach. Still, Knight wanted McCann to fall in line and become a company man—two years later, for a variety of reasons, McCann moved back to the East Coast.

Shortly after McCann arrived in Bloomington, Knight addressed a large gathering of fans and discussed media coverage, especially as it pertained to *The H-T's* new man. "I think as soon as I get him trained he'll be just fine," the coach said.

Hammel's writing bordered on brilliance unless readers were opposed to 87-word sentences and a generally favorable outlook toward Knight and the Hoosiers. Bob was a prolific writer, usually turning out a lengthy game story, column, and at least two side stories on Indiana football games. Sometimes his basketball pieces were almost as long, partly because of a phantom deadline. While other IU beat writers were required to submit their work between 10:15 PM and midnight, Hammel sometimes didn't start writing until 10:30, following his exclusive visit with Knight. Even after switching to a morning edition, *The Herald-Times'* deadline for Hammel's work was "whenever he got it in."

In Hammel's defense, there was minimum negative reporting to do about Indiana during most of Knight's tenure. There was a brief and minor probe by the NCAA after Indiana coaches made an unauthorized trip to Louisville to see Lawrence Funderburke, a top recruit. However, cheating wasn't going to happen on Knight's watch, so most negative reporting about the school involved the coach himself.

Hammel didn't ignore Knight's frequent transgressions, but he often sugar-coated them. When the IU awards banquet was canceled in 1992, it became a brief mention in the last paragraph of a column. It was the lead sports story in *The Courier-Journal* and *The Indianapolis Star*. When Knight had run-ins with a Puerto Rican policeman and a Louisiana State fan, the stories were reported but not glamorized.

Most Indiana fans didn't have a massive interest in reading about Knight's coaching cronies such as Pete Newell and Hank Iba, but Hammel wrote frequent columns about them.

Hammel also went along with a ploy orchestrated by his friend during the 1993 season. Knight reported on his television show that the Hoosiers were about to recruit a tall Yugoslavian named Ivan Renko. There was no Renko, nor even a country called Yugoslavia at that time, and Indiana had no scholarships available. Quickly deciphering that Knight wasn't serious, other reporters called his bluff on the fraud.

Knight was attempting to learn the source of recruiting leaks about his program, and he thought the Renko story would pin down the violator. Obviously aware that there was no Renko, Hammel played along for a couple of days, even reporting an alleged rumor that Renko had been spotted on a U.S. Air flight.

In 1987, Knight's son, Pat, played for Coach Mike Lord at Bloomington North, and Lord was fired after the season. Weeks later word of a conflict reached *The Courier-Journal*, and reporter Pat Forde was sent to investigate.

Accurate or not, the story was that Knight's interference was a major factor in Lord losing his job. The IU coach was reported to have verbally attacked the prep coach after a game. Forde, barely out of college, not only reported the conflict but wrote that nothing about the incident had appeared in the Bloomington paper.

The soft-spoken Hammel was hurt and upset by the story, so much so that he asked one of his reporters to quit calling in high school scores to the Louisville paper. Reportedly, Hammel's reasoning was that he wouldn't report it if any other parent got into it with a high school coach, so why should he with Knight?

At some point in his career, probably after some early differences with the coach, Hammel made a choice. If he wanted to spend his career in Bloomington—and he did very much—he would have to write mostly positive things about the irascible coach and his program. If he had taken a different stance, and thus found himself at odds with Knight, he might have found it easier to move on to another newspaper.

The *H-T* sports editor found many advantages to being Knight's friend. He always knew in advance about Indiana recruits, who were difficult for other reporters to identify. *The Courier-Journal* once checked a report that a Louisville-area recruit was about to commit to Indiana only to have the high school senior say, "I've been told I can't tell anybody until Bob Hammel writes it."

In Knight's later years as coach, news about potential recruits flourished in newspapers and on websites, but there was no recruiting news in *The Herald-Times* until Knight received a verbal commitment. If the Hoosiers were chasing a recruit and he opted for another school, that fact would be ignored, or greatly underplayed, in *The Herald-Times*.

Hammel is well liked by most sportswriters who respect his ability and hard work. His schedule was so prolific that co-workers said he often came to the office by 9:00 AM and didn't leave until 11:00 PM at night. His companionship with Knight certified that he always knew what was going on and wouldn't write inaccurately. In addition, he had frequent access to Knight's feelings, yet he seldom used quotes that weren't obtained with other writers present.

Hammell was revered by most of his readers, although many of them were relieved when *The Herald-Times* later opted to sometimes be critical of the Hoosiers and their coaching.

33 Valentine's Day in Bloomington

Ted Valentine is generally recognized as one of the best college basketball officials in the land. He has worked multiple Final Fours, and while his arrogant manner is frequently cited by his critics, Valentine calls things as he sees them—and usually that's the way things actually happen.

But in Bloomington, Indiana, providing some police protection for the veteran basketball official wouldn't be the worst idea. The most ardent IU fans still blame Valentine for the Hoosiers' loss to Duke in the 1992 Final Four. Even more Indiana followers carry a grudge for Ted's officiating in the 1998 game against Illinois in Bloomington.

Anyone who saw that game will never forget the confrontation between Valentine and IU coach Bob Knight. For more than a decade following that faceoff, Valentine wasn't assigned to work any Indiana games.

It was Senior Night in 1998, but around Bloomington some think the game was played on Valentine's Day. It was a massacre of sorts or more accurately, it was a battle of big egos.

The drama began when Valentine called a technical foul on Knight in the first half. Then a play occurred in which IU's Luke

Recker drove to the basket and went down in a heap without a foul being called.

Illinois' Sergio McClain grabbed the rim and was called for a technical, one of six in the game. Knight left the bench to check on Recker's condition, or more likely to get closer to the officials for a protest. He confronted Valentine under the north basket and was quickly whistled for his second technical, which called for his automatic ejection.

As all Knight followers know, Bobby wasn't about to leave the court until he had some more words for the officials, who also included Ed Hightower and Tom O'Neill. That resulted in a third technical, whereuon Knight departed for IU's locker room, located in the northeast section of Assembly Hall.

He bypassed the primary route in favor of the scenic path, and made a lengthy power walk in the direction of Valentine, who was standing closer to the south end of the floor. As the partisan crowd braced for a bigger confrontation, the coach walked as close to Valentine as possible without hitting him and turned sharply toward another entrance to the locker room.

Valentine later told Jim Arehart of Referee Enterprises Inc. that he saw the coach approaching out of the corner of his eye.

"I made up my mind that if he says something, then it's going to have to be a technical foul," Valentine told Arehart. "He walks to me and he walks as close as he can to me without touching me. He starts walking around me. He's not saying anything, but this whole show is to bring the crowd down on top of me."

Following Indiana's 82–72 loss, Knight said, "I've been coaching 33 years, and that's the greatest travesty I've ever seen in basketball." The Big Ten fined Knight $10,000 for his remarks.

Thirteen years later the Fighting Illini again played at Assembly Hall, and again Valentine was an official. Knight of course, was long gone, and most of the Indiana students apparently had no recollection of past history.

"It wasn't like that happened and suddenly I had a name," Valentine told the *Charleston Gazette*. "I worked Final Fours from 1991 through 1995 and I worked national championship games in '94, '95 and '97, so people already knew who I was."

There were rumors of a longtime feud between Valentine and Knight, which were fueled by a technical against the IU coach against Duke in the 1992 Final Four. IU lost that game 81–78.

34 Hoosier Earned Duke's Respect

Mike Davis was like Rodney Dangerfield. He believed he lacked the respect of many people, and when his Indiana Hoosiers reached the Sweet Sixteen of the 2002 NCAA Tournament, he felt his basketball team faced the same dilemma.

The Thursday night game pitted the underdog Hoosiers against No. 1 Duke in the South Regional in Lexington, Kentucky. IU was the co-champion of the Big Ten and had advanced to the Sweet Sixteen with wins over Utah and North Carolina–Wilmington in Sacramento, California.

However, Duke was a horse of another color, and few gave IU a legitimate shot at beating the Blue Devils. Davis knew that, but an unidentified Duke administrator lit a fire under him at a pregame meeting by asking what time the Dukies should arrive for Saturday's Elite Eight game. The incident occurred Wednesday during an organizational meeting for administrators and coaches to announce the times for press conferences, band locations, and other such incidentals.

Davis didn't like the way the Duke official just assumed his school would beat the Hoosiers, and he told his players about the oversight. They went out and beat the region's top-seeded team 74–73, coming from 17 points behind to do it.

After tournament games it is typical for the winning coach to meet the media first, and Davis felt the Duke official was assuming Devils coach Mike Krzyzewski would fill that time slot.

"I was really upset about that. It was totally disrespectful," Davis said. "He's making all these arrangements. What time do they play on Saturday? I wanted to stop him and say, 'You guys are not going to play on Saturday,' but I didn't have the nerve to say that because we're playing Duke. I'd look really bad saying that and then go out and get beat by 40."

Davis told the Hoosiers, "When someone disrespects you and me like that at a meeting in front of other coaches, we've got to go out and fight."

Indiana's victory set the stage for a win over Kent State that gave the Hoosiers a berth in the Final Four. They eventually fell to Maryland in the Championship Game.

Watching IU win on Kentucky's home floor was even more surreal because Rupp Arena was turned into a sea of red from supporters of the Hoosiers. The crowd was so loud that one sportswriter who had covered Kentucky for an entire season said he had never seen Rupp that loud.

The Hoosiers erupted from a 17-point deficit but still trailed 61–55 with 7:20 to play. They closed within 63–62 when Jared Jeffries converted a missed foul shot by A.J. Moye. Then, in what has become a footnote in IU history, the 6'3" Moye went up and blocked a shot by 6'9" Carlos Boozer.

The IU fans went crazy, chanting Moye's name, but Duke built its lead to 70–64. With just less than two minutes to play, IU's Tom Coverdale tied the game with two free throws. A minute later he hit a baseline jumper that gave Indiana its first lead. After Duke missed at the other end, Moye was fouled and made two shots for a 74–70 IU lead with only 11 seconds remaining.

IU fans were delirious with joy, except that their celebration was premature. Duke All-American Jason Williams made a three-point bucket as Dane Fife fouled. Davis bent over to the floor in disbelief, but Williams missed the free throw that would have tied the game. Still, Boozer nearly converted the missed shot with Jeffries getting a partial block on his attempt.

Jeffries, who would turn professional after the season, had 24 points and 15 rebounds, including nine under his own backboard. IU had trailed by 17 in the first half and by 13 at halftime, at which time the team had 16 turnovers and only 12 baskets.

"They just hung in there the whole time," Krzyzewski said. "We had some opportunities to lengthen the lead at the start of the second half, but we couldn't stop them. They were relentless on the boards, and we just couldn't get that defensive stop to get a bigger lead."

Dick Vitale was among many media members who had predicted a Duke national championship, leading Fife to remark, "Dickie V is finally going to be silent. We can't run, and we can't jump. All we've got is a tremendous will to win."

There were numerous reasons why many felt IU had little chance of beating Duke:

- Guard Tom Coverdale had an ankle injury that limited his production. He was both a solid scorer and one of Indiana's best defenders against quick guards.
- IU's top defender, Fife, stood 5" shorter than Mike Dunleavy, the Duke player he would have to guard.
- Freshman Donald Perry was probably going to have to guard All-American Jason Williams.

None of these concerns proved to be fatal, and when IU had prevailed and the Duke administrator made plans to be home on Saturday, Davis responded to the win by running wildly around the court.

35 Kitchel Nears Perfection Against Illini

Other Indiana players have scored more points in one game than Ted Kitchel did on January 10, 1981, but perhaps no Hoosier has been as hot a shooter as the 6'9" forward was against Illinois.

Two months before IU would win the NCAA championship, Kitchel scored 40 points while making all 18 of his free throws and hitting 11-of-13 from the field. Quick arithmetic tells you that Ted made 29-of-31 attempts at the basket in Indiana's 78–61 victory.

In 1981 Kitchel was a sophomore forward who was fifth on the team in scoring at 9.2 points per game while making 47 percent of his shots on the season. However, in an era when the three-point shot wasn't yet in effect, he was a talented perimeter shooter who blended with Randy Wittman and Isiah Thomas to give the Hoosiers a strong outside threat.

Led by Derek Harper and Craig Tucker, Illinois was among the strongest teams in the Big Ten. Kitchel had been redshirted his first season following back surgery and had averaged only 1.8 points as a redshirt freshman.

"I didn't have any pregame notions that I would be hot," Kitchel said. "First of all, I was not a scorer on that team. I was looking to get Isiah Thomas open because a lot of times we would put Isiah in what we called the triangle. At that time Landon [Turner] was not playing; he was in the doghouse, so it was myself and Ray [Tolbert] inside and Isiah and Randy [Wittman] at the guards who were playing all the time. Then it might be Steve Bouchie, James Thomas—you never knew."

Those who played and coached around Kitchel said he was as tough as they come, especially on defense. "I was a farm kid. I played football through high school—I was a defensive tackle and

Jared Jeffries gestures late in the second half of the NCAA South Regional semifinal game against Duke at Rupp Arena in Lexington, Kentucky, on Thursday, March 21, 2002. Duke players, are from far left, Jason Williams, Daniel Ewing (5), Mike Dunleavy, and Carlos Boozer. Indiana beat Duke 74–73 to advance to the regional championship game. (AP Photo/Al Behrman)

offensive tight end. I was used to getting stepped on and banged up and didn't mind it at all," he said. "When they put me at defensive center, I didn't care if the guy was 7' tall. I just did what I was taught to do."

Kitchel is certain the Fighting Illini weren't programmed to stop him on his hot night. Not with Isiah Thomas playing. "In the first half they were set up to stop Isiah, so a lot of times we would screen him and he'd come off screens. They would jump to him and if you stepped to the basket you'd wind up getting easy buckets. You were going to get the ball; he was going to find you. He was as great a player as I ever played with, and he didn't care who scored as long as we won.

"Early on I was screening and stepping to the basket, and he would find me and I hit some pretty easy shots, either layups or 10' bank shots or things like that. I think I had 16 points at halftime, and we really ran up the score on them. We were up about 20 points in the first half. They were a really talented team, and we were running them out of the gym."

Former IU assistant Jim Crews described Kitchel as a "stubborn personality" who had that "bull-type inside game." Ted was the rare player who could bully his way around inside while retaining a feathery shooting touch.

Crews believes Kitchel's worth to the '81 team was not so much on offense as it was on defense. After 6'10" Landon Turner emerged from a funk to become a starter, the Hoosiers won their final 10 games to win the national championship. With Turner in the lineup Coach Bob Knight put Kitchel on post defense and defended the forwards with Turner and 6'9" Ray Tolbert.

"There were a lot of days in high school where I scored a lot of points and I would know it. Your mind has an idea of what you're doing, but in that game I had no idea because I was so focused on winning. I knew I had had a good day, but I came out of the game with a couple of minutes left and Steve Skoronski, one of the managers, gave me my warm-up and said, 'Do you have any idea how many points you had?'

"I said, 'I don't know, maybe 20 or 22,' and he said, 'You had 40.' I had no idea that I had that many. A lot of guys will tell you that but they know, but I had no idea I had that many points.

"I knew I hadn't missed any free throws, but I didn't know I had hit that many. I think at that time Larry Siegfried had the Big Ten record of 16, and I broke that. For the year I probably averaged eight or 10 points per game, and I scored 40.

"The next game we played Iowa, and we lost at home as I made 14-of-18 free throws. So in two games I shot 36 free throws and was 32-of-36. That's a lot of free throws, especially for a guy that the offense isn't going through much."

36 A Temporary Home for 11 Years

The Harry Gladstein Fieldhouse sits innocently at the corner of Seventeenth Street and Fee Lane in Bloomington and is used for indoor track and field meets and an assortment of other athletic activities. Yet it has a history predating the younger generation of Indiana fans.

Between 1961–71 Gladstein, then known simply as the IU Fieldhouse, was the home of the Hurryin' Hoosiers. George McGinnis played there in his only season with IU. Jimmy Rayl scored 56 points there, winning the game against Minnesota with a mid-court basket. Gladstein was where Indiana beat Ohio State's soon-to-be NCAA champions by 16 points in 1960. It was the site of Walt Bellamy's Big Ten–record 33 rebounds against Michigan in 1961.

On a sadder note, it was where the IU football team was practicing in 1969 when a boycott by African American players threw the program into a lengthy tailspin.

The IU Fieldhouse was constructed to serve as a temporary home pending the building of Assembly Hall next door. Until 1960 IU had played its games in what is now Wildemuth Center, where the Hurryin' Hoosiers fielded teams that won national championships in 1940 and '53.

This was a time when all the Big Ten teams played in fieldhouses, all of which had similar setups for basketball, yet each claimed an atmosphere all their own. The smell of hot dogs and popcorn permeated the air, which by the second half was filled with so much cigarette smoke that it provided a hazy look from the higher seats.

In many cases the portable playing floor was elevated 2' or 3' in order to provide fans with a better view. The benches were below floor level, and coaches had to jump up on the floor to protest officials' calls. The floor was elevated 30" in the Seventh Street field house but only 18" off the ground on Seventeenth. As with others around the conference, IU had removable bleacher seats.

When a hustling player couldn't stop at the end of the court, he would have to leap off the edge of the floor, then clean his feet of the dirt and sawdust that made up the outer floor.

Most of the old buildings remain on their various campus sites, but only Williams Arena in Minnesota remains in use. It still has the elevated floor, but it has more seats than the others.

Wisconsin used its old fieldhouse until the Kohl Center was built in 1998. Wisconsin Fieldhouse had about 10,000 permanent seats, including a balcony that surrounded the floor. The Wisconsin band, one of the most popular in the Big Ten, built a reputation partly because its loud strains were accentuated by the small building. Wisconsin's old building abuts the football stadium, and end-zone seats are built against the fieldhouse wall.

One reporter examined the balcony amid some of the rafters and found a seat where neither the basket nor the scoreboard was visible.

Michigan's Yost Fieldhouse was converted into the school's hockey rink, but the most unique of the old fieldhouses was located at Michigan State. Jenison Fieldhouse was so cramped that the press box hung from a wall behind the bleachers and reporters had to climb to their seats. Box scores and other pertinent material were passed to the press box via a basket that was pulled on a wire from the other side of the gymnasium.

The current Gladstein Fieldhouse had few of these idiosyncrasies, but the floor was an apparent mixture of sawdust and dirt and the locker rooms were off the hallway that now connects Gladstein and Assembly Hall.

The university laid the plans for a new athletic complex by purchasing land north of campus in the late 1940s. At that time all facilities were near the center of campus, including the basketball fieldhouse on Seventh Street. The football stadium was on Tenth Street, and baseball games were at Jordan Field, which became a parking lot that serves the Indiana Memorial Union.

During World War II the Cincinnati Reds held spring training in Bloomington, using Jordan Field.

In 1949 the university drew up plans for a new athletic center north of campus, which would house a new football stadium, a basketball arena, and a fieldhouse. However, by 1957 work still hadn't started on the buildings, and after considerable soul-searching, IU decided to ditch its plans for one contractor to do all three buildings and chose to do each independently. Football, which was the bigger money-maker, took priority over basketball, and Memorial Stadium was opened in 1960.

When the blueprint for the new fieldhouse was finished, it called for a 200' x 400' concrete structure that would be used for indoor football, golf, and baseball practice, plus wrestling and gymnastics. It was meant to be the temporary home for basketball with a seating capacity of 10,300. There would be 20 rows of seats on the north and south sides of the court, 28 rows to the west, and 32 to the east.

The press box, a more-than-adequate 120' long, was built at the top of the north bleachers. Officials first considered moving the playing floor from the older building on Seventh Street but ended up purchasing a new floor for $18,000.

The cost of the new building was $1,684,725.

The first game played there was on December 3, 1960, against Indiana State, and fans saw Bellamy score 20 points in an 80–53 IU victory.

37 Hoosiers Did Their Part in War

World War II played a significant role in Indiana basketball. Even the coach left his position to serve as a lieutenant in the U.S. Navy. Harry Good stepped in to replace Branch McCacken, who became coach before the 1938–39 season and continued through the 1942–43 season.

McCracken not only won the school's first NCAA championship in 1940 but won 87 games while losing only 18 during this five-year term. Good had coached at Indiana Central (now the University of Indianapolis) and posted a 190–52 record from 1928–43. He was available to coach at IU because Indiana Central had discontinued basketball.

Indiana Central had enjoyed a period of domination, including one stretch with 30 straight victories, but Good's first Indiana team won only 7-of-22 games. His second year the Hoosiers went 10–11, but in 1945–46 IU was 18–3 and had a 9–3 conference record.

Good's final team set a school scoring record of 1,183 points.

The war was playing havoc with rosters at every school and the IU players included Ray Brandenburg, who was 4-F in the military draft. Gene Harris, at age 18 the Hoosiers' leading scorer, carried a 1-A label and was called to active duty in early February.

Five days later backup forward Del Russell, who had also been a backup quarterback on Bo McMillin's football team, was called into the service.

Indiana didn't have a letterman beginning the 1943–44 season, and Good started five freshmen in the opening game, a 40–28 victory over Camp Atterbury. On the floor were George Tipton, Paul Shields, Don Earnhart, Bob Rowland, and Sam Young. A day later four IU players, including 1940 Mr. Basketball Ed Schienbein, entered the navy.

The schedule also showed the result of the war as Indiana played Camp Atterbury five times during Good's three seasons. Bunker Hill, a northern Indiana Air Force base, was on the 1944 schedule.

Early in the season IU played DePaul, which had All-American George Mikan at center. Mikan and Indiana's Charley Radcliffe each scored 27.

The year before Good's arrival, Indiana had won its first 16 games and reached a No. 2 ranking nationally during a time when polls were less prestigious. Nonetheless, the Hoosiers played second-fiddle to Illinois' highly touted Whiz Kids who went 12–0 in the conference. Because of wartime travel restrictions, neither Indiana nor Purdue were able to play the Illini in 1943.

When McCracken returned to IU, so did Ward Williams and Ralph Hamilton, two of his all-conference players from three prior seasons. But the most notable returning player may have been Lou Watson, a 6'4" forward from Jeffersonville who had been a gunner's mate and took part in the Normandy invasion on D-Day. Watson became McCracken's assistant and Indiana's head coach from 1966–71.

Hamilton turned in a 31-point game against Iowa before leaving for the military. He played at the Atlanta Army Service Depot and scored nearly 1,000 points in 30 games, including outbursts of 60 against Fort Oglethorpe, 46 against Hunter Field, and 39 against the professional Fort Wayne Zollners.

Williams was a bombardier and flew missions in Corsica during the war.

After World War II, the Hoosier players returned to the hardwood, having a variety of experiences to share. Murray Mendenhall Jr. had played as a navy V–12 guard at Rice Institute. So had Dick Wehr, an Ohioan who was the only out-of-state player on the team. Charley Meyer had played basketball at Camp Grant. Bob Armstrong, who had teamed with Mendenhall to lead Fort Wayne Central to the 1943 Indiana high school championship, had played collegiate at Indiana State as a V–12 trainer. Don Ritter won a freshman numeral at IU before taking part in 28 bombing missions over Guam and Okinawa. With McCracken back in the saddle, Indiana posted a 12–8 record in 1947.

38 Haston Shot Trips No. 1 Spartans

For a change there was a No. 1-ranked team playing in Assembly Hall, and it wasn't Indiana. In fact, IU hadn't carried the top rating since 1993.

On January 7, 2001, the nation's top college team was also its defending champion—Michigan State. Tom Izzo's Spartans had won 23 straight games dating back to an overtime loss in Assembly Hall the previous season. That Indiana team had been coached by Bob Knight and was bailed out by a late bucket by Lynn Washington. This IU team was coached by Mike Davis, and a lot of things had happened in the prior 12 months.

For one thing, 6'9" center Kirk Haston had discovered he was a very good outside shooter. Recuited by Knight, Haston didn't make a three-pointer in his first two seasons on the team. As a junior, he became one of the best three-point shooters in the Big Ten.

On what would be his most spectacular moment, Haston took a pass from Kyle Hornsby and launched a 20' shot from the right wing that gave the Hoosiers a 59–58 victory over the No. 1 Spartans. Haston threw his hands in the air and ran toward a rapidly growing crowd of IU students rushing the court in celebration. Coach Mike Davis fell on his hands and knees for several seconds, pounding his right hand into the floor and rising in time to avoid being mashed by the celebrants.

Davis said he wanted to win the game in regulation, and his thinking was to get Hornsby, a good outside marksman, in position for a lengthy bucket.

"It's a standard play we run for Hornsby," Haston said. "I'm kind of the back-up option. It's Hornsby's choice. He might have hit a two, but I'm glad he made the choice he did."

Haston led all scorers with 27 points, and neither team held more than a six-point lead. There were 14 ties and 16 lead changes in the game.

"I was the goat of that game about 55 seconds before I hit the winning shot because I had missed a block-out on Zach Randolph that allowed him to get a rebound. I went from the doghouse to the penthouse really quick," Haston said.

Haston's outside shooting and deft hook shot increased his chances of playing professionally, and after his junior season he made himself available for the NBA Draft. The Charlotte Hornets selected him in the first round, and his decision to leave Indiana early was questioned not only by IU fans but by Haston himself when the Hoosiers reached the NCAA's championship game the next season.

Haston played two seasons with the Hornets, one in Charlotte and one in New Orleans.

Kirk claims his biggest game as a Hoosier wasn't against Michigan State; rather it was a 108–88 win over George Washington in which he claims to have escaped Knight's doghouse. Most importantly, his mother, Patti, was at that game and about a month later she and her boyfriend, Hollis Hinson, were killed when a tornado swept away her home in Linden, Tennessee, on May 6, 1999.

Patti was so enthused by Kirk's career that she and his grandfather, Hoyt Kirk, shared the costs of a Bloomington apartment where they could stay during visits for IU games, which were six hours away from her home.

39 IU Teams Practice in Style

For years Indiana's Assembly Hall was multi-faceted, a facility shared not only by the men's and women's basketball teams but by visiting squads having their shoot-arounds. Over the years the "home of the Hoosiers" was also home to the circus, concerts, graduations, press conferences, and at least one fight between IU players—the scuffle in which Sherron Wilkerson broke Haris Mujezinovic's nose.

If a varsity athlete wanted to practice his jump shot, he might have to wait until his female peers left the floor. Most Big Ten schools had an extra floor on which to practice, but Indiana didn't even have an anteroom in which to shoot free throws.

About three coaches ago, it was determined that the Hoosiers needed a special place to practice, yet it took until 2010 before one was completed. Now Cook Hall stands as an example of how practice facilities should be done.

Not only does it provide the ultimate floor on which to practice, but it becomes a first-rate recruiting tool, one that expounds on IU's past success and details it from wall to wall in pictures and memories.

Cook Hall, located at the southeast corner of Assembly Hall, is connected with court level of the older building through a pedestrian tunnel lined with graphics that detail the iconic stature of the school's basketball program. The modern architecture of the 67,000-sq. ft. Cook Hall blends with that of its 40-year-old neighbor, yet its contemporary design provides a look to the future. It was built with the consideration that a new Assembly Hall might someday be built in the area.

The practice floor inside bares almost total resemblance to the court in Assembly Hall, with red lines, a map of the state at center court, and the words "Indiana" at the ends of the court.

The project cost $16.5 million, of which $15 million was donated by Bloomington's Gayle Cook and her late husband, Bill. Additional funding came through contributions by the "For the Glory of Old IU" campaign. The dedication was held in April 2010.

The new facility provides not only practice courts but locker rooms, a strength and conditioning area, coaches offices, a sports medical center, study areas, and meeting/video rooms. Cook Hall is also home to the Pfau Shine Legacy Court, a unique museum/exhibit space that chronicles the history of IU basketball with photos and memorabilia that celebrate the school's championships and basketball traditions.

Both the men's and women's teams have use of the hall.

Ground was broken for the facility in 2007, and architectural work was headed up by Populous, assisted by Moody-Nolan of Indianapolis. The name of the structure honors Bill and Gayle Cook, who founded Cook Group in 1963 in a spare bedroom in their Bloomington apartment. They produced medical products such as wire guides, needles, and catheters, and Cook was the first company in the world to develop and manufacture coronary artery stents.

Cook Group is honoring past and present employees with permanent plaques placed in Cook Hall to recognize the thousands of people who compose their workforce.

"For the Glory of Old IU" is a campaign by the athletics department with a goal of raising $80 million in private support for new athletic facilities, endowments, and annual support of athletic scholarships.

Visitors enter Cook Hall through Legacy Court, a hall of interactive displays and tributes, including an illuminated two-story tower highlighting IU's five national championship trophies.

"Cook Hall honors the hard work and determination of those who have made IU great," athletic director Fred Glass said, "and it represents a renewed commitment to elevating both our men's and women's basketball programs into a new era of excellence."

40 Sampson's Hiring Shakes IU

Former Indiana athletic director Rick Greenspan can keep a secret. Every time he hired a new coach he was tight-lipped about it. No leaks to the media. No Deep Throat out there.

Nonetheless, when IU was looking for a new basketball or football coach, Greenspan couldn't prevent reporters from speculating—or from writing about the speculation of others—but the inner circle was small and impenetrable.

As a result, the name of Kelvin Sampson as a likely successor to Mike Davis in 2006 never came up until an announcement was eminent. There was premature conjecture that it might be Marquette's Tom Crean. Mark Few of Gonzaga was always viewed as a possibility. Late in the search the name of John Calipari of Memphis was mentioned.

Suddenly, we had Kelvin Sampson, a 51-year-old coach at Oklahoma who already had a sketchy record with NCAA investigators. He was introduced at one of the strangest press conferences ever seen at Assembly Hall. Sampson walked in alongside Greenspan, who waved his arms toward the assembled students while urging them to cheer louder. Seats normally assigned to reporters were occupied by trustees and other dignitaries.

The Kelvin Sampson era had begun.

Either Indiana didn't know what it was getting, or it looked at Sampson's season average of 23 wins at Oklahoma and no longer cared about anything else. For instance, the Sooners' graduation rate ranked 269th out of 317 Division I schools from 1996–99. During a four-year period, Sampson and his staff made more than 500 impermissible phone calls to potential recruits; Oklahoma was awaiting sanctions from the NCAA.

Sampson came from Native American heritage, a member of the Lumbee tribe, and that reportedly impressed IU president Adam Herbert, an African American. Herbert and other IU dignitaries apparently looked favorably at replacing the school's first African American coach, Davis, with another minority candidate.

But within two months of Sampson taking the job, the NCAA barred him from recruiting off campus and from making phone calls to recruits for one year. Indiana had not run afoul of the NCAA since 1960, and sanctions at that time involved football. Prior coaches Bob Knight and Davis were above board with the rules, and IU was considered an example of how to do things right.

Sampson's hiring brought out the skeptics, such as former IU star Ted Kitchel, who said he "wouldn't hire that guy to coach [my daughter's] fifth-grade team."

For a year Sampson had things going in the right direction, posting a 21–11 record, graduating his three seniors, and speaking often of the Indiana tradition. The basketball team was awarded a community service award by the athletic department.

Meanwhile, Sampson was losing friends quickly in the state of Illinois, where Indianapolis North Central star Eric Gordon had long since committed to play for the Fighting Illini. Sampson raised eyebrows by adding Jeff Meyer, a friend of the Gordon family, to his staff. Sampson also added some players who were academic risks and a couple whose characters were in question.

Gordon didn't reverse his verbal commitment until October, and Illinois coach Bruce Weber was irate that Sampson didn't give him a courtesy call and discuss his own recruitment of Gordon. Weber had built his recruiting class around Gordon and didn't have time to replace him for the upcoming season.

When Gordon made his only appearance at Illinois, both Sampson and Gordon were booed heavily, and students waved a placard reading "Cheater! Cheater!" in Sampson's direction. A pregame handshake between coaches was brisk.

Sampson's biggest problems arrived in October when someone in the IU compliance office came upon records of impermissible three-way phone calls involving recruits, an assistant coach, and a cell phone issued to the head coach. The incident paralleled irregularities at Oklahoma involving Sampson.

Assistant Coach Rob Senderoff was made the fall guy and resigned at the university's request. The university hired a firm to look into the phone allegations. Acting on its own, IU forfeited a basketball scholarship for the 2008–09 season, and Sampson's scheduled $800,000 raise was negated.

Its off-court problems aside, IU fielded its strongest team in several years, going 25–8 including four losses in its last five games. By then Sampson had resigned under pressure, and Dan Dakich was interim coach. Players had already undergone a series of suspensions and rumors of drug use, and team grade-point averages dropped significantly amid reports of skipping class.

Sampson left on February 22 with a $750,000 buyout after agreeing that he would not sue the university. Dan Dakich was named interim coach, although many of the players asked for Ray McCallum. Five players boycotted Dakich's first practice, and when Armond Bassett and Jamarcus Ellis refused Dakich's discipline, they were dismissed from the squad.

Gordon reportedly didn't get involved with the improprieties of some of his teammates, but long before Sampson was forced out, he made his decision to leave Indiana after his freshman year. He had led the Big Ten in scoring at 21.5 points per game and was a first-round pick of the Los Angeles Clippers, who traded him to the New Orleans Hornets in 2012.

By the time the 2008–09 season rolled around, only former walk-on players remained.

41 Frank Cut His Teeth as IU Manager

They make up the majority of people at an Indiana basketball practice. They are dressed alike in red T-shirts and shorts, scurrying about Assembly Hall while retrieving missed shots, operating the

Lawrence Frank was once a manager for the Hoosiers. Here he is in 2009 as the head coach of the New Jersey Nets. (AP Photo/Bill Kostroun)

scoreboard during scrimmages, and doing chores for coaches and players alike.

They are the managers, an ambitious, hard-working crew of students who are so important to the program that all former managers are listed in the IU media guide.

Some of them were former players in high school. Some simply love being around the game, and a number of them aspire to be coaches and want to learn from IU's staff. One man who served as a manager two decades ago went on to become head coach for two NBA teams.

Lawrence Frank, the current coach of the Detroit Pistons, roomed with Indiana players Calbert Cheaney and Chris Reynolds at Indiana. He enrolled at IU bent upon learning as much as possible from Hall of Fame Coach Bob Knight, and Frank is now considered to be one of the finest young basketball minds in the NBA.

"He was always saying he was going to be a coach and we'd kind of laugh it off and say, 'Whatever,'" Cheaney recalled. "There are a lot of guys out there who really haven't played the game and don't know the game, but he was around Coach Knight and the whole IU program, and that's why he's where he is. He's such a great individual and has a great mind for the game of basketball. What sets him apart from a lot of people is he really burns the midnight oil and works hard, looks through a lot of film."

Frank, born in New York City and raised in Teaneck, New Jersey, was an NBA head coach at age 33. He failed to make his high school team but played for a Jewish Community Center team and was a player-coach for a Catholic Youth Organization squad.

He spent four seasons as a manager for the Hoosiers, earning a Bachelor of Science degree in education in 1992. He was awarded a Master of Science degree in education administration from Marquette University.

Frank then served three years as an assistant at Tennessee under Kevin O'Neill after first being an aide to O'Neill at Marquette.

Lawrence then spent three years as an assistant to Brian Hill with the Vancouver Grizzlies. Hill would later be Frank's assistant with the New Jersey Nets, where Lawrence was the head man from 2004–10.

New Jersey won its first 13 games under Frank, which set a record for consecutive victories by a new head coach in all four major professional sports. However, he was fired after the Nets dropped their first 16 games of the season in 2009–10.

Boston Celtics coach Doc Rivers hired Lawrence as an assistant in 2010, and Frank was named head coach of the Pistons in August 2011. The other finalist for the Detroit job was former IU star Mike Woodson, who later in the season was named interim head coach of the New York Knicks.

42 Hoosiers Dominate List of Top Marksmen

Like gunslingers in the Old West, the Big Ten's reputation was built on its marksmen. Arguments about which one was the best will rage as long as nets are hung on rims.

The sharpshooters have been around almost since John Wooden played at Purdue, and as scores have gotten higher, the men who put shots in the basket have established their legacies around the conference. In the vintage days most of the marksmen shot high-arcing two-handed set shots, which were long and extremely beautiful when they fell true.

In 2010 the Big Ten Network selected the top 10 shooters in Big Ten history and, not surprisingly, all of them played in the 1960s or later. Indiana's Steve Alford was No. 2 on the list, and Jimmy Rayl was No. 10. Rick Mount of Purdue was named the best of them all.

IU was well represented on the list with Calbert Cheaney ranked fifth and Jay Edwards sixth. Others on the list were Michigan's Glen Rice (third), Michigan State's Scott Skiles (fourth), Michigan State's Shawn Respert (seventh), Illinois' Eddie Johnson (eighth), and Michigan State's Steve Smith (ninth).

The state of Indiana produced six of the top 10; Mount is from Lebanon, and Skiles is from Plymouth.

Many Indiana fans who recall Rayl twice scoring 56 points in a game would protest that he was rated too low. Rayl averaged 25.3 points per game as a senior and often has been compared favorably with Mount, who had a 61-point game against Iowa. Both players preceded the three-point basket.

Left off the list were such outstanding IU shooters as Steve Green, Mike Woodson, Brian Evans, Scott May, and Ted Kitchel. Others around the Big Ten who were great shooters included Ohio State's Jay Burson and Jon Diebler, who once scored 77 points in a high school game. Penn State had two great marksmen in Pete Lisicky and Joe Crispin. In 2000, Penn State beat Kentucky in Lexington as Crispin scored 31 points and his brother, Jon, added 26.

Older fans will remember Robin Freeman of Ohio State, who averaged 39.5 points per game as a high school senior and 32.9 as a senior at OSU. At 5'11", 160 pounds, he was reportedly the first Buckeye to include the jump shot in his repertoire.

The St. Louis Hawks selected Freeman in the 1956 NBA Draft, but he never played in the league after severing the tips of two fingers while chopping wood.

Another player known for his range was Iowa's Chris Kingsbury in the mid-1990s. He set school records with nine three-pointers in one game and 117 in a season, but he skipped his senior season to turn professional. No NBA team picked him, and Chris only played in lesser leagues.

43 Lou Watson Was Sandwiched Between Legends

Like the coaches before and after him, Lou Watson had a winning record as Indiana basketball coach. However, his 62–60 slate pales alongside the 364 victors of his predecessor, Branch McCracken, and the 662 wins by his successor, Bob Knight.

McCracken served two terms as IU coach, but he retired for good in 1965 he was replaced by his assistant, Watson. Watson held the job until 1971, although assistant Jerry Oliver served as acting coach in 1970 when Watson had surgery to remove a cancerous growth from his back.

Watson was a disciple of McCracken's fast-breaking style, but when Branch retired he basically left the cupboard bare. Future pros Dick and Tom Van Arsdale and Jon McGlocklin were members of McCracken's last team. However, Watson took the remaining players and won the Big Ten in 1967 with a team that included Butch Joyner, Vern Payne, Jack Johnson, Bill DeHeer, Irv Inniger, and Bill Russell.

Still called the Hurryin' Hoosiers, the '67 team earned the nickname Cardiac Kids because of the manner in which they won close games. The team was 18–8 overall but went 10–4 in the Big Ten and tied Michigan State for first place. Advancing to the NCAA Tournament for the first time since 1958, IU lost to Virginia Tech in Evanston, Illinois, and then defeated Tennessee in the consolation game.

Indiana won six straight games in the middle of the Big Ten season before losing at Michigan State. IU also dropped two games to Iowa and one to Illinois before wrapping up a share of the title with victories over Michigan and Purdue.

The previous year IU had struggled through an 8–16 season in which it won only four conference games. In 1968, Watson's team went 10–14 and in '69 it was 9–15. The 1970 season saw Watson sidelined by cancer and Oliver taking over. Oliver coached Indianapolis Washington High to the 1965 state championship with a team led by future Purdue star Billy Keller.

"I was fairly lucky. I was taking over for a guy who won two national championships," Watson said in 2006. "My first year we didn't have one player who had started a Big Ten game, but we won the Big Ten my second year."

Oliver joined Watson's staff in 1969, having coached George McGinnis and Steve Downing at Washington High. Both players enrolled at IU after leading their team to the '69 high school championship but couldn't play until the 1970–71 season when Watson returned to the bench. McGinnis left for the pros the year Knight arrived, while Downing led IU to the Final Four in 1973.

Oliver's one season at the helm saw IU go 7–17.

"McGinnis is by far the most mature kid I ever coached. He was a man. He was by far the best all-around player I ever had," Watson said.

Watson's last team had McGinnis, Downing, and John Ritter, but that team never showed the chemistry needed to be a big winner. Watson felt unrest created by a boycott by some football players in 1969 carried over to the basketball program.

Watson was from Jeffersonville, Indiana, and played for McCracken, making the 1950 All-America team. He was an IU assistant in basketball and baseball before becoming head basketball coach at Huntington High, later to return as McCracken's aide.

Watson died in May 2012 at age 88.

44 A Tale of Cerebral Reversal

On March 15, 1992, the Indiana Hoosiers were knocked out of a Big Ten championship by losing a 61–59 game at Purdue. The fallout may have been unprecedented for an IU team.

The Hoosiers not only lost to their archrivals but probably lost a No. 1 seeding in the upcoming NCAA Tournament. The trip home reportedly was climaxed by Bob Knight's walking to his residence from the Monroe County Airport, which is a couple of miles outside of Bloomington. The upcoming week would be full of unique responses by the head coach.

It started on Monday when Knight canceled the team banquet, a tradition that covered 41 successive years. "I'd like to see banquets reserved for a celebration when a team really achieves something," the coach explained.

The banquet was sponsored by the local Suburban Kiwanis Club and traditionally drew about 1,000 people. It was less than a month away and tickets had been sold, caterers had been hired, and public service announcements had been arranged.

Craig Tenney, the president of the sponsoring organization, wasn't amused and publicly criticized Knight, leading to a press release from the university, backing the coach's decision.

"The basketball program has been reviewing for some time the format for its award banquet. At the same time, the athletic department has been considering a banquet honoring all sports since some of the teams do not participate in such an event," the statement read.

Various IU offices received more than 100 calls complaining of the late cancelation. Also, Knight bypassed his weekly radio appearance on the *Bob Knight Talk Show*, sending assistant coaches instead.

Presumably because of the loss to Purdue, the NCAA Selection Committee made the Hoosiers a No. 2 seed and sent them to play in the West Regional site of Boise, Idaho. It was a blow to IU fans because a plane ticket to Boise ran in the $1,300 range.

If reporters thought Knight's actions in Bloomington were unique, they arrived in Boise to an even weirder scenario. Tournament coaches are bound to hold news conferences before their games, as well as to speak to reporters afterward. Writers ran into a coach who filibustered through his required session without saying anything worthwhile about his team or the upcoming game. Even when Indiana won two games in Boise and two more in Albuquerque, New Mexico, Knight's press conferences were full of non-basketball tales.

Taking the microphone before IU's second-round game against Louisiana State, Knight rambled on about Chinese water torture, guerrilla training, and threats he claimed to have used to evoke better play from the Hoosiers. He claimed a friend was involved, "one of the foremost authorities in the nation on the function of the brain."

"There's a process—and I won't get into all of it—it's too complicated and I'm not sure I understand enough about it—called cerebral reversal."

"Cerebral reversal" became a catch phrase for the next three weeks, a term Knight mentioned frequently in lieu of how IU should stop Shaquille O'Neal or how he hoped to reverse an early season loss to UCLA.

His "best" explanation of cerebral reversal went like this:

"Cerebral reversal is about when an athlete gets into a contest that has a little different tone to it than the last contest he played in, or the majority he has played in. There are portions of his nervous system, which obviously is controlled by portions of the brain, that speed up. His actions, his reactions get him going a little quicker than he normally would go and perhaps, in many cases, get him going too fast. There's a complicated medical term for it, but cerebral reversal reverses that trend."

Eyes wandered skyward, and pencils and pens were unused as the coach rambled on. No one bothered taking notes as the filibuster continued.

"This morning we got our kids up early and had each kid sit with his feet in buckets of ice," Knight continued with a wry grin. "This is a cooling process for the entire body. Then we talked to them about certain things and re-iced them.... Moved to different parts of the body. It was a fascinating thing. I'll have some interest in pursuing this to a greater extent."

Knight's required time at the podium was growing short, but the weirdness continued:

"I forgot to tell you. We put two of our players in chains. We just didn't think they performed as well as they should have last night. I woke them up at 4:00 and put them in chains. We didn't let them use the chains, though, when we got them in the ice buckets."

Writers unaccustomed to covering Indiana mostly chuckled, and some went on to write about the wit, and perhaps the craziness, of Coach Knight. Writers assigned to the IU beat who were expected to write daily stories about basketball were less amused.

45 The Call Could Have Gone Either Way

Steve Downing arrived at Indiana University as the second best player in his recruiting class. George McGinnis was the best, as he had been throughout most of Downing's teenage years.

McGinnis was the No. 1 player on Indianapolis Washington's state championship team, leaving Downing as No. 2. McGinnis

Steve Downing accepts his induction to the Indiana University Athletics Hall of Fame during a ceremony in Bloomington, Indiana, on Friday, November 6, 2009. (AP Photo/AJ Mast)

was the best player on the Indiana All-Star team, of which Downing also was an integral part.

And after his sophomore season at IU, McGinnis signed a contract with the Indiana Pacers and, suddenly, Downing was the man. On the night of December 11, 1971, he showed everyone what a big man he was.

The game was Indiana vs. Kentucky at Freedom Hall in Louisville, a rivalry that stirred emotions up and down the Mason-Dixon Line. In two overtimes the Hoosiers beat the seventh-ranked Wildcats 90–89.

Making the performance even more outstanding was the fact that Downing was battling a knee injury suffered a week earlier. Despite being slowed by the problem, he never left the game.

Downing led the way with 47 points and 25 rebounds. The 47 points remains tied for the fourth-highest total in school history (Jimmy Rayl 56 twice and Mike Woodson 48). Downing's 25 rebounds is tied for seventh on the all-time list and wasn't even Steve's personal best; he grabbed 26 rebounds 10 days earlier against Ball State.

Among the top 17 rebounding games in Indiana history, five of them belong to Downing. Four others belong to McGinnis, who played only one year at Indiana. Among the top 24 rebounding performances, 19 belong to players under Branch McCracken. McCracken's Hurryin' Hoosiers traditionally put up more shots than Bob Knight's Hoosiers, who played more deliberately.

Downing had a banner senior season in 1973, averaging 20.1 points and 10.6 rebounds per game while making 52 percent of his shots and earning the Big Ten's Most Valuable Player award. The Hoosiers had a 22–6 record, coming on late to overcome Minnesota for the Big Ten title and reaching the Final Four before losing to eventual champion UCLA 70–59.

Downing averaged 24 points during the Hoosiers' last eight games of the regular season, including 41 against Illinois. He scored

20 in a season-ending victory over Purdue, one that was sweetened when Northwestern upset Minnesota to assure Indiana of the Big Ten title.

The Hoosiers upset Marquette in the NCAA Tournament at Nashville, Tennessee, behind 29 points by Downing. Then they upended Kentucky 72–65 as Downing scored 23 to send IU to the Final Four in St. Louis against top-rated UCLA.

The team returned to Assembly Hall as the state high school final game was being played and marched across the court with the victory nets during a break in that game.

UCLA's John Wooden had one of his greatest teams, featuring Bill Walton, Keith Wilkes, Greg Lee, and Dave Meyers. Downing outscored Walton 26–14 in the semifinal game that featured a call that could have gone against either of the centers. Walton had four fouls at the time, Downing had three, but the call went against Downing, and the Bruins went on to a 70–59 victory.

The Hoosiers led 18–13 midway through the first half, but after Downing picked up his third foul, the Bruins completed a 29–4 outburst that led to a 20-point lead with 13:14 to play.

Suddenly, Indiana unleashed a 17–0 spurt that started while Walton was on the bench with four fouls. The big redheaded center returned when IU got within 54–47; and with the score 54–51, Walton started to drive for the basket. Downing intercepted him, and a foul was called on the IU center who picked up his fifth foul moments later.

Two days later, Walton put on perhaps the greatest individual show in Final Four history, making 21-of-22 field-goal attempts as the Bruins beat Memphis State 98–85. IU won the consolation game over Providence and finished sixth in the final Associated Press poll.

Downing made the All-Tournament team and was the No. 1 pick of the Boston Celtics in the 1973 NBA Draft. He was a

Celtic when they won the NBA championship the next season. Downing went on to become a longtime administrator at IU and Texas Tech. He is presently the athletic director at Marian College in Indianapolis.

46 Turning Over a New Leaf at IU

Tates Locke and Norm Ellenberger had many things in common. Both were from small Indiana towns, Locke from Batesville and Ellenberger from New Haven. Both had been successful head coaches but had blemished resumes with the NCAA when Bob Knight hired them as assistant coaches with the Hoosiers.

Knight was the standard bearer for running a clean basketball program, which made these hirings mysterious to some people. In any event, both Ellenberger and Locke were major additions to the IU coaching staff, and neither one's time at Indiana was marked by anything outside permissible behavior.

Locke's background with Knight went back to the U.S. Military Academy where Tates was the head coach and the youthful Knight, barely out of Ohio State University, became his assistant. When Locke resigned to take the job at Miami University of Ohio, the 24-year-old Knight became Army's head coach. From Miami Tates advanced to become head coach at Clemson in 1970.

Locke would have success with the Tigers, winning 43-of-58 games on Clemson's home court and taking his team to the school's first Top 20 rating in 1975. Clemson had a 20-win season and was led by center Wayne "Tree" Rollins. Locke later wrote a book called *Caught in the Net*, a self-incriminating description of the methods used to recruit Rollins and other high school standouts.

In retrospect, Locke said he simply became tired of losing. "I didn't cheat because the Jones did or because it made me a big man. I did it because I didn't want to get my brains beat anymore. That's all," Locke said.

Among the methods used by the Clemson coach was establishing a fictitious fraternity for black students, an attempt to help recruit the intercity African American players. The NCAA launched a year-long investigation that led to Clemson spending three years on probation and setting up Locke's dismissal at the school. The investigation concluded that Locke, his staff, and boosters had bought players, changed grades, and purchased cars for players.

He later coached at Jacksonville but was fired from that job and assumed his college coaching days were over. "It would take a college administrator with a lot of guts to touch me," Locke admitted.

However, on the heels of IU's 1987 NCAA championship, Knight brought in his former mentor as an assistant. Still hoping for a college head coaching job, the 52-year-old Locke was hired by Indiana State in 1989.

The movie, *Blue Chips*, was made in the early 1990s and, according to some sources, was based on Locke's career. Knight and several former Hoosiers appeared in the movie.

As with Locke, Ellenberger enjoyed major success as a head coach before running into trouble with the NCAA while coaching New Mexico. In his seven seasons there he wore flamboyant modern clothing, was fiery on the sideline, and enjoyed an almost iconic status with Lobo fans, who knew him mostly as "Stormin' Norman."

Under Ellenberger, who had been a three-sport star at Butler University, New Mexico won Western Athletic Conference titles in 1974 and '78 and became a fixture in the national rankings. Ellenberger established a reputation as an outstanding defensive coach as his teams posted a 134–62 record in Albuquerque.

Then the trap door opened for the UNM coach when the NCAA uncovered evidence of forged academic transcripts and 56 other alleged violations. Stormin' Norman wound up as an assistant to Don Haskins at Texas–El Paso and was there when Knight brought him to Bloomington in 1991. Joining with fellow assistants Dan Dakich and Ron Felling, Ellie helped IU field one of its last great teams in the early 1990s when the Hoosiers had Calbert Cheaney, Greg and Pat Graham, Damon Bailey, and Alan Henderson.

Ellenberger eventually left Indiana to become an assistant coach with the Chicago Bulls.

47 IU's Campus Loved Nationwide

Many a basketball recruit has committed to play at Indiana University and been asked his reasons for choosing IU. In most instances, he will reply that the college campus was one of the things he liked best.

Princeton Review, a group that rates colleges in various categories, agrees. The New York–based company, which has no connection to Princeton University, rated the nation's 50 most beautiful campuses and listed Indiana at No. 15.

Another in-state college, Notre Dame, was No. 16 in the unscientific rankings.

Princeton Review elaborated by writing, "The town of Bloomington, Indiana, is the ultimate college town. A campus filled with 1,200 miles of biking and running trails, this quaint town not only encourages students to embark on a sense of community, it nearly demands it. Students can visit off-campus stores, restaurants, and coffee shops just a few steps from the limestone buildings in which they will live and learn. The Student Union Building on campus is listed on the National Historic Registrar. The Sample Gates welcome students onto the campus. Most of the campus is made of Indiana limestone sourced locally and was built during the Great Depression."

The list of beautiful campuses was headed by Elon University in North Carolina. Second was Kenyon College in Ohio, followed by Suwanee, Pepperdine, Lewis & Clark College, Emory, Loyola Marymount, William & Mary, Dartmouth, Hawaii at Manoa, Harvard, Furman, Mount Holyoke College, Chicago, IU, Notre Dame, Virginia, the U.S. Naval Academy, Stanford, and Washington.

48 *Breaking Away*, an IU Classic

A trip to Bloomington should include visits to sites where the 1979 classic movie, *Breaking Away*, was filmed. The movie describes the coming of age of four teenage Bloomington boys who are looking for their spot in life alongside the more affluent university students who degradingly refer to them as Cutters (a reference to the limestone-cutting companies in the area.)

The boys spend much of their time swimming in an abandoned stone quarry, a longtime Bloomington tradition. Dave Stoller (Dennis Christopher) is a retired stonecutter's son who frustrates his father with his love of the Italian culture. Dave courts a coed (Robyn Douglass) while masquerading as an Italian exchange student. His aspirations to compete against top European cycling teams vanishes when he is bumped off the road by one of the Italians while racing near Bloomington.

Dave finally confesses to his girl that he is from Bloomington and, following some brawling with IU students, joins his friends in fielding a team for the Little 500 bicycle race, a longstanding campus tradition. Wearing T-shirts with "Cutters" across the front, the team wins the race behind Dave's courageous effort. In so doing he earns the respect of his once-dubious father.

The movie was ranked eighth on the List of 100 Most Inspiring Movies compiled by the American Film Institute in 2006. Writer Steve Tesich won the 1980 Academy Award for Best Original Screenplay. Barbara Barrie, who played Dave's mother, was nominated for Best Actress in a Supporting Role. The movie also earned Academy nominations for best director, best original score, and best picture.

Breaking Away won the 1980 Golden Globe award for Best Film (comedy).

Much of the film was shot on the IU campus with glimpses of the Indiana Memorial Union and the university library. A pizza restaurant featured in the film is no longer in business on the east side of the courthouse square. The house used for Dave Stoller's home is on the corner of South Lincoln and East Dodds streets.

The bike race was filmed at the old track on Tenth Street that once circumvented the school's football field. Tesich based the plot on the 1962 Little 500 in which Phi Kappa Psi featured champion rider and Italian enthusiast Dave Blasé. In the 1962 race Blasé rode 139 of the 200 laps and crossed the finish line first, much as Dave Stohler did in the movie. The race was reenacted at the old stadium, which was demolished shortly after the filming.

A Cutters team now competes annually in the Little 500.

49 Sending Shaq Off to the Pros

The task facing the Indiana Hoosiers on March 22, 1992, was monumental. Shaquille O'Neal stood in their path like the Colossus of Rhodes, a 7'1", 295-pound bulkhead who throughout his career at Louisiana State University had proved that size does matter.

Shaq stood in front of the Hoosiers like Goliath in the path of David, and in an astonishing display of fortitude, Indiana's smaller kids took him down without a slingshot.

Not that the future NBA star would go quietly. O'Neal produced 36 points, 12 rebounds, and five blocked shots, but as one observer wrote, "Boy, can the Hoosiers take a punch."

Indiana's 89–79 victory in the second round of the NCAA Tournament in Boise, Idaho, probably reflected one of Bob Knight's best coaching jobs. The Hoosiers' ball movement that night seemingly put every IU shot a few inches from O'Neal's finger tips. When Shaq was drawn away from the basket, Indiana went inside. When he was screened away from a passing lane, the Hoosiers threw the ball where he wasn't. When Shaq scored or rebounded, Knight's kids made certain his LSU teammates didn't.

Shaq scored 27 points in the second half alone. Calbert Cheaney's 30, spaced over 40 minutes, led the Hoosiers.

It would be the final college game for the burly All-American. Eight years earlier the Hoosiers had ousted North Carolina from the tournament in Michael Jordan's last game as a Tar Heel.

Assigned to stop O'Neal were Eric Anderson and Matt Nover, each about 4" shorter and 65 pounds lighter than the LSU star. "He's a tremendous player. So huge," Anderson said. "I couldn't stop him. I was just out there hacking him up. He put on a pretty good show."

Nover set the stage by making three jumpers early in the game that were just out of Shaq's reach. However, the Tigers began hitting outside shots and took a 27–13 lead.

Knight called a timeout and, according to Cheaney, said, "They can't keep shooting like that. Just keep playing."

After the timeout Anderson broke out and scored five straight points, setting up a perfect shooting night in which he scored 12. "Coming in, we felt we could get a lot of open shots on the baseline. Coach Knight told us that," Anderson said. "Their diamond-and-one and triangle-and-two defenses are pretty susceptible there."

"We tried five defenses," LSU coach Dale Brown lamented. "We couldn't cover everything."

Indiana had shot less than 40 percent in its three previous games, which included a tournament opening win over Eastern Illinois and a season-closing loss at Purdue.

Brown and Knight had been involved in a confrontational relationship over the years but both appeared to have resolved those issues after the 1992 game.

When their teams had met in Cincinnati during the 1987 NCAA Tournament, the Tigers built a 66–57 lead with about five minutes left. During a late timeout Knight said he was concerned about whether his team had a chance to pull out a win. "Then," he said after the game, "I looked down the floor and saw Dale Brown. Then I knew we had a chance."

Indiana followed the win over Shaq and LSU with victories over Florida State and UCLA in Albuquerque, New Mexico, before losing to Duke in the Final Four.

The loss at Purdue, which cost Indiana a share of the Big Ten title, sent shock waves all over the state. Knight canceled the annual awards dinner, irritating the sponsoring service club president, and Knight failed to appear on his weekly radio talk show. When he arrived in Boise, he filibustered through the required news conferences by talking about his team camping out by the Snake River and constantly referring to something he called "cerebral reversal."

As for O'Neal, he soon announced that he would bypass his senior year at LSU and enter the NBA Draft. He was that year's first pick, going to the Orlando Magic and playing for six teams during a 19-year-professional career. He earned four NBA championship rings.

About a year after the game against IU, O'Neal appeared in the movie *Blue Chips* and made the winning shot in a mythical game against Indiana for the national championship. Knight and several former Hoosiers were cast in the movie; Nover played one of Shaq's teammates.

50 Have That Seat in the Corner

John Feinstein came to Bloomington in the fall of 1985 as a 29-year-old sportswriter on leave from *The Washington Post.* He left a few months later as a rich man and the envy of countless other reporters who couldn't even get a five-minute interview with Indiana's head coach.

How Feinstein survived a winter in which he was almost as close to Knight as his deodorant probably marked the height of diplomacy for a sportswriter. During the 1985–86 season, the young reporter lived, breathed, and slept Indiana basketball. He sat on the IU bench during games, went to the locker room at halftime, and was present at almost every practice.

During an era when Indiana players were often afraid to be quoted, most of them spoke freely with Feinstein. Much more amazingly, so did Knight. The result was *Season on the Brink*, one of the best-selling sports books of all time. It offered an inside view of Indiana basketball that Knight's closed practices had never granted. It described coach-player conflicts that previously become public only via the rumor mill.

The sporting nation, which previously knew only that Coach was volatile, now had documented incidents of what it was like to play at Indiana. While other writers, especially Bloomington *Herald-Times* sports editor Bob Hammel, had enjoyed close relationships with the coach, they were less likely to describe anything Knight didn't want published.

Only Knight knows how Feinstein gained such confidence, but positive references from Duke coach Mike Krzyzewski and *Washington Post* writer Dave Kindred played a big part. Krzyzewski had played for Knight at West Point, and Kindred had gained the coach's confidence while a columnist for *The Courier-Journal* in Louisville, Kentucky. Fortunately for the reporter, Knight reserved any conflicts with Feinstein until after the season. He claimed he and Feinstein had an agreement that cursing wouldn't be included in the publication. He also said he thought the book was to be about IU basketball and not himself. Personal information was to be avoided, Knight ruled.

After *Season on the Brink* was in print, and after Feinstein had deposited numerous hefty checks, the budding author said there was no agreement about profanity and added that it would be impossible to write such a documentary without the foul language.

After the book came out, the coach and writer didn't speak for months, and when Feinstein made his first return to Bloomington, he wasn't graciously received. The Maryland-based writer was told no press seats remained, and he was assigned to watch the game from a small portable table well up in a corner of Assembly Hall. Feinstein sat there among the fans, signing autographs.

On only one prior occasion had a writer been placed in the same location. *Indianapolis Star* columnist Robin Miller, who had written that he hoped Knight died like a chicken flapping his wings in the middle of the basketball court, was placed among the cheap-seat fans.

Had Feinstein chosen to do the book a year earlier, he could have titled it *A Season Over the Brink* because the 1984–85 season was probably the most frustrating of Knight's career. Besides Bob's fabled throwing of the chair in February of '85, the season saw the Hoosiers lose 11 games in the Big Ten, including seven at Assembly Hall. The year began with Knight taking away the scholarship of forward Mike Giomi and benching regular Winston Morgan. It also featured a loss at Illinois in which the disgruntled coach started center Uwe Blab and four freshmen.

One year after *Brink* was published, the Hoosiers won their fifth NCAA championship.

Season on the Brink was made into a television movie that generally wasn't well received by those familiar with the IU program. It starred Brian Dennehy as Knight and marked the first television movie made by ESPN.

Uniquely, it was filmed in two versions. One containing profanity was telecast on one channel, and another without foul language was shown on another ESPN circuit.

Feinstein launched a noted career as an author with that season in Bloomington. His long list of credits include *A Good Walk Spoiled*, a story about golf, and *Hard Knocks*, an inside look at the professional tennis world. He makes frequent appearances on the Golf Channel and other television networks.

Born in New York, Feinstein's family background was in the arts world. His father was the first executive director of the Kennedy Center and was general manager of the Washington National Opera.

51 Old Hoosier Classic Was Popular

Competition involving Indiana, Purdue, Butler, and Notre Dame had a special attraction for fans in the 1940s and '50s, so some 50 years later the four Indiana schools decided to try it again.

The original Hoosier Classic—not the one in which IU traditionally pounded two patsies annually—began in 1948 and was staged seven more times over the next 11 years. All of the games were played at Butler Fieldhouse—now Hinkle Fieldhouse—on 49th Street in Indianapolis.

The four schools played the two-day event for the last time in 1959, after which Indiana withdrew when Coach Branch McCracken tired of playing every year on Butler's home court. Illinois replaced IU for the 1960 Hoosier Classic, won by Butler, and the event disbanded thereafter.

Because Big Ten members Indiana and Purdue already met during the Big Ten season, they were prohibited from playing each other in the Hoosier Classic. Thus both Big Ten schools would meet Butler and Notre Dame each year, and a champion was crowned only when a single team won both games.

Indiana beat the Fighting Irish but lost to Butler in the inaugural Classic, with identical results the following year. The Hurryin' Hoosiers rebounded to beat both in 1950, '51, and '52, but the Classic wasn't held between the 1953 and '57 seasons. It was revived in 1958 and Purdue, led by Jake Eison and Willie Merriweather, won both games. Indiana lost to Butler and Notre Dame but rebounded to win the Big Ten championship. A year later, IU lost again to both Classic opponents. That Butler team was led by Bobby Plump.

In 1959, Indiana beat Notre Dame by 11 points and beat Butler by five. The latter game featured a 36-point outburst by the Bulldogs' 6'4" center, Ken Pennington, against 6'10" Walt Bellamy.

The name Hoosier Classic was revived in 1983 and was staged as a four-team tournament each year in Indianapolis with IU as the host. The opposition generally was inferior, at least in comparison to Indiana's strong teams of that era, and IU won 39 straight Hoosier Classic games before Butler won 66–64 in 2002 on Joel Cornette's follow-up jam with 3.4 seconds left.

The Classic's renewal was designed to give non-season ticket holders an opportunity to see the Hoosiers, especially in Indianapolis where the events were staged at Market Square Arena. The event also gave Coach Bob Knight an opportunity to schedule games against coaches he admired.

In 1975, Knight had launched another four-team event to be held every December in Assembly Hall. It was called the Indiana Classic and provided a similar level of competition. The Hoosiers didn't lose an Indiana Classic game until Indiana State beat them in 1999. Eight years earlier the Sycamores had received a 50-point shellacking from Indiana.

A revival of the original Hoosier Classic, now named the Crossroads Classic, occurred in December 2011 when Indiana played Notre Dame and Purdue met Butler at Conseco Fieldhouse in Indianapolis. Purdue athletic director Morgan Burke instigated the renewal after quickly getting the blessing of fellow athletic directors Fred Glass of Indiana, Barry Collier of Butler, and Jack Swarbrick of Notre Dame.

Between the original Hoosier Classic and the Crossroads Classic, another doubleheader was held featuring Indiana, Kentucky, Louisville, and Notre Dame.

52 No One Could Tell the Difference

Tom and Dick Van Arsdale are legends in Indiana basketball probably the best twins to ever play basketball in the Hoosier state. From the womb to their desks at a Phoenix real estate firm, they were always side by side.

Not only could you not tell them apart in person, but Tom and Dick were equally identical on the playing floor where they starred from 1963–65 for Branch McCracken's Hurryin' Hoosiers. During their senior season, Dick had 208 rebounds to Tom's 205. The previous season Dick also had three more rebounds than his brother. As juniors, Dick averaged 22.3 points per game to Tom's 21.3; the following season Tom averaged 18.4 points per game to Dick's 17.2

Tom finished his Indiana career with 1,252 points, just 12 more than his brother. Tom also won the rebounding battle by four during their three seasons. Tom made 44.8 percent of his shots to Dick's 44.2 percent.

It was so impossible to differentiate between the two that they shared the state's Mr. Basketball honor in 1961 as well as IU's Most Valuable Player award in 1964–65. For good measure, both were academic All-Americans.

The twins grew up in Greenwood, Indiana, a southern suburb of Indianapolis, but they attended high school at Indianapolis Manual where their mother was employed. Fans may have argued over which one was the better player, but they never reached a conclusion.

"We played one-on-one against each other all the time, and it was almost 50-50," Tom said. "It was always even."

The Van Arsdales' grandfather launched their career by building them a basketball goal while they were in grade school, and some of the fiercest competition in northern Johnson County occurred underneath. If not competing against each other, the boys watched the IU Hurryin' Hoosiers on television and were fascinated by the talent of Oscar Robertson, whose high school exploits were also on TV.

Family members may have been able to tell them apart, but normal fans and even their head coach had less success.

"Branch put different color socks on us at practice. Branch liked to play that up, and it was part of his demeanor. In practice we would wear grey practice shirts and didn't have the numbers that we had in games," Tom said.

Teammate Jon McGlocklin said there were guys in the Vans' fraternity who lived with them for four years and still didn't know who was who. McGlocklin said they'd simply call them "Van."

The state of Indiana had another famous family that predated the Van Arsdales. Terre Haute Gerstmeyer reached the final game of the 1953 state tournment with twins Harley and Arley Andrews starting alongside their uncle, Harold Andrews. Eight years later, the Vans took Manual to the state tournament's final game where they lost to Kokomo.

After graduating from IU, the Van Arsdales faced a unique problem—if they were going to play professionally, they almost certainly would have to play for different teams. If they played for the same team, they would be competing against each other for playing time because both were 6'5" and just more than 200 pounds. Their natural position in the NBA would either be shooting guard or small forward, but there was little chance they would play equally.

Both men were second-round draft choices—Dick by the New York Knicks and Tom by the Detroit Pistons.

"We didn't want to be drafted by the same team because it would be so difficult just to make a team anyway, and we didn't want to be fighting for the same position," Tom said.

Late in their careers the two did play together for the Phoenix Suns after Tom played 2½ seasons in Detroit and also played for the Cincinnati Royals, Kansas City Kings, Philadelphia 76ers, and Atlanta Hawks. Dick left the Knicks to become the Suns' first pick in the 1968 NBA Expansion Draft and is still considered the "original Sun" by Phoenix fans. He scored the first basket for that franchise and twice led the team in scoring.

The pair were partners in a Phoenix real estate company following retirement, and Dick once served as the Suns' general manager. He also had a brief stint as head coach in 1987.

53 Don't Miss Hall of Fame Pictures

A walk into Assembly Hall requires a look upward to study the pictures of past Indiana University athletes who have earned a spot in the IU Athletic Hall of Fame. These pictures are located in both the north and south lobbies.

The university began honoring recipients in 1982 from all Hoosier sports, and each year a group of inductees is honored at an annual banquet.

The most notable and controversial honoree was Bob Knight in 2009. Since his firing in 2000, Knight has not been seen in Assembly Hall, and there was reluctance on the part of many to admit a man who had been outspoken against the university since his dismissal. However, athletic director Fred Glass worked to heal old wounds, and the Hall of Fame coach was among seven welcomed into the group.

Knight chose not to attend, reportedly so he wouldn't detract from other honorees. Included with the man who coached three

NCAA basketball champion teams was former soccer coach Jerry Yeagley who coached six before his retirement in 2003.

Basketball players in the Hall include:

Class of 2011—Clarence Doninger, an IU player in 1957 and athletic director from 1991–2001; **Don Ritter**, basketball letterman in 1947–49; **Ray Tolbert**, IU's starting center from 1978–81 and the Hoosiers' leading rebounder all four years; **Harlan Logan**, won letters in 1924–25 but missed senior year after winning a Rhodes Scholarship. He became editor of *Look* magazine and speaker of the New Hampshire House of Representatives; **Dean Barnart**, won letters from 1909–11; **Bill Menke**, lettered from 1939–41 and played on IU's first NCAA championship team; **Gene Thomas**, won letters in four sports, including basketball in the early 1920s; **Joe Zeller**, won basketball letters from 1930–32.

Class of 2010—Steve Green, leading scorer on top-ranked 1975 team that lost only once.

Class of 2009—Steve Downing, IU's Most Valuable Player on the 1973 IU team that reached the Final Four, first-round draft pick of Boston Celtics; **Bob Knight**, won three NCAA championships and 11 Big Ten championships during 29 years at Indiana. Led U.S. Olympic team to the gold medal in 1984.

Class of 2008—Alan Henderson, started from 1992–95 and made All-Big Ten as a senior. Led IU in rebuilding all four seasons; **Don Luft**, won letter in basketball in 1951 and also won four letters in football and two in baseball. Caught touchdown pass in a 1951 football upset of Ohio State and was later on basketball coaching staff.

Class of 2007—Damon Bailey, four-year starter through 1994 and All-Big Ten as senior; **Ralph Hamilton**, won three basketball letters through 1947 and was team's Most Valuable Player as senior.

Class of 2006—Jon McGlocklin, lettered from 1963–65 and won the Balfour Award as a senior. Played 11 seasons in the NBA.

Class of 2003—Calbert Cheaney, Big Ten's all-time leading scorer with 2,613 points. Won team's MVP four times, and was Big Ten's MVP as a senior, when he was national Player of the Year.

Class of 1998—Tom Bolyard, lettered in 1961, '62 and '63 and averaged 18 points over career. Was All-Big Ten in '63; **Hallie Bryant**, lettered from 1955–57 after starring at Indianapolis Crispus Attucks High. Played 13 years with Harlem Globetrotters.

Class of 1997—Steve Alford, four-year starter and All-American on 1987 NCAA championship team, started for Bob Knight on 1984 gold medal–winning U.S. Olympic team. Currently coach at New Mexico; **Arthur "Cotton" Berndt**, won eight letters in three sports, including two in basketball through 1909. Became mayor of Bloomington in the 1930s.

Class of 1996—Ted Kitchel, forward on three Big Ten championship teams and 1981 NCAA champions. First team All-Big Ten in 1982 and 1983.

Class of 1995—Randy Wittman, won four letters and started for 1981 NCAA champions and played for 1979 National Invitation Tournament champions. Big Ten's MVP in 1983. Played and coached in NBA.

Class of 1993—Isiah Thomas, led IU to 1981 national championship before leaving school early to play professionally. First-team All-American who made NBA first-team all-pro three times.

Class of 1992—Mike Woodson, four-time letterman through 1980 and two-time MVP. Become long-time NBA player and coach.

Class of 1991—Jimmy Rayl, twice scored 56 points in one game, highest output in Indiana history. First-team Big Ten in 1962 and '63.

Class of 1990—Lou Watson, won four letters through 1950, and was team's MVP in 1949 and '50. Named All-American as a senior and was IU's all-time leading scorer when he graduated. Later became assistant to Branch McCracken and head coach from 1966 to 1971, winning Big Ten title in '67.

Class of 1989—Kent Benson, All-America center was Big Ten's MVP in 1977 and was voted best player in the 1976 Final Four, where Indiana became the last team to go undefeated through the regular season and tournament. Played in NBA for 11 years.

Class of 1986—Quinn Buckner, starting guard on 1976 national champions who played on four Big Ten championship teams. All-American in '75 and '76 and starter on gold medal-winning Olympic team. Led football team in interceptions two years, and went on to play and coach in the NBA; **Scott May**, averaged

Hoosiers Run Hot and Cold in Big Ten

Indiana has experienced both hot and cold spells against some of its longtime rivals. For instance, Northwestern lost 56 times in 59 meetings with the Hoosiers between 1971 and 2003. The three IU losses occurred in Evanston, and Northwestern didn't win its first game in Assembly Hall until 2009 when the Wildcats drilled a rebuilding Indiana team 75–53.

However, since 2008 Northwestern has beaten IU six times in eight meetings but still trails in the series 110–48.

Wisconsin also had a long string of disappointments against Indiana, the most obvious being a triple-overtime loss in Madison during IU's championship season of 1987. The Badgers have won the last 10 meetings and still trail 94–65 in the all-time series.

Between 1980 and 1997, Wisconsin dropped 31 straight games to Indiana.

After former Michigan coach Johnny Orr left Ann Arbor to become coach at Iowa State, he was asked the difference between the Big Ten and what was then the Big Eight. Orr reportedly wisecracked, "Northwestern and Wisconsin, and I sure miss 'em."

Since the start of the twenty-first century, Wisconsin has turned around its program to the point where it has won its last 10 meetings with the Hoosiers, along with 16 of its last 19. Indiana hasn't won in Madison since 1998, eight days after Wisconsin opened its new Kohl Center.

Indiana has also been hard pressed to win at Michigan State's Breslin Center. IU has dropped its last 17 games in East Lansing.

23.5 points per game in 1976 when he was named national Player of the Year. Won Big Ten Player of the Year honors last two years at IU. Won gold medal with U.S. Olympic team, and played for three professional teams.

Class of 1985—Bob Dro, starter on 1940 NCAA champions and *Look* magazine All-American. Played professionally in both basketball and baseball. Served IU for 30 years in various capacities; **Dick Van Arsdale**, Co-MVP in 1964 and '65 and academic All-American both seasons. Had successful career in NBA, and made All-Star team three times; **Tom Van Arsdale**, twin brother of Dick with whom he shared MVP honors in 1964 and '65. Was academic All-American as a senior. Played in NBA and was member of All-Star team three times.

Class of 1984—Bill Garrett, first African American player to play regularly in Big Ten. Led IU in scoring and rebounding from 1949–51, and was All-American as senior. Won Indiana high school title as a player (Shelbyville) and coach (Indianapolis Crispus Attucks).

Class of 1983—Ernie Andres, played basketball and baseball from 1937–39, and was basketball All-American. Was head baseball coach from 1949–73, and assistant basketball coach from 1949–58. **Archie Dees**, All-American and two-time Big Ten MVP, averaged 22.7 and 13.4 rebounds from 1956–58.

Class of 1982—Walt Bellamy, All-American in 1960 and 1961 and member of the 1960 gold medal-winning U.S. Olympic team. All-time IU rebounding leader, and his 33 in one game remains Big Ten record; **Everett Dean**, IU's first basketball All-American in 1921, he coached Hoosiers from 1925–38, and in 1942 coached Stanford to NCAA championship; **Vern Huffman**, played football and basketball in mid-1930s and was All-American in both sports; **Bobby Leonard**, All-American guard in 1953 and '54, hit the winning free throw as IU won '53 NCAA championship. Became successful player in NBA and coached in both the

NBA and ABA; **Branch McCracken**, served two terms of duty as IU coach and won NCAA titles in 1940 and '53. Was All-American as player before winning 457 games as coach, capturing four Big Ten crowns; **Don Schlundt**, All-American center who led Big Ten in scoring, free throws, and shooting accuracy.

54 Senior Night Stirs Players' Emotions

Indiana basketball players endure a lot during their four-year careers. They run wind sprints daily and give up late-afternoon naps to be at practice. They work at their skills for hundreds of hours without knowing if they will be rewarded with playing time. They are yelled at by coaches and forced to make up the homework that accumulates during road trips. If they mess up during a game, some television analyst points it out to the world.

What makes up for this?

A full scholarship eases the pain, but there is another benefit; IU players are loved, absolutely taken to the bosom of the Hoosier Nation and doted upon as if they are godlings. And especially after one game in their careers, the players stand there in the spotlight and accept the unbridled love that flows down upon them on Senior Night.

For an Indiana senior, this is his 15 minutes of fame, although some of the speeches are longer than that. This is his chance to speak his piece while 17,000 fans lavish him with applause. Every senior, ranging from the Big Ten scoring champ to the guy who never plays, gets the same opportunity to be loved.

Shy players dread Senior Night more than final exams because they have to speak in public, but some of their peers can't wait to

Forward D.J. White speaks to the fans during Senior Night following a 69–55 win over Minnesota on Wednesday, March 5, 2008. (AP Photo/Darron Cummings)

take the microphone and thank everyone from Mama to Coach to Aunt Alice to those who sell popcorn to their teammates without whom they would be nothing. It sometimes has all the length of the Academy Awards without the revealing dresses or red carpet.

One Senior Night stands out, the one in which Damon Bailey, Todd Leary, and Pat Graham turned the postgame festivities into heartfelt moments. Bailey, a legend anyway, chose the moment to pay tribute to his sister, Courtney, who was battling leukemia.

"The first time I went and talked to her about it, she said she was going to beat it, and she has," Bailey told his fans. Then in an unprecedented move, he called for his sister to come out of the crowd, and he gave her a hug and kiss at center court.

Damon played in 132 games for the Hoosiers, and the state's all-time high school scoring champion failed to score only once. That was against Iowa when he learned shortly before the game that he was not a match to provide bone marrow for Courtney.

"She's an inspiration to me," Damon told the fans. "When I go home she's probably going to beat the crap out of me [for bringing her onto the court], but it was a way to let her know how I really felt about it. It was a way to acknowledge the love that I have for her."

If Bailey had chosen to give Senior Night a medical theme, then teammate Leary chose to add another chapter. First wise-cracking for the crowd and then becoming emotional as he told of another serious situation, Leary related his relationship with an Indianapolis boy who was hospitalized by leukemia. The young man was a newfound friend of Leary's who said he had tried to bolster the young man's spirit over the previous two years.

The next man at the microphone was Graham, whose five-year career at IU had been marked by injuries to his foot and back. Graham's healing was slowed because of his diabetes, and he talked to the fans about that ailment.

"I've been that way since I was 11. Occasionally children will find out that I'm diabetic. I've received a lot of mail from kids or from parents wanting me to write back to kids. It's not a really big deal to a lot of people, but I do appreciate those letters," Graham said.

Graham added that he tried to encourage youngsters with diabetes or other ailments. "Don't ever let anyone tell you you can't do something. I'm living proof of that," he said.

The 1992 Senior Night provided drama of a different kind. Eric Anderson and Jamal Meeks publicly thanked Bloomington businesses and some Purdue fans, who were watching on television, began calling news agencies to see if Anderson was unknowingly disclosing acts prohibited by the NCAA.

Eric's list of thank-yous included one to Newt's Marathon in Bloomington for taking care of his car and to Crosstown Barber Shop for cutting his hair. Meeks also thanked Marathon manager Newt Chitwood as well as doctors' wives for having him out to dinner.

Both Bloomington businesses mentioned said they charged athletes the same rates that other customers received, and David Berst, executive director for enforcement of the NCAA, said he found no problem as long as the players paid for these services and the dinner visits were infrequent.

55 Bracey Came with High Acclaim

Bracey Wright always seemed to be the redheaded stepchild of Indiana University basketball. His impending arrival was overplayed by his coach, Mike Davis, who labeled the youngster as a bit of a savior. His first three college games saw him named the Most Valuable Player in the Maui Invitational.

Unfortunately, things went downhill from there.

Wright's arrival in Bloomington was trumpeted so highly that he might as well have ridden into town on a donkey surrounded by palm branches. Davis, who had coached the Hoosiers to the title game of the 2002 NCAA Tournament, believed Wright and classmate Marshall Strickland would be the building blocks to future IU greatness. While both had credible careers, the Indiana program

Bracey Wright (4) puts up a shot against Wisconsin's Clayton Hanson during the second half in Bloomington, Indiana, on Saturday, January 8, 2005. Wright had 30 points as Indiana defeated Wisconsin 74–61.
(AP Photo/Darron Cummings)

failed to reach Davis' high expectations, and Wright's popularity probably suffered because he was seen as the coach's pet.

A 6'3" guard from The Colony, Texas, Wright averaged 16 points as a freshman and scored 21 points against Virginia as the Hoosiers captured the Maui Invitational at the start of his career. He averaged 19 points over his first seven games, all victories, and enjoyed a 31-point outburst against Vanderbilt. The Hoosiers won their first eight, including a win over defending national champion Maryland, and went on to a 21–13 record.

Wright scored in double figures in his first 14 college games but was perceived as a bit of a gunner by many IU fans. He went 2-of-11 from the field against Maryland and 3-of-10 against Wisconsin. Bracey's skills included a burst along the baseline for baskets, but in time he began relying more on outside jumpers, some from well beyond the three-point line. His big games—such as a 31-point, 11-of-18 shooting outburst against Ball State—seemed to be overshadowed by his lesser performances, and fans who didn't like Davis linked him with Wright.

Wright's problems were complicated by a back injury that reduced his vast athleticism on the court and by teammates who sometimes were caught up watching the Bracey Wright Show. Frequently, as the shot clock wound down with no teammates finding open shots, it was left for Wright to fire up a 22' prayer.

Bracey hit a lot of those attempts, but he was a streak shooter and his critics tended to forget the hot streaks.

Wright committed to Indiana with expectations of being a teammate of future NBA players. Jared Jeffries was an All-American the year before Wright enrolled but turned professional after the 2002 season. For a long time IU expected to land Sean May, Jared's former teammate at Bloomington North, but he decided to attend North Carolina.

Both Jeffries and May had success in the NCAA Tournament and in the professional ranks.

Wright was often the key man in a lineup that included 6'11" George Leach, who never arrived as a prolific college scorer, and 6'3" A.J. Moye, who was undersized as a Big Ten forward. Wright had been a high school teammate of Deron Williams, who played against him at Illinois and went on to become an All-Star in the NBA, while Bracey never reached such professional heights.

Indiana went 14–15 in Wright's sophomore season, the Hoosiers' first losing season since 1970 and the first IU team to miss the NCAA Tournament since 1985. IU went only 15–14 his junior year and lost in the NIT's first round.

Wright decided to forego his senior season and try his luck as a professional. He said goodbye to IU fans by taking out an advertisement in the Bloomington *Herald-Times*. It read:

"Thank you Indiana! I'd like to thank Coach Mike Davis, the entire Indiana University family, and most especially you, the fans, who make Hoosiers basketball the best in the country. I look forward to joining you as we cheer on the 2005–06 Hoosiers to a Big Ten championship. Thank you!"

Wright finished his college career with 1,498 points, which ranks at No. 15 on the school's scoring list, and he averaged 17.6 points per game. Those who rank on down the list in points include such stars as Walt Bellamy, Jimmy Rayl, Andrae Patterson, and the Van Arsdale twins, Dick and Tom. Wright's 186 three-pointers are the fourth most in IU history.

Wright was selected in the second round of the 2005 NBA Draft by the Minnesota Timberwolves who assigned Wright to their developmental league team. He has since played for several European teams and was named second-team All-Europe in 2011. Wright, his wife, and son live in Honolulu, Hawaii.

56 Bird Was in the Hand, but Others Got Away

The list of Indiana lettermen in the IU Media Guide contains some of the most prominent names in the history of the sport. But had the chips fallen in a different direction it might have included the names of Oscar Robertson, Larry Bird, and even Wilt Chamberlain.

Bird's brief time on the IU campus has been well documented, how he got homesick early in his freshman year and went back to French Lick to work on a garbage truck before enrolling the next year at Indiana State, and eventually becoming a Hall of Fame player with the Boston Celtics.

Perhaps nothing could have been done to entice the young Bird to remain in Bloomington, but if he had stayed, one can only surmise how good the 1975 and '76 teams would have been. As it was, the Hoosiers won 63-of-64 games, and no team has been better during the past 37 years.

Bob Knight would have had an interesting if welcome problem in 1975 if he had been forced to pick two starters from among Steve Green, Scott May, and Bird. Green would have been a senior, and simple protocol would have left him in the lineup. May became the national Player of the Year in '76, so one wonders if Bird would have been the odd man out.

There is a bigger mystery surrounding IU's recruitment of Robertson, who led Indianapolis Crispus Attucks to two state championships in the mid-1950s. Oscar eventually went to Cincinnati and is among those discussed in conversations about the best players of all time.

According to Robertson's autobiography, Oscar was leaning toward attending IU. But as he wrote, "I wanted to be a Hoosier. I grew up in Indiana. I was Mr. Basketball in Indiana. Coach McCracken didn't want anything to do with me. I went to Cincinnati, and the rest is history."

Crispus Attucks won three state championships in a five-year period and was runner-up on another occasion. In 1955, Attucks beat Gary Roosevelt for the title in a battle of two African American schools. Yet, despite having one of the nation's top programs at the time, IU didn't get a single player from that game.

Jake Eison and Willie Meriweather starred at Purdue. Dick Barnett went to Tennessee State and became an NBA superstar. Bill Scott starred at Butler, and although Indiana obviously wanted Robertson, he chose the Bearcats.

Crispus Attucks won 179-of-199 games between 1950 and '57, but only Hallie Bryant from that team played for the Hurryin' Hoosiers.

As with Bird, Robertson would have provided a gigantic boost to a great team that already had Walt Bellamy and in 1960 may have been the best team not to make the NCAA Tournament.

Another seemingly logical recruit who went out of state was Clyde Lovellette of Terre Haute Garfield. The 6'9" Lovellette chose Kansas and became national Player of the Year in 1952 when he averaged 28.6 points per game.

Chamberlain reportedly had Indiana on his short list but spurned the Hoosiers for Kansas. In more recent years, Indiana saw in-state talent go elsewhere. Players who might have helped the team win more national titles included Eric Montross, Sean May, Greg Oden, and Mike Conley.

57 Knight's Whip Snaps Back at Him

Bob Knight was out west in March 1992, so he decided to become a cowboy.

Innocently enough, at least for anyone other than Bob, he displayed a bull whip at a press conference before the Hoosiers played Florida State in the West Regional in Albuquerque, New Mexico. It was meant to be a joke, but it was taken in another light by some people.

You could say that Knight whipped up another controversy.

Knight joked about using the whip as an incentive to make Calbert Cheaney play better. Knight is Caucasian, Cheaney is African American, and African American groups saw nothing funny about a white man whipping a black man. The Civil War era connection was fueled by a newspaper picture showing Knight and assistant Norm Ellenberger playfully whipping Cheaney.

Knight's Hoosiers were en route to the Final Four, and during press conferences the previous week in Boise, Idaho, the coach also had gone off on weird subjects, including his team camping outside the city. In Albuquerque he gave descriptions of dripping blood and the effectiveness of a whip after a cold shower.

Most of the IU beat reporters didn't make a big deal of the whip, most of them believing that Knight was no racist. In other elements the coach took a lot of heat.

Derrick Martin, a senior on the UCLA team that IU would defeat during the upcoming weekend, remarked, "If that incident had happened in L.A., probably there would have been riots by now."

Martin expounded on the remark by saying, "I don't know if that was the right thing to do in today's society. I think maybe he could have been more discreet with it, even though it was intended as fun and games. I think that type of thing really doesn't sit well with a lot of people."

UCLA's Gerald Madkins added, "Fear is what comes to my mind when I see a whip. Not motivation."

Cheaney laughed it off, saying white players have also felt the whip. During the game, Cheaney took a towel and mockingly whipped his coach across the back.

58 Hall of Champions Honors All Sports

The end zones at Memorial Stadium sat partly empty for almost 40 years except for a few thousand bleacher seats that really weren't needed. There was ample seating in the sideline seats except for the Ohio State game or maybe when Purdue came in with a good team.

The end zone seats were sometimes available at bargain rates, but that really didn't work because there were no concession or restroom facilities there. Often the grassy slopes at each end of the field provided sliding facilities for youngsters.

So when university officials announced they were filling in the north end zone with more seats, the immediate reaction was to ask why.

No one asks anymore because the creation built at the north end of the stadium represents what has already become one of the major campus landmarks. The four-story limestone edifice blends perfectly with the rest of the 52-year-old stadium. The bottom floor has an ultra-modern weight room far exceeding what Indiana athletes previously used, and above it are a series of offices,

Buckley Was Coach of BSU Cardinals

Indiana assistant coach Tim Buckley spent six seasons as head coach at Ball State University. The Cardinals won the Mid-American Conference's West Division title in 2002 and made the Elite Eight in the NIT. The same season saw Ball State beat No. 3 Kansas and No. 4 UCLA in the Maui Invitational.

Buckley was an assistant under Tom Crean at Marquette University, where he served two terms on the staff. He was also on the University of Iowa staff under Steve Alford and was on the Wisconsin staff in the mid-1990s.

Buckley played two seasons at Wabaunsee (Illinois) Community College before completing his eligibility at Bemidji State.

including a large one assigned to head coach Kevin Wilson that looks out onto the field.

While the stadium seating is about the same as before the construction, the north end zone was a major step in a lengthy plan to upgrade the school's athletic facilities. The 138,000-sq. ft. facility was designed by RATIO Architects of Indianapolis, assisted by another Indianapolis firm, Moody-Nolan.

The rooms and hallways of the north end zone features pictures and memorabilia of various IU sports and provides the most modern of offices, training rooms, meeting rooms, and areas of relaxation. It also includes a team auditorium and underground walkway to the practice fields.

Ground was broken in June 2007 and completed in August 2009.

The showpiece of the facility is the Henke Hall of Champions, a large meeting and dining area that opens up to the third and fourth floors. The Hall of Champions is an entertainment area that will eventually add more permanent museum displays celebrating great achievements by all 24 IU athletic teams.

The Hall is named for Indiana alumnus Steve Henke of Carmel, Indiana.

59 IU History Lies in the Weeds

Indiana University owns and operates its own golf course, an 18-hole championship course on the east edge of the campus. The course, which is open for public play, was built in 1957 and also includes a nine-hole par-3 layout and a driving range.

Yet, the most famous item at the IU course has nothing to do with golf. In fact, a golfer could experience 18 holes there and not even notice a link to the school's famous basketball program. The basket standards that held the goals at Assembly Hall during Bob Knight's 29 years as coach go almost unnoticed in a weeded area left of the first green.

The two metal standards were once a bright red and white and marked the color scheme of the Hoosiers' basketball home. Now the red is faded, the paint having rusted while peeling from a decade of Central Indiana winters. The Plexiglas backboards are intact, although also scuffed and weathered, but the rims and shot clocks have been removed. The standards no longer stand proudly 10' in the air but are laid flat near trees that separate the first green from a maintenance building in the woods.

The basket standards were unlike any others in the nation during Knight's tenure. Long after most schools had switched to a fold-away type standard, Knight continued to stick with the wider, less-mobile units that often restricted the view of fans seated at the end of the court. The goals mounted on them provided the targets for some of the nation's greatest players, and when a fan tuned in on television, he immediately recognized the standards as being those in Assembly Hall.

The basket standards were so heavy they couldn't be wheeled around like the more modern ones, and some IU administrators thought they were unsafe. It was mentioned to Knight that perhaps they should be switched but not until Mike Davis was named coach in September 2000 were they changed. It wasn't Davis' idea as the decision was made by school officials.

The golf course grounds also include the former scoreboards, including the one that hung above center court. The giant scoreboard now hanging above the center circle has many bells and whistles not featured earlier, including player scoring totals, advertisements, and JumboTron replays.

It would have seemed logical for the university to auction off the basketball relics, assuming many wealthy fans would love to have the original Assembly Hall goals along their driveway. Associate athletic director Chuck Crabb says that remains a possibility.

"We've talked about it, but we've just never moved forward on it," Crabb said. "There has been talk of them being in online auctions, but there's nothing active on them right now. They're just being held."

The golf course itself was cut from heavily wooded land and demands straight shots down narrow fairways. It is a winter favorite of cross-country skiers and features many deer wandering across the fairways to more secluded spots in the trees.

The IU golf course is where Ohio State's Jack Nicklaus won the Big Ten championship in 1961. It was also the home course of 2003 PGA Championship winner Shaun Micheel, a former Hoosier, and current tour star Jeff Overton.

A golfer from Memphis, Tennessee, Micheel also finished second to Tiger Woods in the 2006 PGA Championship at Medinah Country Club in Chicago. In 2010, he became only the second player in U.S Open history to make a double eagle.

Overton established himself as one of America's leading amateurs while playing for the Hoosiers. His six top-10 finishes in 2010 helped him obtain a berth on the U.S. Ryder Cup team where he was one of the American standouts in a losing effort.

Indiana's Randy Leen was a first-team All-American in 1997 and played as an amateur in the 1996 U.S. Open at Oakland Hills Country Club near Detroit where he was low amateur in the field. One of the amateurs trailing Leen was Tiger Woods.

60 Hoosier Fans Loved Moye

Sometimes there's a single second in one's lifetime that defines the rest of his years, a fleeting moment that remains etched in the memories of thousands of people.

For A.J. Moye that moment occurred on March 21, 2002, in Lexington, Kentucky, the site of Indiana's stunning removal of top-seeded Duke from the NCAA Tournament. As the game wound down into its final minutes, the IU forward came out of the depths to reject a short shot by the Blue Devils' muscular center, 6'9", 280-pound Carlos Boozer.

The block was instrumental in the Hoosiers' 74–73 upset victory in the Sweet Sixteen. Indiana trailed 63–62 when Moye, who probably stood about 6'2", buried Boozer's attempt back into his face.

The film clip, still visible on YouTube, along with a 4½ minute film of Moye's various exploits at IU, has become legendary among IU fans. Moye's name became a byword in the Hoosiers' march to the NCAA Tournament's final game, with fans chanting it both in Lexington's Rupp Arena and in Atlanta's Georgia Dome, site of the Final Four.

Moye had already become one of the most popular Hoosiers, a testament to his intensity and especially to the myriad of emotional expressions that earmarked his play. Nobody pumped his fists

A.J. Moye blocks the shot of Duke's Carlos Boozer (4) as Indiana's Dane Fife (11) watches during the second half of their NCAA South Regional semifinal game at Rupp Arena in Lexington, Kentucky, on Thursday, March 21, 2002. (AP Photo/Ed Reinke)

harder after a big basket. Nobody extolled his teammates more following their triumphs. Nobody was more animated when called for a foul. Nobody played to the fans more than A.J. Moye.

No one sacrificed his burly but vertically challenged body more than A.J. No one tried to take a charge more often, and no one got more out of rudimentary skills than the Indiana forward. He didn't necessarily trash talk, but he was always talking. Teammates didn't always know how to take A.J., who they felt was cut from a different cloth, but the fans never tired of them.

The other Hoosiers could only look perplexed when Moye described his block against Boozer.

"I thought he was going to try to go up and dunk it, and I said, 'I'm going to jump as high as I can and probably foul him,'" Moye said. "And then I realized I was higher than him, so I thought I might as well block it."

Coach Mike Davis could only respond by saying, "You thought of all that in a split second?"

Moye was a strong offensive rebounder, which he explained through another wordy epistle: "Like Moses Malone said about rebounding, if you've got 10 shots, most guys will only go for five or six rebounds, but if you go for all 10 you've got a chance to get all 10. If you only go for five, you've only got a chance to get five."

Moye was a man of many tattoos, including one that read, "It's not easy being me."

During his sophomore season, A.J. referred to himself as a young leader, which drew a chuckle or two from the team's older leaders.

Jared Jeffries, who was the same age but a bigger star, responded to that by saying, "He talks. He communicates. If you want to call him a young leader, I guess you can."

Added Moye, "I'm the butt of a lot of jokes." Besides his famous block, Moye made two critical foul shots that gave Indiana a four-point lead late in the game.

Following his IU career, Moye played professionally in Europe, playing first in Iceland and Portugal before finding a more stable spot in Germany. In November 2010 A.J. collided with a teammate and was knocked out cold by a blow to the temple. Later that day he was taken to the hospital, and it was determined that he had suffered a stroke.

Moye, whose full name is Ajene Malaki Moye, told peegs.com writer Jeff Rabjohns that the right side of his body continues to react improperly.

Moye told Rabjohns that basketball, which now may be totally in his past, buffeted him from many other personal problems. He said his mother had children by three men, and his father had children by four women.

"I always felt like everything in the world would be okay because I got a basketball game tomorrow. No matter what happened, I can go play ball," he told peegs.com.

61 This Is No Dungeon

The hallways under Assembly Hall hardly match the catacombs of Rome, but they have a history of their own, much of it is unknown to the general public.

The IU locker room is a few feet off the court at the northeast end of the arena where a black-painted door reminds you that the public isn't welcome. Inside the door is a small entry way that opens to a modest-sized room with red carpet and lockers lining the walls.

At one time reporters were allowed entrance for a few minutes of postgame interviews. Players would sit or stand in front of their lockers, fully dressed, as reporters and cameramen crushed closer to hear. Since many players spoke softly, there was a full complement of tape recorders pushed toward their faces as writers tried to avoid being smacked by the large television cameras.

Not surprisingly, the game's outstanding player often had the locker in the corner where space was even more limited.

Outsiders, with the possible exception of high-ranking school officials, were restrained. When Mike Davis was coach, his three-year-old son, A.J., talked a reluctant babysitter into entering the closed quarters. "It's okay. You're with me," the outsider was told.

The men's locker room can also be reached via a door at the southeast section of the Hall. That apparently was the one used by Associated Press reporter Beth Harris when she somehow found her way into the locker room when it was off limits. That gave Coach Knight an opportunity to close the locker room on a permanent basis. Instead, the coach opted to bring a couple of players to the press room after the game.

A tough loss often meant no players were coming, or perhaps the two players selected by Knight to be interviewed had made only cameo appearances in the game.

With players' quotes at a premium, many reporters stood outside the locker room doors, awaiting their chance to talk when the players left. After a time Knight tried to quell that by hanging curtains across the hallway and limiting those areas to the players' families.

One day after A.J. Guyton made a game-winning shot, he was unavailable to the media. About an hour later a Bloomington *Herald-Times* writer located Guyton in the parking lot and got a few quotes. Incensed, Knight sent word to the reporter that even the parking lot was off limits.

The most private area of Assembly Hall is known as "The Cave" and is located a few feet from the southwest entrance to the floor. Although the official basketball offices are located on the

Sport Started in Nineteenth Century

The first college basketball game was reportedly played about six years before Indiana played its first competition. The game featured nine players on a side and saw Minnesota School of Agriculture beat Hamline College 9–3 in February 1895. A few weeks later, Haverford College defeated Temple 6–4.

According to Mike Douchant, author of *Inside Sports College Basketball*, Amos Alonzo Stagg reportedly sent his University of Chicago team against a YMCA team made up for students from the University of Iowa in 1896. This time only five players made up a team, and Chicago won 15–12. The University of Pennsylvania believes the first "real" game was held in 1897 when Yale beat Penn 32–10, also with five on a team

Yale reportedly fielded teams in 1898, 1899, and 1900, and in 1900 made a swing through the Midwest and played Ohio State and Wisconsin. As more colleges began to field teams, many of them had to construct gymnasiums, and a number of schools played their games outdoors.

mezzanine level of the Hall, The Cave is where the coaches hang out before and after practices and games. The windowless concrete walls give the room its name, and the most obvious ornaments are television sets and tape machines.

If a reporter gained Knight's confidence, a requested interview would probably be done in The Cave. If in the proper mood, Knight might talk an hour or more with his guest or guests, often not taking many questions but rambling at length about whatever was on his mind. Once, a reporter started to leave when the coach's wife, Karen, entered the room. Knight told him, "No, hang around. I enjoy having you here."

The visitors' dressing room is located under the seats on the west side of the arena. It was once just off the floor in the southeast corner, but that area was revitalized and turned into the IU women's team quarters. Most of the traffic through the lower hallways heads toward an IU gift shop on the east side of the floor.

Adjacent to the gift shop is the press room, a concrete walled fortress where the opposing coaches address reporters following the game. Usually, the visiting coach goes first and the Indiana coach will follow as soon as the spirit moves him, which has varied from a few minutes to more than an hour.

The best known public areas at court level are at the north end of the court where a refreshment stand and restrooms are located.

62 Students Push Social Skills to No. 1

In 2002, Indiana University delighted its administration by finishing second in the NCAA basketball tournament. That same year IU finished first in another national category, and the administration was less enthused.

In a highly unscientific ranking by the *Princeton Review*, the Bloomington school was rated the No. 1 "party school" in the country.

If those within the school who value public images were a bit embarrassed, most of the students themselves were overjoyed. The *Princeton Review* has annually ranked a variety of aspects about colleges, and IU has continued to be represented in the "party school" category, ranking No. 16 in the 2012 listing. Indiana was followed in the 2002 rankings by Alabama, Penn State, and Florida.

IU surged to the top after failing to be listed in the 2001 ratings. During the year in which the school climbed to the top of the charts, Indiana had five fraternities suspended or expelled for violations of alcohol policies.

The *Princeton Review*, which has no connections with Princeton University, began ranking colleges in 1992 in 63 different categories, reportedly based on personal or computer interviews with 100,000 students. *Princeton Review* is a test-preparation and college admissions company. Among the other categories is "Stone-Cold-Sober Schools," a list of colleges and universities where there is little drinking. In 2002, Brigham Young University held that title.

The 2012 top party school was Ohio University, followed by Georgia, Mississippi, Iowa, and California–Santa Barbara. Indiana's No. 16 ranking was one step below DePauw University of Greencastle, Indiana. Georgia, where the campus is surrounded by about a hundred bars, also topped the rankings in 2010.

63 Little 500 Known Nationwide

The Little 500 was launched in 1951 as a means to finance scholarships, and during the past 63 years, it has marked one of America's classic college weekends.

The Little Five, as it is often called, matches up competitors representing Greek and other IU organizations and is held every April on the quarter-mile cinder track at Bill Armstrong Stadium. The event, which was originally for men only, has expanded to include a women's race and is the centerpiece of a massive party weekend on campus.

The original men's race was patterned after the nearby Indianapolis 500, and like the Indy 500 features 33 competing teams starting in 11 rows of three. The women's race is for 25 miles, or 100 laps, and the men's race is for 50 miles. The riders are amateurs and are full-time undergraduate students at IU. As with the Indianapolis race, starting positions are determined through qualifying. As many as four riders can comprise a team.

Originally, the race was staged on the quarter-mile track at the now-demolished Tenth Street football stadium. The event has enhanced Bloomington's reputation as a cycling center, and in the months leading up to the race, the teams train on the streets and roads around the city.

64 Only Rayl Outscored Mike Woodson

If there is an underrated player in IU history, it might be Mike Woodson. The 6'5" forward from Indianapolis Broad Ripple was among the very elite Indiana players, yet he played during an era when the Hoosiers didn't win the NCAA or even make the Final Four.

Woodson, who went on to play and coach in the NBA, did lead IU to the 1979 NIT title and was selected to the gold medal–winning Pan American team. There was a span of five seasons during which Indiana produced 11 All-Americans, including Woodson.

Indiana teams were prolific when Woodson was playing, posting an 80–39 record during his years in Bloomington. As good as Mike was, he undoubtedly would have been better had he not suffered a herniated disc in his back that required surgery during the 1980 season. IU had a 5–0 record at the time but lost five of its 12 games without him. When Woodson returned, the Hoosiers took six in a row and won the Big Ten championship while Mike won the league's MVP award.

Rayl Wasn't the Top Gunner

There are shooters and then there are gunners in basketball, and sometimes they are one and the same.

Surprisingly, the all-time record for shots taken in a game wasn't done in modern times when scores have been higher. Illinois guard Andy Phillip, a member of the touted Whiz Kids of Champaign, put up 54 shots in a 40-point game against the University of Chicago in 1943.

That was eight more than IU's Jimmy Rayl launched in a 56-point game against Michigan State and seven more than Purdue's Rick Mount tried in his 61-point game against Iowa in 1970.

Rayl launched 39 shots in his other 56-point game against Minnesota in 1962.

Most Hoosiers fans are well aware that Jimmy Rayl had a pair of 56-point games but fewer remember Woodson collecting 48 in a 1979 game at Illinois. It's the third-highest scoring effort in school history, exceeding the 47 points by Steve Downing and Don Schlundt (twice).

"In that particular game I couldn't miss," Woodson said.

Woodson's junior season in 1979 marked some of college basketball's greatest days. Magic Johnson had become a major rival of Woodson's in the Big Ten, and one hour west of Bloomington Larry Bird was leading Indiana State to the NCAA Tournament's title game where the Sycamores would lose to Johnson and Michigan State. Also the IU roster not only had Woodson but a promising freshman named Isiah Thomas.

Woodson prospered in Bob Knight's motion offense, which he called the best offense he ever saw. Woodson had a knack of working behind screens, and the offense gave him the freedom to make things happen.

The morning before he scored 48 points, Woodson picked up a newspaper and read how he had made the All–Big Ten second team. Upset at being left off the first team, Woodson's timing for the 48-point game was perfect, although he claimed he was motivated most by the fact that IU was still trying to live up to its potential.

"I didn't know exactly where I was in the game. One thing as a player that I never did, either in college or in my 11 years as a pro, was search for points," Woodson said. "I was given the ability to score for some reason. It wasn't something I felt I had to do, it just came naturally to me. During that particular game, I had no idea how many points I was scoring. All I was interested in was trying to keep the lead and win a ballgame, which we did. That enabled us to get an NIT bid.

"Eddie Johnson, who played for Illinois, walked over to me as we were leaving the floor and said, 'Hey Woodson, how many points do you think you got?' I don't count my points when I play and I said, 'I have no idea,' and walked off the floor. From that day on until we became teammates in 1981 in the NBA in Kansas City, I had no idea that he didn't like me at all. He thought I was an asshole.

"I was just being honest. Today, he and I are the best of friends."

Woodson made his first four shots in his 48-point game, missed two, and made three more in a row before missing another. Then he closed the first half by hitting his last six shots.

The IU forward would have scored 49, but a teammate stepped into the foul lane on one of his free throws and a point wasn't allowed.

65 Cuban Made Use of IU Degree

If the Dallas Mavericks are playing in Indianapolis, there's a decent chance you could run into Mark Cuban at a Bloomington watering hole. If you see him, he won't be looking like the typical Madison Avenue executive, but he will probably be dressed like the normal party animal.

The only difference is that Cuban is possibly Indiana University's wealthiest alum—his worth valued at $2.5 billion.

Cuban is also among the most visible of IU graduates, often yelling at officials working the Maverick games. Cuban owns the Mavericks, Landmark Theatres, and Magnolia Pictures.

For all his major investments, he is best known for purchasing a majority interest in the Mavericks for $285 million in 2000. At the time the Mavs had a winning percentage of 40 percent during the prior 20 seasons, but in the next 10 years they won almost 70 percent of their regular season games. The 2011 Mavs also won the NBA championship.

The 54-year-old Cuban has repeatedly expressed interest in owning a Major League Baseball franchise, and in 2008 he submitted an initial bid of $1.3 billion for the Chicago Cubs. Two years later he offered a bid to purchase the Texas Rangers, and in January 2012 he entered a bid to buy the Los Angeles Dodgers.

Cuban, born in Pittsburgh as the son of an automobile upholsterer, made his first business venture at age 12 when he sold garbage bags to pay for a pair of basketball shoes. While at IU he held a variety of jobs, including disco dancing instructor, bartender, and party promoter. He helped pay for college by collecting and selling stamps.

Cuban, married and the father of three, started MicroSolutions after being terminated as a salesman for a software retailer in Dallas. MicroSolutions was an early proponent of technologies such as Carbon Copy, Lotus Notes, and CompuServe. In 1990, he sold MicroSolutions to CompuServe for $6 million.

Cuban and another IU alumnus, Todd Wagner, started Audionet in 1995, and it became Broadcast.com three years later. By 1999 it had grown to 330 employees and had a second-quarter revenue of $13.5 million. In '99 Broadcast.com was sold to Yahoo for $5.9 billion in Yahoo stock.

In 2011, Cuban was listed as No. 459 on Forbes' list of the world's richest people.

Cuban's investments are so varied they include one in Brondell Inc., which developed a high-tech toilet seat called a Swash, which works like a bidet but mounts on a standard toilet. In other ventures he published a children's book titled, *Let's Go Mavs!* He wrote another e-book called *Win at the Sport of Business: If I Can Do It, You Can Do It.*

Cuban flies his own Gulfstream V to Mavericks road games. He has been fined more than $1.5 million by the NBA for a string of 13 incidents, mostly involving critical remarks about the team and officiating.

In 2006, Mavericks star Dirk Nowitzki said about Cuban, "He's got to learn how to control himself as well as the players do. We can't lose our temper all the time on the court or off the court, and I think he's got to learn that, too. He's got to improve in that area and not yell at the officials the whole game. I don't think that helps us.... He sits right there by our bench. I think it's a bit much. But we all told him this before; it's nothing new. The game starts, and he's already yelling at them. So he needs to know how to control himself a little."

Cuban has said he matches his fines by giving equal amounts to charitable organizations.

Cuban once criticized the NBA's manager of officials, Ed T. Rush, by saying he wouldn't be able to manage a Dairy Queen. Company officials were offended and invited Cuban to manage a Dairy Queen restaurant for a day. He accepted and worked one day at the Dairy Queen in Coppell, Texas, which did a banner business that day.

Cuban's antics include rushing onto the court and criticizing officials in a playoff game against the San Antonio Spurs. He reportedly cursed Spurs forward Bruce Bowen during the same game and was fined $200,000 by the NBA. He was also fined $250,000 for misconduct following the Mavericks' loss to Miami in Game 5 of the 2006 NBA finals.

Cuban has appeared in numerous television shows, ranging from *The Simpsons* to *WWE Raw*.

66 Bellamy Owned the Backboards

Walt Bellamy came upon the basketball scene during a high-water mark for pivotmen. The 1950s produced Bill Russell and Wilt Chamberlain. The Big Ten had Jerry Lucas and Terry Dischinger. However, Bellamy was as big as any of them—and almost as good as the best of them.

Bellamy came to Indiana in 1957 out of New Bern, North Carolina. He wore knee pads and carried his proud body upright, which somehow made him look regal when he ran the court. His arms were as long as Plastic Man's, and his dunks resounded from Bedford to Martinsville.

Big Walter followed two All-America centers at Indiana, Don Schlundt and Archie Dees. When he arrived his game was so ragged few could foresee him equaling their achievements, but after three seasons at IU and 14 in the NBA, Belamy became a Hall of Famer.

Bellamy was listed at 6'11", but some opponents believed he topped 7'. He averaged more than 22 points per game during his last two seasons, making more than 50 percent of his shots and averaging 15.5 rebounds during his IU career.

Bellamy's last game as a Hoosier was his best. Teammates Tom Bolyard and Jimmy Rayl said Big Walter set his sights on the Big Ten rebounding record during an 82–67 victory over Michigan.

Rayl said he sat on the bench with a small piece of paper and wrote down each of Bellamy's 33 rebounds that day. Walter also scored 28 points.

Bellamy's last rebound of the game broke the five-year-old record of Ohio State's Frank Howard.

Bellamy was a member of the United States Olympic team that won the gold medal in Rome in 1960, winning all eight games by a margin of 42.4 points. Ten of the 12 college players on the American team went on to play professionally, including Oscar Robertson, Jerry West, Jerry Lucas, and Terry Dischinger. Bellamy, Robertson, West, and Lucas are members of the Basketball Hall of Fame.

Bellamy was the first overall pick in the 1961 NBA Draft and had an incredibly successful first year with the Chicago Packers, an expansion team. His solid play was rewarded when he was named Rookie of the Year. "Bells" averaged 31.6 points per game that season, which was the second highest rookie output in history and trailed only Chamberlain's 37.6. Bellamy also had 19 rebounds

Bellamy: King of the Double-Double

The term double-double is a byproduct of modern basketball, but it has become an excellent measuring stick for rating players. It represents someone who has both scored and rebounded in double figures or has produced double figures in rebounding-assists or scoring-assists.

The most double-doubles by an Indiana player were the product of Walt Bellamy who had 59 of them during his three-year career. Bellamy's predecessor, Archie Dees, had 56 and Alan Henderson had 49.

Others among the top ten are Steve Downing 43, Kent Benson 42, Tom Van Arsdale 38, Dick Van Arsdale and Ken Johnson 34, Joby Wright 30, Bill DeHeer and Kirk Haston 29.

The most double-doubles in one season belongs to Dees, 23 in 1958, followed by George McGinnis, 22 in 1971; Bellamy, 21 in 1961; Downing, 20 in 1972 and Bellamy in 1959; and D.J. White, 18 in 2008, Henderson in 1994, and Bellamy in 1960.

a game, which among rookies trailed only Chamberlain's 27 and Russell's 19.6. The IU product also led the NBA in field-goal percentage and had 23 points and 17 rebounds in the 1962 All-Star Game.

The Chicago Packers eventually became the Baltimore Bullets and then moved to Washington, D.C. Bellamy was traded to the New York Knicks during the 1965–66 season and to the Detroit Pistons for Dave DeBusschere during the 1968–69 season. Because of scheduling differences, Bellamy played in 35 games for the Knicks and 53 with the Pistons, setting a record of 88 games in one year that still stands. Walter later played for the Atlanta Hawks and finished his career after one game with the New Orleans Jazz. He is one of only seven NBA players to score more than 20,000 points and grab 14,000 rebounds.

Bellamy settled into the Atlanta area and became a proponent for several causes. Twice he was a delegate at the Democratic National Convention and was a longtime worker for the National Association for the Advancement of Colored People (NAACP). He was the first African American to serve as sergeant-at-arms for the Georgia General Assembly, the result of an appointment by then Lieutenant Governor Zell Miller in 1977.

67 IU Scores 122, 74 in the Second Half

The Hurryin' Hoosiers of Coach Branch McCracken took a lot of shots, made a lot of them, and often ran up a lot of points. But until Groundhog Day 1959, they had never played a game like the one at Ohio State. That night Indiana beat the Buckeyes 122–92 in St. John Arena.

IU's numbers from that game are staggering. The Hoosiers made 50-of-79 shots, setting records for the number of field goals and field-goal percentage (.633). The teams combined for 214 points and 84 field goals, both records.

Although IU took an early 10-point lead, Ohio State led 38–35 with 4:43 left in the first half. That was the only lead the Bucks enjoyed, but it was 48–48 at halftime despite Indiana shooting 54.4 percent in the first period.

The 74-point second half was something to behold. Herbie Lee, a sophomore guard from South Bend, made his first seven shots of the second half and finished with 25 points. Lee made 12-of-18 shots, while sophomore Gary Long made 11-of-20 from the field and, while shooting underhanded, made 7-of-8 at the foul line. Leroy Johnson made 9-of-15 shots for 20 points and added 11 rebounds.

Frank Radovich, the only non-sophomore who started, added 13 points and 13 rebounds. The IU bench, led by Gene Flowers' perfect four-for-four, made 7-of-8 shots.

The three-point shot was still almost three decades away, but Long recalls that a number of IU's shots would have been from the present three-point distance.

Ohio State coach Fred Taylor said his team played its best game of the season, adding, "Ninety-two points is nothing to sneeze at, and we still lost by 30 points. I never in my life saw anything like it. It was fantastic."

Indiana had won four of its last five when it went to Columbus, including a 75–69 victory over DePaul two days earlier. The Hurryin' Hoosiers beat Michigan in a follow-up game to the 122-point outing but lost five of their next six within the conference.

Ohio State was led by guard Larry Siegfried and forward Joe Roberts, who would start the following season for Ohio State's NCAA champions. Freshmen Jerry Lucas, John Havlicek, Mel

Nowell, and Bob Knight were ineligible to play until their sophomore season.

Three years later, the Hurryin' Hoosiers would score 122 points again, this time beating Notre Dame 122–95. McCracken's 1962 team broke 100 points on four occasions.

68 Hoosiers Honored as Conference MVPs

The *Chicago Tribune* has honored the Big Ten's Most Valuable Player annually since 1946, and the award has gone to an Indiana player on 16 occasions.

Don Schlundt was the first Hoosier to win it in 1953, and his successor in the pivot, Archie Dees won it twice, in 1957 and '58. No Hoosier won it again until Steve Downing in 1973, but the Hoosiers owned the trophy from 1975–77 when Scott May won it twice and Kent Benson followed during his senior season.

Indiana's Mike Woodson received the honor in 1980, and Ray Tolbert followed the next year. After Ohio State's Clark Kellogg won in 1982, the honor again went to a Hoosier, Randy Wittman.

Six IU players have been the conference's MVP in the past 25 years. Steve Alford captured the honor in 1987, Calbert Cheaney in 1993, Brian Evans in 1996, A.J. Guyton in 2000, Jared Jeffries in 2002, and D.J. White in 2008.

Ohio State's Jerry Lucas won the award three straight times between 1960–62, and his successor as the Buckeyes center, Gary Bradds, won it the next two years.

Schlundt was the first sophomore to win the award, but in his junior season the honor went to Schlundt's major rival, John "Red"

Jared Jeffries dunks the ball over Iowa's Glen Worley during the first half on Sunday, January 13, 2002, in Iowa City, Iowa. Worley was called for a foul on the play. (AP Photo/Charlie Neibergall)

Kerr of Illinois. When Schlundt was a senior, Minnesota's Chuck Mencel was the MVP.

Dees' back-to-back wins in 1957 and '58 saw him averaged 25 points per game as a junior and 25.5 as a senior. Downing's senior season he averaged 20.1 points per game and was highlighted by a 47-point, 25-rebound game against Kentucky. May carried a 16.3 points per game scoring average as a junior and 23.5 as a senior when he was national Player of the Year.

Benson averaged 19.8 points per game as a senior when he was plagued by injuries, and Woodson was a 19.3 scorer the year he won the honor. As with Schlundt and May, Alford captured the honor on the heels of an NCAA championship, and Cheaney duplicated May's senior season by being named national Player of the Year. Evans was the top Big Ten player in 1996 when the left-hander averaged 21.2 points per game, and Guyton carried a 19.7 mark in 2000.

Jeffries was a sophomore when he was honored, moving on to the NBA after the season. He came within one game of playing for an NCAA champion. White, who was recruited to IU by Mike Davis, won his MVP while playing for Kelvin Sampson.

Hoosiers Honored for Final Four Play

Sixteen Indiana players have been named to the NCAA All-Tournament team, almost twice as many as any other Big Ten school. Michigan State is second highest with nine, six of those in the twenty-first century. Michigan has had seven players honored, including Chris Webber twice, and six Ohio State Buckeyes have made the All-Tournament team, including Jerry Lucas three times.

Indiana players honored were Marv Huffman, Jay McCreary, and Bob Menke in 1940; Don Schlundt and Bob Leonard 1953; Steve Downing 1973; Kent Benson, Scott May, and Tom Abernethy 1976; Isiah Thomas, Landon Turner, and Jim Thomas 1981; Keith Smart and Steve Alford 1987; and Dane Fife and Kyle Hornsby 2002.

69 Staring Down an Adversary

Bob Knight is 6'5", Russ Brown is closer to 5'6". Knight is total evidence that a big man can be intimidating. Brown is proof that a little man doesn't have to be intimidated.

Early in Knight's 29-year term as Indiana basketball coach, he was confronted by Brown, a reporter for *The Courier-Journal* in Louisville, Kentucky, who had been assigned the IU beat. It was to become a 14-year head-butting contest between two men destined to dislike each other.

When Brown was assigned to cover Knight's team, he asked a co-worker what to expect. John Flynn, who had covered Knight when he was a high school coach in Ohio, gave a classic answer.

"Calling Bob Knight 'Bobby' is like calling Atilla the Hun 'Tilly,'" Flynn told him.

Brown recalled his first interview of Knight, which was on the phone, and Russ asked about the possibility of IU's George McGinnis turning pro. The coach's response would be predictable now, but wasn't then, "That's a dumb [bleeping] question!"

Brown said everything went downhill from there.

Brown said he was jolted by Knight's response, but it didn't deter him from doing his job. Over the years Brown would sit in the front row and frequently ask the first question while more timid reporters sat on their hands or offered creampuff questions that were unlikely to draw a fiery answer. On many occasions, Knight would respond to Brown's query by saying, "Does anyone here have an intelligent question?"

Brown said there were occasions when the coach would call his home in New Albany and Russ's wife would answer to a charming voice.

"He'd be real nice. 'Hi, Mrs. Brown, how are you? Could I speak to Russ?' Then I'd come on the phone. 'You little SOB. You [bleep]. Don't you ever come up here anymore! I'll ram your [bleeping] head through the locker room wall' Oh, he threatened me on a number of occasions," Brown said.

The Knight-Brown faceoff came to a peak in the late 1970s when the television show *60 Minutes* came to Bloomington to do a piece on the coach. Dan Rather was there, and Knight was on a high about the situation. As usual, Brown sat in the front row during the postgame press conference, and Knight looked his way and said, "I really feel good. I feel so good, Russ, that I'm even gonna shake your hand and ask you how your family is and how you're doing."

Suspicious, Russ remarked in a clip that made the *60 Minutes* show, "Well, you must be feeling pretty damn good then."

When Brown left the press conference, he walked past Knight in the hallway without either remarking. When Brown was about 15 yards past the coach, he heard a voice, "Hey, Russ."

Brown turned around and Knight had a pistol pointed toward him, and the coach fired it—with blanks. "You missed," Brown said, basically unshaken.

"Wait until you shake your head," Knight said.

Brown took the incident as a joke, but considering that Knight had threatened him in lesser ways, many subordinates felt otherwise. *The Courier-Journal* asked Brown if he wanted to take legal action. Russ said no.

In 1984, Brown was taken off the Indiana beat and assigned to the University of Louisville. He felt like the world was lifted off his shoulders, and he enjoyed a close relationship with U of L coach Denny Crum.

Perry Farrell, a young African American reporter with *The Courier-Journal*, was offered the chance to succeed Brown. Farrell said he would love to cover Kentucky or Louisville, but he wanted no part of Bobby Knight.

"There is no job in America tougher than covering the IU basketball team," Brown said. "You have little access to the coaches and players. You've got to put up with his bullshit all the time."

Brown, who grew up in Salem, Indiana, about an hour's drive from Bloomington, admits to being an IU fan until he was assigned the beat. Because of Knight, he claims he wanted Indiana to lose every game.

Brown said *The Courier-Journal* was supportive of his ordeal with the coach. Former publisher Barry Bingham Jr. wrote a letter complaining about Knight's threats against the reporter. Knight returned a letter signed by Mickey Mouse with copies to Donald Duck, et al.

Brown said his major fault with Knight was the way the coach treated people. He cited an example that involved the death of Russ' sister in an auto accident. Brown said the coach encountered his parents shortly after that and offered his condolences, but upon seeing Russ later Knight chided Russ for a story he didn't like.

"Why would a guy be nice enough to my parents to say something like that, and then see me, and knowing that I'd just lost a sister, treat me like that?" Brown said.

70 Turn an Ear to Dakich's Talk Show

The Dan Dakich Show can be heard from noon to 3:00 PM on weekdays at 1070 on your AM radio dial. The host tries to be an authority on many subjects—the Indianapolis Colts, Indiana Pacers, golf, auto racing and, yes, college basketball.

Dakich, the former IU basketball player, can be boisterous, repetitive, and often cocky. He has a swagger in his voice and doesn't object to shooting down an opinion by one of his callers. Still, celebrity guests enjoy being on the show because conversations with Dakich have the atmosphere you find in a bar an hour before closing time.

Not surprisingly, listeners accuse Dan of loving the Hoosiers too much—or even of hating the Hoosiers because he was bypassed for the head coaching job when Tom Crean was hired. Most Purdue fans accept him because he genuinely likes Matt Painter and seems to follow the Boilermakers as closely as they do. It's the same thing with Butler fans because Dan highly praises Brad Stevens and doesn't look down on the mid-major school.

Dakich's talk show is best when its host enlightens a controversy by falling back on his years of college coaching. Dan has opinions about how coaches still handle certain situations, and it's worth listening for three hours to catch a few minutes of such insight.

Because of his connections while coaching, Dakich has a long list of friends and acquaintances he can tap for interviews. Those include new Ohio State football coach Urban Meyer, who was at Bowling Green during Dan's days there. Frequent guests include IU radio voice Don Fischer, *Indianapolis Star* columnist Bob Kravitz, and various coaches from around the state.

Some of Dakich's best shows involve controversies in his community, such as Peyton Manning's future and the Colts basically throwing away a perfect season in order to prevent injuries before the playoffs. One of Dakich's best interviews was with Bill Polian a few days before the Colts' executive was fired.

One day Dakich explained how, as a coach, he handled parents who complained that their kids weren't playing enough. It's the kind of stuff most talk-show hosts can't touch.

Dakich had done some radio work while at Bowling Green, and after his brief stint as IU coach in 2008, a friend in the radio business asked if Dan would be interested in such a venture. Dick Vitale was his first guest.

"I'll never forget driving up there my first day and thinking, 'What the hell am I going to talk about?'" Dan recalled. "It's one thing to sit with your buddies and talk for three hours. But this is me, a mic, and hopefully some callers."

The former Hoosier said he spent a long time preparing for dull moments and trying to make certain he knew something about the subjects being discussed. If he stumbles, he isn't hesitant to admit this isn't his area of expertise.

His former preparation as a coach serves him well now, he said early in his new venture.

"I've got stacks of [reference] stuff. I'm afraid that I'm going to be there and the phone lines will go dead with no guests and now it's me. So I make sure I'm ready for it."

Dead air space has been no problem for Dakich, who can talk with the best of them.

71 School Song a Century Old

The melody Indiana fans have grown to love turned 100 years old in 2011, and it was first written not to inspire basketball fans but to create a circus atmosphere.

Karl King, a famous composer of march songs, includes "The Viking March" among his long list of musical credits. A year later, Russell Harker put the song to words, starting with "Indiana, Our Indiana", and at the 1912 football game against Northwestern it was first played as an IU fight song.

The song has been played at every home football and basketball game since. The words:

Indiana, our Indiana
Indiana, we're all for you,
We will fight for
The Cream and Crimson
For the glory of old IU.
Never daunted, we cannot falter.
In the battle, we're tried and true.
Indiana, our Indiana
Indiana, we're all for you!

Dave Woodley, Indiana University director of athletic bands, thinks the song is a perfect fit for IU. "Since Indiana is sort of a weird word, I think it fits well. Plus, it's pretty singable. Obviously, when we listen to it at basketball games, everybody will sing along. I think it's a great tune," said Woodley, an Iowa native who has been at IU for 19 years.

While "Indiana, Our Indiana" plucks the heartstrings of IU fans everywhere, it isn't the school's only fight song. Woodley describes "Indiana Fight" as a secondary school fight song.

"It was written by Leroy Hinkle, and I think Leroy was an IU graduate. In the middle of the fight song everybody yells, 'Go IU! Fight! Fight! Fight!'" Woodley said. "As much as the students and crowd love singing "Indiana, Our Indiana," they will always sing, 'Go IU! Fight! Fight! Fight!' in the middle of the secondary fight song."

The words to "Indiana Fight" are:

Fight for the Cream and Crimson,
Loyal sons of our old IU.
Fight for your Alma Mater
And the school you love so true.

Fight for old Indiana;
See her victories safely through.
Go IU! Fight! Fight! Fight!
For the glory of old IU.

Since IU's music school is highly acclaimed, some will be surprised to learn that about 90 percent of the school's Marching Hundred aren't music majors. "The marching band was formed in 1896, but the term Marching Hundred band came in the 1920s," Woodley said. "We were one of the first bands in the Big Ten to march—with a 10 by 10 block of men. That's where the name Marching Hundred came up. We have 300 members now."

The basketball pep band for men's games has about 90 members, and another band of about 55 plays at women's games. "Our kids from the Marching Hundred audition for the pep bands, and they make either the women's or the men's," the director said. "We take everybody from the marching band who wants to play. If we had all 300 members of the marching band wanting to play, we'd take them all."

The pep bands consist of a full range of trumpets, which project very well. There are also trombones, French horns, four tubas, two drummers, and an electric bass. "You can hear the bass throughout the arena," Woodley said.

The drum line is the most competitive section of the marching band, according to Woodley.

"Most of the kids from the drum line have spent many years learning from a teacher and have also marched drum corps in the summer. They've done a lot of extra things to get to that level. By far, the most competitive part of our band is the drum line. Even more competitive is the basketball band's drum section. We take only two people but they have to be just outstanding," he said.

Woodley likes to build a list of songs that inspire the crowd, especially the students.

"Obviously, their favorites are the two fight songs, and they like a little timeout song that we play called 'Seven Nation Army.' We added that last year, and it is a really big favorite," the director said. "We play 'Zombie Nation,' where they all do arm movements and sing along with that. Those are probably the two most popular.

"The other song that was popular for a long time was 'Doctor Hoosier,' but the students like to yell bad words in the middle of it, so we don't play it anymore. They'd love it if we did."

A few years ago students became attached to the theme from the Pee Wee Herman movie, and Woodley says he is alert to adding songs that might add to the atmosphere and spirit of the crowd. He claims he gets suggestions from fans "every day of the year" and occasionally puts one into practice.

"I don't know if any of our songs inspire the team. I think a lot of our songs inspire the crowd," Woodley said. "Part of inspiring a team is getting the fans on their feet and cheering."

Woodley, a graduate of the University of Iowa, said the evening's music generally starts out with "Sweet Georgia Brown."

"That's been played first here forever, and I want to keep that because it's something unique," he said. "After that I kind of judge by the audience. If the students are here early, I know by playing this certain song I'll get them a little more riled up. I try to increase the excitement of the songs closer to tip-off."

Indiana bands perform not only for men's and women's basketball and football, but also for men's and women's soccer and women's volleyball.

"Not all the same kids do everything, but a lot of them do. They love to play," Woodley said.

The NCAA and Big Ten both have rules that bands can't play when the game is active, which includes during free throws. "Although some bands have cowbells and other stuff going on," the IU band director noted.

Woodley says Assembly Hall is perfect to emit the band's sound throughout the building. In general, smaller arenas project more sound, and the Wisconsin band probably lost some of its volume when the Badgers left the small UW Fieldhouse for the larger Kohl Center.

"They loved the old place, but when they went to the new place they were smart enough to put them at the end of the court, so they still have a very strong presence. It was kind of like when Ohio State was in St. John Arena," Woodley said.

The IU band director believes IU and Michigan State have the best bands in the Big Ten, with Wisconsin ranking third "because they rile the place up.

"Michigan State built its new arena, so it's almost straight up and down, a boxy kind of thing. You get a lot of sound trapped in an arena like that," Woodley said.

IU does have an alma mater song, "Hail to Old IU," that was first performed on March 10, 1893, in Indianapolis. The words were composed by J.T. Giles who organized the IU Glee Club and needed a school song for a performance at a state contest. The melody comes from an old Scottish song. The lyrics:

Come and join in song together,
Shout with might and main;
Our beloved Alma Mater,
sound her praise again.
Gloriana Frangipana.
E'er to her be true.
She's the pride of Indiana,
Hail to Old IU!

72 No Cheering on the Microphone

Most people probably don't notice, but when Chuck Crabb speaks over the microphone at Indiana basketball games, he never cheers for the home team.

He pronounces every syllable and probably can recite the roster of the Czech Republic national team without a blemish. He is the author of *"Your Indiana Hooooosiers,"* which is an Assembly Hall tradition unlike any other, and he seldom says IU if he can say In-di-an-a U-ni-ver-si-ty, which has seven more syllables.

A beloved figure who has been with the athletic department since 1977, Crabb also fills the position of assistant athletic director for facilities.

Crabb does not slip into a mold that entraps many public address announcers. He doesn't go into hysterics when the Hoosiers do something special. He doesn't slowly roll the IU starting lineup off his tongue until it sounds like he is screaming while eating. He gives us the facts. Nothing more, nothing less.

"I'm kind of a background person, and that's the way any announcer should be," Crabb said.

Crabb has been on the microphone at IU basketball games for 35 seasons and football for 24. He also does women's basketball and men's and women's track and field.

Crabb says if he ever shows emotion it's probably at a track and field event. "It may sound crazy for a Hoosier, and even a little bit sacrilegious, but I have a greater love of doing track and field than any other sport," he said.

"Announcing, to me, is reporting. It's simply relating what you're seeing and then stepping aside and letting the fans enjoy it," Crabb said. "I purposely watch the inflection of my voice. I'm not one who's going to do what I affectionately call 'NBA announcing.' I'm not going to get enthused and excited. There are cheerleaders in college who do what professional basketball announcers do. I've had more than one basketball official thank me for the way I present a basketball game."

The IU public address announcer doesn't speak multiple languages, as some suspect when he enunciates the names of foreign players. It isn't that simple, he says, adding, "I have no second language. I have enough trouble sometimes with English."

What he does have is a university where more than 125 different languages and dialects are taught.

"I was always able to call particular departments and ask to sit down with either an agent from that country or a professor who would spend some time with me," he said. "I could put a tape recorder in front and ask them to review the basic principles for a language. Like where is the emphasis on a syllable? Is it the first syllable or the second syllable? We simply would record whatever names I was reading, and I would try to mimic what the speaker was saying. For the most part, it worked out."

A native of Brazil, Indiana, Crabb's original desire was to be a journalist.

"My hope coming out of college in 1973 was to be the next Grantland Rice. I always had that aspiration of writing. I started doing the internal public address announcing in the football press box, a service that gives statistics to the writer so that everything is consistent," he said.

The press box announcer reports who carried the football and who made the tackle, along with the yards gained, the downs situation, and other such information. Sometimes he must say, "No cheering in the press box."

"Sid Hartman of the *Minneapolis Star-Tribune* challenged that frequently," Crabb said, chuckling.

Crabb began that announcing job as an IU junior and continued for three years, by which time he was a desk editor and managing editor for two afternoon newspapers. In March 1976, sports information director Tom Miller asked Chuck if he would like to succeed Bert Laws as public address announcer. Laws was planning to retire the next year after 39 seasons in the position.

"That was a great thrill. Ironically, before Bert retired, I came to work for Indiana University athletics in the athletic fundraising area.

As Laws' departure loomed, Crabb was interviewed by athletic director Paul Dietzel and told his boss of the plan to replace Laws.

"I still remember him kind of smiling and saying, 'Well, Charles, I'm not sure that's something you can accept. Would you like a fulltime job with me, or would you like to have this game-by-game opportunity?'" Crabb recalled.

In the spring of 1977, the university publicly honored Laws, and Dietzel's mailbox was besieged by tape recordings from people wanting the public address announcer's job.

"He really didn't want to go through an audition process, and he called me in one day and suggested that Tom Miller had given me a very positive referral, and he said, 'That's good enough for me.' He said, 'You start this fall.'"

Laws offered Chuck three pieces of advice: "Don't repeat what's on the scoreboard. Don't cheerlead, and don't listen to yourself."

In many ways it is up to Crabb to run the game from his announcer's position. Sometimes it is his call when a television network wants extra time during timeouts to finish a promotion or commercial.

"Every network has moments when it wants time to tell a story, and five or ten seconds doesn't really make a difference," Crabb said. "We did have a problem this year with a freelance producer who was doing the game. He had Jim Jackson doing the color, and Jim had some stories he was trying to tell. Unfortunately, we had a couple of timeouts that went maybe 2:40.

"The Big Ten encourages timeout coordinators not to give extra time. There are some things within reason, but what I experienced on the two extended timeouts was very awkward. I would hope the conference would work more with its TV partners and stress the need to stay within time limits."

Crabb admitted that what the networks are showing during the long timeouts are often good promotions for the university. But he is less enthralled with them taking extra time to show a chair sliding across the floor.

"I really don't want to watch that again," he said.

Sitting a few feet from Bob Knight during games could be an experience, including several in which the coach grabbed the microphone and spoke to the crowd. That's a practice not allowed since the late 1980s.

"He obviously had moments when he would get on the crowd for not cheering. He also would get on the crowd for maybe some antics that he didn't consider appropriate," Crabb recalled. "The most difficult thing was the Northwestern game where he said something and then his first wife, Nancy, came down and grabbed the mic and tried to say something to the crowd. She said, 'You fans don't understand how hard these players work and get ready to represent you, and now you're booing them.'

"And the crowd booed her. That was the last time that the wife of a coach was permitted those options."

73 The Grinch Actually Stole This Game

Christmas 2004 was three days away, and Indiana's basketball team was desperately in need of a victory. Mike Davis' Hoosiers had won their first two games before dropping their next five. Never mind that three of those losses came against Top 10 teams, North Carolina, Connecticut, and Kentucky.

Indiana played host to the University of North Carolina at Charlotte on December 22, and Pat Ewing Jr. had seemingly given IU fans a big Christmas present when he tipped in a missed shot by D.J. White with seven tenths of a second remaining. However, there was to be a Grinch in the picture.

The 49ers inbounded the basketball from under their own basket, and Brendan Plavich caught it at midcourt. Plavich pivoted, dribbled once, and fired a 45' shot that went in.

Charlotte 74, Indiana 73.

Officials Ed Hightower, Paul Janssen, and John Higgins went to the television monitor at midcourt to determine if the shot was launched in time. Within moments, the officials decided that the shot counted. Former IU star John Laskowski, who was doing the game on television, saw the same monitor and agreed.

"It beat it," Laz admitted.

Later, evidence would surface indicating the shot shouldn't have counted. Unfortunately for Indiana, the game remains in history books as a loss.

"Obviously, technology becomes more a part of officiating all the time. The officials have allowances from the NCAA when videos can be used for reviews," said Chuck Crabb, IU's public address announcer. "Any scoring in the last five seconds is reviewable if it's a close game."

The television replay used by the officials was incorrect, although at that time the flaw hadn't been detected.

"The technology being used in that game had a camera on the shot clock," Crabb said. "The camera, in order to do the graphics for ESPN, had to go through what's called a video converter where the video image is converted into digital and then goes through those programming moments for a graphic on the screen. A video converter adds time. That's just a fact of operation."

"We had video that was not usable at that particular time, shot from a platform high above the court, that showed the full court and the lights on the basket. It clearly indicated that the shot was still in his hand as the light went on," Crabb said.

The flaw in the system was changed by the NCAA and can't happen today.

There have been many instances in basketball where the official timer is blamed for last-shot controversies, but this wasn't the case in the Charlotte game.

"A lot of people wanted to say it was Carl Harrington, our 28-year timer. Well, it wasn't Carl," Crabb insisted. "We use what's called Precision Timing, a company out of North Carolina that created a system where the officials wear a belt pack. They have a small microphone where when they blow their whistle, it stops the clock.

"Three officials can blow whistles. You also have Carl, who still has the on-off switch on the control panel. In the same respect, you have four people with belt packs who can start the clock by punching that, or Carl can start it. It's the first response."

The loss to Charlotte almost prevented Indiana from having a winning season, but the Hoosiers won four of their last five regular-season games and finished 15–14 after an NIT loss to Vanderbilt.

74 A Blow to International Diplomacy

November 21, 1987, was already a banner day on the Indiana University campus when the IU basketball team took the court for a night game against the Soviet National team. Earlier that afternoon Bill Mallory's IU football team had completed its most successful regular season in years with a 35–14 victory over Purdue in Memorial Stadium.

Then, as often was the case at Indiana, the basketball program upstaged football. Sunday newspapers across the land revealed the latest Bob Knight controversy—the pulling of his team from the court.

There were two principals in the story: Knight and a rising young official named Jim Burr. While Knight went on to win more than 900 games, Burr became one of the most recognized referees in the country, appearing multiple times a week on televised games and forever a figure of authority on the court.

Indiana was coming off a national championship, and while losing Steve Alford, Daryl Thomas, and Steve Eyl from the 1987 team, it retained Dean Garrett, Keith Smart, Joe Hillman, and Rick Calloway. The crowd anticipated the Hoosiers to administer a lesson in basketball to the touring Soviets.

What happened instead was hard to believe—and for IU fans hard to accept. The Hoosiers were never in the game. Although Indiana got within five points of the Soviets early in the second half, the more experienced USSR team led 66–43 with 15:05 remaining when the game was forfeited.

Public address announcer Chuck Crabb was as close to the game as anyone.

"It was one of those games where calls started going crazy during the game. We were supposed to be playing college rules, and the Russians were invariably falling back into using some FIFA rules," Crabb recalled. "Some of them went unnoticed, but then Coach Knight started getting more frustrated with some of the lane violations.

"Obviously, it finally reached a point where he got very hot. Jim Burr was calling the game. Coach and Jim locked horns and really started arguing the issue pretty intensely. Jim called Coach for two technicals. Then there was a point where Bob walked to the end of the visiting team's bench where Bill Walls was sitting. Bill was the longtime administrator of USA Basketball, the national governing body."

According to Crabb, Knight told Walls that he needed to try to set the officials straight on how the game should be called.

"It finally built up to some discussion in front of the bench between Burr and Knight," Crabb continued. "I remember Bob saying something like, 'If we don't get this straightened out, I'll pull my team. We don't need to go through this.' So Burr finally turned the scorebook and said, 'The coach refuses to comply with the officials' request that he leave the court for the number of technicals that have been called. So this game is forfeited.'"

Knight had been assessed a third technical along the way, and after the coach said he wasn't leaving the floor unless his team did, too, Burr asked if his decision was final. When Knight said it was, Burr declared a forfeit.

The first two technicals were called after Knight came onto the court protesting a lane violation against a Soviet player when the Russians' Sarunas Marciulionis was shooting two free throws with 15:38 to play.

In the confusion that followed, *Indianapolis News* reporter Dick Mittman asked a Soviet player if he spoke English.

"Not very good," the player responded.

When Mittman asked what had happened, the Soviet responded, "Crazy coach."

75 Assembly Hall Goes High Tech

For almost 35 years Assembly Hall lacked the frills of modern-day arenas. There was no advertising. No paint on the playing floor except the required lines and a white map of Indiana. The scoreboard above midcourt carried minimum information: the score, time left in the period, timeouts remaining, and team fouls.

Bob Knight never was a bells-and-whistles type of guy. He opposed advertising in the arena, names on the uniforms, and the modern lighting and noisemakers that became commonplace in the NBA and eventually settled into the college game. When the university installed a mammoth new scoreboard in 2005, IU fans realized what they had been missing.

To some ticket-holders, the game has almost become secondary. The 35,000-pound scoreboard has increased the basic information to include the points scored and personal fouls of those in the game. Pictures of players are flashed when that player enters the game, and highlights by the Hoosiers are replayed.

However, the major purpose of the scoreboard is to solicit support for the Indiana team. It encourages fans to applaud, cheer louder, and basically raise the roof. For the most part, the idea has been successful.

In the minutes prior to tip-off, the scoreboard screen displays a highlight film of IU's championship teams. Often the score isn't even on the big board, but fans can refer to smaller scoreboards in the four corners of the arena.

Assistant athletic director Chuck Crabb launched preparation for the big board three years before Daktronics Inc. of South Dakota was hired to create the improved system.

"The desire was to start showing video in the stadium and have LED panels that would allow statistics to be shown," Crabb said. "We had to do a $1 million investment in the roof structure in order to hold 35,000 pounds of dead weight. That work was done shortly after the IU commencement, and then we covered the court with three-quarter inch plywood, crisscrossed, and had a boom truck that sat in the northwest corner. It hoisted the pieces from the garage door around to the center. Then the board was bolted together.

"We built the scoreboard from the top down and kept raising it through a hoist system we had installed. We kept raising it a number of feet at a time in order to accommodate the next section that was being added."

The scoreboard is four stories high and features nine screens. Four of those have a resolution only slightly duller than high definition. Four more scoreboards have a slightly lesser resolution and are used largely for statistics.

"Then we have a ring around the bottom that is kind of our cheerleading board," Crabb said. "We can use it for advertising. We can use it for messages, chants such as 'Stand Up' or 'Make Noise.' In a sense, there's a 10th LED board, and that's the five-section scorer's bench where we also have the ability to have photos."

Operating the scoreboard, which involves taking shots of people in the stands, doing video replays, etc., requires a crew of about 20 people.

"Indiana University performs a very novel concept with our videos," Crabb said. "We don't depend on the originating television network. We work with the Indiana University Radio and Television Service. Of those 20 people, probably 12 to 24 are IU students. They're getting hands-on experience."

76 Nick Nailed It from Midcourt

You live by the sword, and you die by the sword—even in basketball.

During Indiana's magical 1989 season, which saw the Hoosiers rebound from an embarrassing start to win the Big Ten championship, Indiana both won and lost a game on a last-second three-point shot. Jay Edwards provided the dramatics February 19 when his outside jumper hit the cords almost at the exact moment the time clock expired, giving IU a one-point victory.

Edwards was primed for more heroics less than a month later when Illinois came to Bloomington for a critical Big Ten game. The lithe sophomore drilled a difficult jumper from the baseline that tied the game at 67 with two seconds left in the game.

The Fighting Illini's Stephen Bardo immediately called a timeout, and the visitors contemplated how to get off a decent shot in the time remaining. Bardo took the ball out of bounds at the north end of Assembly Hall and, instead of placing a defender on Bardo, Indiana coach Bob Knight used all five players upcourt against the Illini's four remaining players.

Bardo was left with a clear path to throw the basketball inbounds. He fired it 50' with precise accuracy, and the 6'6" Nick Anderson went up for the ball near the Illinois bench, catching it cleanly and turning for a shot that fell cleanly through the net. The game clock didn't start until Anderson touched the basketball and, unlike Edwards' game-winner against Michigan, the shot was clearly made before the final buzzer.

Illinois 70, Indiana 67.

The Hoosiers had hoped to clinch a share of the Big Ten title in the game, but the Fighting Illini retained hope with the victory. IU left the court with a 14–2 record and two conference games remaining. Illinois had a 12–4 record and was ranked No. 8 in the Associated Press poll, five spots below IU. Knight defended his strategy of not defending the inbounds passer, saying, "We don't do that here."

Even before the late dramatics, the game had all the earmarks of a classic collegiate battle. Indiana led 27–25 after a tight first half in which the Illini's Kenny Battle made a three-pointer three seconds before intermission. However, the Hoosiers struck quickly when play resumed and took a seven-point lead 72 seconds into the second half.

Senior Joe Hillman, who scored 24 points, pushed IU's lead to 11 with a three with about 8:30 to play, but Lou Henson's Illini weren't done and with 17 seconds left held a two-point lead. Everyone in the arena knew IU would try to get the ball to Edwards, who in the previous month not only had beaten Michigan at the buzzer but had hit the winning basket in a 64–62 win over Purdue.

"We definitely wanted to double-team him. We were just trying to keep it from him," Henson said.

At that moment no double team was good enough to stop the IU guard, who got the ball with about 10 seconds left and scrambled toward the left baseline in an attempt to find a good angle for the shot. Unable to do so, he launched a difficult shot over two defenders that fell true.

"I didn't think it had a chance to go in because he put too much arc on it," the Illini coach said. "But it came down through, and with two guys on him. It was a great shot. I don't think I've ever seen a player in this league do the things that he has done."

Knight was rational about the loss, noting that IU had won similar games in similar ways. "You don't win all of those," he said.

A few months earlier, Anderson had been named Illinois Mr. Basketball after his senior season at Simeon High School on the south side of Chicago. The previous year IU forward Eric Anderson had won the honor at St. Francis De Sales High School.

Indiana's Anderson went on to play two seasons with the New York Knicks of the NBA and Illinois' Anderson played 13 seasons in the NBA, most of them with the Orlando Magic. Nick Anderson left college to enter the 1989 NBA Draft and was the 11th pick in the first round.

Nick Anderson's biggest game as a pro came in 1993 when he scored 50 points against the New Jersey Nets.

77 IU Women Win Big Ten by a Neck

The most dramatic victory by an Indiana University basketball team may not have been provided by the men's team but by a group of women in 2002 who caught lightning in a bottle and won a Big Ten Tournament championship for their coach.

Kathi Bennett was on her way to work on a morning that was almost like any other morning. The exception was that on February 8 she didn't fasten her seat belt and was involved in an accident barely a half mile from her office in Assembly Hall.

Coach Bennett suffered a broken neck that doctors said could easily have been fatal. For weeks she wore a brace that had four screws in her skull. She could barely sleep, couldn't shower, and couldn't hug people.

At the time her senior-oriented basketball team was wallowing in the middle of the Big Ten standings. For lack of a better nickname, Bennett could have been coaching the Indiana Underachievers at the time of her wreck. IU had an 11–12 record, including a 5–7 slate in the conference. Thrilled to be alive, Bennett arranged for associate coach Trish Betthauser to take over the team.

Senior center Jill Chapman, the Hoosiers' leading scorer and rebounder, said while hospitalized Bennett was trying to motivate her players to beat Purdue. Her father, former Wisconsin and Washington State men's coach Dick Bennett, and mother, Anne, spent several days visiting her in the hospital.

The Hoosiers were only the fifth seed in the upcoming Big Ten Women's Tournament in Indianapolis. A glance at the pairings made it look like a one-and-done situation. IU's first opponent was Iowa, a team that had beaten the Hoosiers 11 of the past 12 meetings.

However, with a somewhat immobile Bennett on the bench, the Hoosiers beat the Hawkeyes and advanced against the regular season champion Purdue Boilermakers. The chances of Indiana winning didn't look much better because Purdue had won the last nine meetings with its archrival.

But the revamped Hoosiers advanced to the championship game against Penn State, which had defeated IU in 16 of their prior 17 games.

Penn State had All-American Kelly Mazzante, who had averaged 25.1 points per game that year and scored 49 against Minnesota, but Indiana had a better reason to win. Senior guard Heather Cassady led the Hoosiers to a 75–72 victory before a crowd of 9,221 mostly IU fans. Some crowds at Assembly Hall had numbered in the hundreds, but the bandwagon was full after wins over Iowa and Purdue.

Cassady was named Most Outstanding Player, and Chapman added 14 points and 13 rebounds.

"They saw greatness and then went out and got it," Bennett said.

78 Chronology of IU Basketball, etc.

Basketball at Indiana University has been around more than a 100 years, and the university was founded itself in 1820 as the State Seminary. The name was changed to Indiana University in 1838.

Picking through the website, Chronology of Indiana University, one can view the major occurrences in basketball over the years as they occurred within the framework of other historic events at IU.

1824: Classes begin at the State Seminary with 10 men enrolled.

1829: Andrew Wylie named first president.

1830: Construction of first building started at Seminary Square.

1854: First college building destroyed by fire.

1867: IU becomes one of the first state universities to admit women.

1883: First intercollegiate game (baseball) played by an IU team.

1885: Mitchell Hall (named Maxwell Hall until 1894) constructed on new campus.

1886: Football team started.

1894: Kirkwood Hall constructed.

1896: Men's Gymnasium constructed (renamed Assembly Hall in 1917, razed in 1938.

1898: Men's basketball team started.

1900: Kirkwood Observatory constructed.

1910: IU hosts homecoming event for alumni in conjunction with IU–Illinois football game.

1912: "Indiana, Our Indiana," the most recognized of IU's fight songs, is first performed in November at a football game against Northwestern. The song has been played at every basketball and football game since.

1925: Memorial Stadium (renamed Tenth Street Stadium in 1971) completed. Old Oaken Bucket makes first appearance during IU–Purdue game at which the stadium is dedicated.

1928: Fieldhouse is completed, renamed Ora L. Wildermuth Intramural Center in 1971.

1932: Indiana Memorial Union completed (additions made in 1939 and 1946) becoming the world's largest college union building.

1940: Men's basketball team, coached by Branch McCracken, wins school's first NCAA championship by beating Kansas in final game.

1945: Indiana wins first Big Ten football championship.

1946: IU zoologist Hermann J. Muller wins Nobel Prize.

1947: Alfred C. Kinsey and his colleagues establish the Institute for Sex Research, now called the Kinsey Institute for Research in Sex, Gender, and Reproduction.

1949: Men's Quadrangle (renamed Joseph H. Wright Quadrangle in 1959) and University Apartments are completed.

1951: IU holds first Little 500 bicycle race, which will become an annual tradition.

1953: Men's basketball team wins second NCAA championship, again beating Kansas.

1954: One hundred twenty acres north of campus purchased from Faris estate.

1956: Beck Chapel constructed and School of Law Building completed.

1959: Biddle Continuation Center opens.

1960: Seventeenth Street Football Stadium (renamed Memorial Stadium in 1971) and Athletic Fieldhouse completed.

1961: Showalter Fountain completed.

1968: Indiana football team shares Big Ten title and plays in Rose Bowl.

1971: Assembly Hall on Seventeenth Street is one of four new buildings completed on campus. The others are Musical Arts Center, Glenn A. Black Archaeological Laboratory, and Publications/Printing Services Building.

1972: Men's swimming team wins NCAA championship. Hoosier Mark Spitz wins seven gold medals at Munich Olympics.

1976: Men's basketball team wins NCAA championship while going unbeaten under Coach Bob Knight. Hoosiers defeat Michigan for third time in season in championship game.

1978: Movie Breaking Away is filmed in Bloomington and on IU campus.

1981: Men's basketball team wins school's fourth NCAA championship, beating North Carolina in final game.

1987: Keith Smart's baseline jumper beats both the buzzer and runner-up Syracuse as IU wins its fifth NCAA championship in New Orleans.

1987: Sample Gates dedicated on west end of campus.

1996: John Mellencamp Pavilion, the IU Advanced Research and Technology Institute, and the IU Research Park open.

2000: University Chancellor Herman B Wells dies at 97.

2003: Coach Jerry Yeagley leads Hoosiers to sixth NCAA soccer championship in final season.

2004: Indiana wins seventh NCAA soccer title under new coach Mike Freitag.

2005: IU School of Music renamed Jacobs School of Music in honor of donors Barbara B. and David H. Jacobs.

79 Bloomington Home to Mellencamp

Go to an Indiana basketball game, and you might see a celebrity sitting somewhere in Assembly Hall. Rock singer John Mellencamp is a big Indiana fan, so much so that his contribution enabled the university to build an indoor football practice facility that is used by several athletic teams.

Mellencamp's musical hit, "Small Town," applies to Seymour, Indiana, a city of 17,000 southeast of Bloomington. He now lives near Bloomington and is frequently seen around town and at various IU events where his nephew and namesake formerly played on the soccer team.

The Mellencamp Pavilion was dedicated in 1996 and was made possible by a $1.5 million gift from the Indiana singer. The building, located adjacent to Memorial Stadium and Assembly Hall, is used by the field hockey team for varsity games and by the football, baseball, and softball teams for practice. The building covers more than 100,000-sq. ft. and was built at a cost of $6 million. The surface is covered by artificial turf, and the height of the building is sufficient to allow kicking and batting practice.

Several members of Mellencamp's family are IU graduates, and he has lived along Lake Monroe, five miles south of Bloomington, for several years.

After growing up in Seymour, Mellencamp moved to New York City to launch his music career. He cut his first album in 1976 and had his first hit, "I Need a Lover," in 1979. Mellencamp reluctantly allowed his professional name to be changed to Johnny Cougar, and upon becoming a star, he returned to his birth name.

Mellencamp has been nominated for 13 Grammy Awards, and he has won one. He sold more than 40 million albums while

Meg Ryan and singer John Mellencamp during the second half of a game between Indiana and Ohio State on Saturday, December 31, 2011, in Bloomington, Indiana. The Hoosiers won 74–70. (AP Photo/Darron Cummings)

recording 22 Top 40 hits. He was inducted into the Rock and Roll Hall of Fame in 2008.

Mellencamp is also one of the founding members of Farm Aid, an organization that began in 1985 with a concert in Champaign, Illinois, designed to provide financial aid for struggling farmers. These concerts have continued and have raised more than $30 million to promote agriculture.

Mellencamp was the commencement speaker at IU's 2000 ceremonies and received an honorary doctor of music degree from the university.

80 Writer Set Screen for Player

It was a typical Indiana-Purdue game, full of emotion, pressure, and competitiveness, and after 40 minutes the score was tied.

Overtime is a nasty word to most sportswriters, whose upcoming deadlines are tough enough without the game being lengthened an extra 10 minutes or so.

Curt Cavin, a reporter for *The Indianapolis Star*, faced an even bigger dilemma on the night of February 18, 1997. Seated along what was then press row on the east side of McCracken Court, Cavin watched with great concern as the tip to start the extra period came bouncing his way. A couple of feet in its wake was the always-hustling Purdue forward, Brian Cardinal.

Cardinal was one of the hardest-nosed players in the Big Ten, and as the basketball bounced directly over Cavin's left shoulder, Cardinal came leaping over press row in an attempt to retrieve it.

He failed and crashed into Cavin's computer screen, leaving it shattered and unworkable. Most of Curt's story was already written, and somehow he managed to send that portion to the office, then dictated the lead paragraphs after play ended with Purdue winning 89–87.

The shaken Cavin felt fortunate to have survived the night with a story unlike any other he had written, but he was more pleased when his managing editor congratulated him on his work without knowing the difficulty involved.

81 Recker's Leaving Stirs the Fans' Wrath

Sometime after midnight, when the final edition of most newspapers were on the presses and the last editor was en route to his favorite watering hole, the story of the day broke.

It came over the fax machine and details probably weren't to be noticed before the morning shift arrived. The fax out of Auburn, Indiana, revealed that Indiana University basketball star Luke Recker would transfer to another university.

Several hours later, as Bloomington residents sipped their first cup of coffee, the news quickly spread across the town. At first the natives were stunned; then they were outraged. Luke Recker, the Golden Boy of IU basketball, was bailing out on Bob Knight.

Bailing out because of Bob Knight, more than likely.

Plenty of Hoosiers had transferred elsewhere: Derek Holcomb, Mike LaFave, Delray Brooks, Rick Calloway. Only two years earlier, Jason Collier had left for Georgia Tech.

But Luke Recker was different. He came with a four-year warranty. On Flag Day 1999 he waved the white flag after only two years as a Hoosier. No one with such a golden image had rejected the Hoosiers in midstream.

Recker averaged 16.1 points per game during his final season at IU. He was a sophomore at DeKalb High School when he committed to Indiana, and as Hoosier fans salivated for his long-awaited arrival, they clutched him to their bosoms. But when he decided to get out of town, they virtually ran him out of town.

Recker's late-night statement, released while Coach Knight was traveling, said he wasn't satisfied with his development as a player. He wrote that he appreciated the opportunity Knight gave him and implicated no one but himself.

The negative response to Recker's departure was immediate. *The Indianapolis Star* conducted a poll on its website and reported 500 responses in the first two hours.

Star columnist Bill Benner wrote, "Be prepared, Luke. When the Big Red spin-meisters are done, you won't recognize yourself. Instead of the emotional, fire-em-up leader of enormous potential, you will be cast as a selfish, me-first player who was thinking more about your NBA career than you were about leading the Hoosiers."

Recker made no mention of a future college in his middle-of-the-night release, but he eventually said it would be Arizona. Then Recker's entire life changed the night of July 10, 1999, when the car in which he was riding collided with a vehicle operated by a drunk driver.

Recker was in the back seat with his girlfriend, Kelly Craig, and her brother, Jason. Three friends, including driver John Hollberg, were in the front seat of the 1990 Ford Taurus. At about 9:40 PM, a 1977 GMC pickup truck roared along County Road 240 near Durango, Colorado, crossing the center line. It sideswiped another pickup truck loaded with 11 people, nine of them riding in the truck bed, before continuing into the path of the Hollberg vehicle.

Moments later another vehicle approached, this one carrying a nurse named Margo Philpott. She stopped and headed for the first victim she saw, Luke Recker, whose temporal artery had been sliced. His left wrist was smashed, and bones adjoining his thumb were fractured.

Philpott called for someone to apply pressure to Recker's neck because the chance of him bleeding to death was a real possibility. Nearby, Kelly Craig couldn't move because of a broken neck. One person was dead, and 14 were injured. Jason Craig was in a coma, and John Hollberg was about to die.

Bob Hardwick Jr., the 21-year-old driver who initiated the accident, suffered only cuts. He was charged with vehicular homicide, vehicular assault, driving causing injury, and driving under the influence of alcohol.

As Kelly struggled with her injuries, Luke recovered and proceeded with plans to attend school in Arizona. But upon arriving in Tucson, Recker was lonely and talked to Kelly daily on the phone. Finally, he asked Arizona coach Lute Olson for permission to transfer closer to Kelly and his family. Olson told him to do what was best for him.

Recker already knew Iowa coach Steve Alford and eventually wound up with the Hawkeyes, not far from where Recker's father lived. IU fans who had grown to accept him playing thousands of miles away were less enchanted with him returning to Assembly Hall as a Hawkeye.

Kelly Craig faced a mountain of struggles in her rehabilitation, but she persevered and received a degree from Southern Indiana. She and Luke eventually parted and both married other people.

Sixteen months after he last played for the Hoosiers, Luke returned to action as a Hawkeye.

82 Long, Son Have Roles in *Hoosiers*

When the credits roll across the screen at the end of the movie *Hoosiers,* viewers might recognize the name of former Indiana guard Gary Long. Recognizing Long's face is harder to distinguish because his cameo role as an opposing coach in the regional final provided no closeups.

Gary was supposed to have one speaking line in the picture, but it failed to materialize when he was too far away from the bench. He was supposed to have yelled, "Foul the runt!" in reference to Hickory's smallest player.

Long got the role because Angelo Pizzo, a Bloomington resident who wrote the script for the movie, recalled retrieving balls for Long while Gary was playing for IU in the early 1960s. When

Enberg Started Describing IU Games

Before Don Fischer ever announced an IU game, there was a Voice of the Hoosiers named Dick Enberg.

Enberg, who went on to nationwide fame as an announcer of many sports, described Indiana games in the late 1950s and '60s. His most famous line was, "Here come the red shirts," which he used frequently when the Hurryin' Hoosiers were in the midst of a fast break.

A native of the Detroit area, Enberg first attended Central Michigan University before transferring to IU. After graduation he moved to Los Angeles and eventually became the play-by-play announcer for the Los Angeles Rams, the California Angels, and the UCLA Bruins. He rose to become NBC's top play-by-play announcer during the 1970s. His assignments included major tennis tournaments, baseball, and football, including eight Super Bowls. He even has his own star on the Hollywood Walk of Fame.

Gary's son, Brad, won a major role in the movie, Pizzo told him to get his dad for a lesser role.

Brad played the part of Buddy, a starter for Hickory who was kicked off the team during one of the early practices. Later he is back on the squad with no explanation of how he was reinstated. According to his father, Brad had a two-minute scene with Coach Norman Dale, portrayed by Gene Hackman, in which Buddy apologizes for his indiscretions. Hackman told Brad he did a great job, but the scene ended up on the cutting-room floor.

Brad won the acting part over several thousand candidates, according to his father, and had played at Center Grove High School and Southwestern College in Kansas.

The building that represented Hickory's home gym is in Knightstown, Indiana, and remains a popular visiting place for fans. The old high school building in Nineveh, Indiana, became the site of the Hickory school, and Hinkle Fieldhouse on the campus of Butler University in Indianapolis was the site of the state finals.

83 Indiana Won NIT Once—Over Purdue

Indiana has made four appearances in the postseason National Invitation Tournament (NIT), winning it in 1979 when it defeated Purdue in the Championship Game 53–52. The Hoosiers, who won four games in the NIT, finished with a 22–12 record.

IU began tournament play with a 78–59 victory at Texas Tech, then returned home to beat Alcorn State 73–69. That advanced the Hoosiers to New York's Madison Square Garden where they beat Ohio State 64–55. IU played the Buckeyes twice during the regular season, winning at home 70–62 after losing 66–63 in Columbus a week earlier.

Indiana had a 10–8 conference record in 1979 and finished fifth, three games out of first place. Michigan State, Purdue, and Iowa tied for the championship, all with five losses.

The Hoosiers' top scorer that season was Mike Woodson at 21 points per game. Others on the team included Ray Tolbert, Butch Carter, Randy Wittman, Steve Risley, and Landon Turner.

Two years later IU won the national championship.

Indiana's first NIT appearance coincided with Bob Knight's first season in Bloomington. The 1972 Hoosiers went 17–8 but finished the regular season with nine wins in their last 10 games. They lost their NIT opener to Princeton in New York 68–60.

That Indiana team won eight of its first nine, the loss coming at Ohio University, but dropped five straight in January. Major victories included a double-overtime win over Kentucky in Louisville, a home win over No. 14 Kansas, and a neutral-court victory over No. 8 Brigham Young. The Hoosiers also stomped all over Notre Dame 94–29.

Indiana's third appearance in the NIT was in 1985 when the Hoosiers ended an otherwise disappointing season by reaching the tournament's final game. Reggie Miller led UCLA to a 65–62 win over IU in Madison Square Garden.

As was the case in 1979, the Hoosiers won the NCAA two years later.

Indiana lost 13 games in the regular season, including 11 in the Big Ten, but began playing well in the tournament. IU beat Richmond by 22 in Assembly Hall, but the Hoosiers were fortunate to overcome Marquette in double overtime. They beat Tennessee 74–67 in New York.

After that IU became an NCAA Tournament fixture until 2004 when a 14–15 record under Mike Davis made them ineligible for postseason play. Their 15–14 record the next year got IU into the NIT, but it lost in the first round to visiting Vanderbilt, 67–60.

Indiana has also played in the preseason National Invitation Tournament. In 1988, both Syracuse and North Carolina scored more than 100 points in New York wins over the Hoosiers, who then bounced back to win the Big Ten.

Things were better in 1992 when IU won the preseason tournament with wins over Florida State and Seton Hall in New York. They won the preseason NIT again in 1996 as Andrae Patterson scored 39 points to beat Duke 85–69 in the title game.

Mike Davis' first IU team reached the preseason final four but lost two games there to Temple and Texas. The Hoosiers were back in the preseason tournament in 2006–07 but were beaten at Conseco Fieldhouse by Butler, which won the tournament.

84 Hoosiers Recognized in State Hall

Approximately 40 miles east of Indianapolis rests the town of New Castle, a basketball-crazed community of 18,000 that houses not only the nation's largest high school fieldhouse but the Indiana Basketball Hall of Fame.

New Castle was the home of two former Indiana Mr. Basketballs, Kent Benson in 1973 and Steve Alford in '83. Marv Huffman, a standout on IU's 1940 NCAA champions, was from New Castle. So was Ray Pavy, one of Chrysler High School's greatest players, who was paralyzed in an automobile accident after his sophomore year at Indiana.

Other New Castle natives who played at IU included Jerry Ellis, a two-sport star, Vernon Huffman, and Harry "Butch" Joyner, a standout on IU's 1967 Big Ten championship team.

The Hall of Fame, located off State Road 3 on the south side of town, is a must see for any IU fan—or any basketball fan for that matter. Its museum is a timepiece of the sport across the state and honors former players, coaches, and others who contributed to the game.

New Castle was the site of perhaps the most famous scoring duel in state history. Played in what was then the Trojans' bandbox gymnasium, New Castle's Pavy outscored Kokomo's Jimmy Rayl 51–49 in 1959. They would become teammates with the Hurryin' Hoosiers.

That bandbox was long since replaced by the world's largest high school gym, located near the Hall of Fame. There are 9,325 seats in the fieldhouse, but crowds have exceeded 10,000.

The fieldhouse is where Alford practiced his jump shot when he wasn't watching the teams coached by his father, Sam. In recent years New Castle has sent several players to Butler, including Zach Hahn and Chase Stigall from the Bulldogs' successive national finalist squads.

The 81,000-sq. ft. fieldhouse was built in 1959, and the Hall of Fame was moved to New Castle in 1990. Nine of the nation's 10 largest gymnasiums are located in Indiana, including the one used by New Castle's longtime rival, Muncie Central. Muncie, which is about 20 miles north of New Castle, has a gym seating 6,500.

Perhaps the most famous gym in the state is the Wigwam in Anderson that seats 8,996 but was closed in 2011 for financial reasons. East Chicago Central, Seymour, and Richmond also have gyms exceeding 8,000 seats, and ten other high schools have gyms with more than 7,000.

More than a hundred men and women with IU connections have been inducted into the Indiana Basketball Hall of Fame. They include former players, coaches, administrators, media members, and contributors to the game. Those with IU connections follow, in alphabetical order:

Steve Ahlfeld, Sam Alford, Steve Alford, Ernie Andres, Jimmie Angelopolous, Paul Armstrong, Mildred Ball, Ray Ball, Jim Barley, Dick Baumgartner, Kent Benson, Tom Bolyard, Steve Bouchie, Cinda Rice Brown, Hallie Bryant, Phil Buck, Jeannie Butler, James Campbell, Robert Cowan, Don Danielson, Everett Dean, Ed Denton, Steve Downing, Bob Dro, Elder Eberhart, Jerry Ellis, Dick Farley, Ron Ferguson, Scott Fisher, Gene Flowers, Chet Francis, Bill Garrett, Guy Glover.

Steve Green, Jim Gridley, Gary Grieger, Charlie Hall, Ralph Hamilton, Bob Hammel, Byard Hey, William Holzbach, Marvin Huffman, Vernon Huffman, Charlie Jenkins, Bill Johnson, James Jones, Harry Joyner, Willard Kehrt, Roy Kilby, Ted Kitchel, Bobby Knight, Dave Krider, John Laskowski, Bob Leonard, Gary Long, George Marshall, Bob Masters, Debra McClurg, Branch McCracken, Lawrence McCreary, H.T. McCullough, George McGinnis.

Jon McGlocklin, Tom McKinney, Jerry Memering, Murray Mendenhall, Bill Menke, Robert Menke, Amy Metheny, Charles Meyer, Robert Mygrants, Gordon Neff, Pete Obremskey, Ray Pavy, Vernon Payne, A.L. Phillips, Joe Platt, Paul Poff, Richard Polk, Dave Porter, John Porter, Wayne Radford, Frank Radovich, Jimmy Rayl, Gene Ring, Earl Roudebush, Herman Schaefer.

Don Schlundt, Ed Schienbein, Jim Schooley, Burke Scott, Tom Schwartz, Sam Simmermaker, Melinda Sparkman, Bill Stearman, Arnold Suddith, Donna Sullivan, Ray Tolbert, Bill Tosheff, Landon Turner, Dick Van Arsdale, Tom Van Arsdale, Markham Wakefield, Lou Watson, Woodrow Weir, Cliff Wells, Randy Wittman, Andy Zimmer, Steve Redenbaugh, Mike Woodson.

85 Big Ten Tournament Unkind to IU

Bob Knight had few opinions stronger than how he felt about the Big Ten holding a postseason tournament. For years he was a bulkhead of determination when others pointed out the popularity of other tournaments, especially the Atlantic Coast Conference.

Knight's reasoning made sense. When an 18-game regular season schedule already has determined the Big Ten champion, why do we need to determine another champion over a four-day period?

The reason was simple—money. The gate receipts and television money from a Big Ten shootout would fill the conference coffers like nothing else, and the fans would love the competition and the pre-NCAA Tournament atmosphere.

One argument from the Knight supporters was fatigue, pointing out that three or four extra games before the national championship would be a hindrance. The other side of the argument was the theory that the extra games would toughen them for the NCAA.

More coaches whose backgrounds involved conference tournaments were hired by Big Ten schools, and Knight's once-strong position was weakened. In 1998 the Big Ten voted to hold its first league tournament. Knight reluctantly took his Hoosiers to the United Center in Chicago as the No. 6 seed, and the Hoosiers opened with a 78–71 victory over Ohio State. However, in the second round IU lost to Purdue 76–71.

Michigan, which had finished fourth during the regular season, won the tournament over Purdue, which had finished third.

After 15 conference tournaments, the Hoosiers still haven't won a Big Ten Tournament. They've had only marginal success

Always a Doctor in the House

Whenever the Hoosiers play a game, there is a doctor close by to administer medical assistance and help longtime trainer Tim Garl.

Dr. Larry Rink, a Bloomington cardiologist, has looked over the IU program for the past 33 years and initiated cardiovascular testing for Indiana players in 1980. Dr. J.D. Heady has been with the men's basketball program for the past 12 seasons.

Dr. Steve Ahlfeld has spent the past 27 years as the team's orthopedic surgeon. He was an IU guard from 1972–75 and his son, Adam, was on the Indiana squad from 2004–08. Another son, Chris, was on the IU football team.

For many years Bloomington physician Brad Bomba sat alongside Bob Knight during every basketball game. Now retired, Bomba was an end on the IU football team in the 1950s.

over these years during the regular season, sharing only the 2002 regular season championship in the 15 years.

Indiana also lost first-round games in 1999, when 11th-seeded Illinois bumped off the No. 3 Hoosiers, and in 2000, when IU fell again to the Fighting Illini. In 2001 the Hoosiers beat Wisconsin before upsetting top-seeded Illinois 58–56 in the semifinals.

However, No. 6 Iowa stunned No. 4 IU 63–61 in the title game. That was the deepest the Hoosiers have gone into the tournament, and they were victimized by Indiana native Brody Boyd, who scored 22 points in the upset.

Boyd, from Dugger, Indiana, grew up as a big IU fan but was averaging only five points per game and shooting only 39 percent. Against Indiana he made eight of 12 shots, including four of eight three-pointers.

A year later IU beat Michigan State but lost again to Iowa in the semifinals, this time on a last-second bucket by former Hoosier Luke Recker.

Recker, who had announced he was leaving IU via a middle-of-the-night fax, first announced plans to attend Arizona but then decided upon Iowa. Recker came into the Indiana game playing a hot hand—he scored 25 in the opener against Purdue and had 28, including 24 in the second half, against Wisconsin.

One of Indiana's worst losses came in the 2008 Big Ten Tournament after Dan Dakich had been named interim coach to replace Kelvin Sampson. Most of the players had wanted Ray McCallum as their interim coach, and their effort in the first-round game against Minnesota was suspect.

Although D.J. White had a 23-point, 13-rebound game, the Hoosiers fell behind 24–8 at the start and somehow were in the hunt when the Gophers' Blake Hoffarber threw in a spinning last-second shot to beat them.

86 It's Intense Behind the Scenes

Competition within IU's Assembly Hall isn't always confined to the playing floor. There have also been some battles in the press room where competition to get a story, or even a quote, is intense.

Newspaper editors don't like to read something in a competing paper that hasn't appeared in their own, and in such situations on-the-scene reporters are often called on the carpet. The guy typing on his computer 6' away may be writing something that will spoil everyone else's day.

Usually, the concrete-walled room adjacent to the school's gift shop is a picture of tranquility, a spot where reporters can get away from the crowd, talk sports, and enjoy the food that is brought in before the game. Sometimes after a game it is a war zone.

The area consists of about 75 chairs with armrests where writers may take notes as the coaches or players speak at the podium.

Along the side walls are about 25 more seats with a built-in desk where stories are compiled, often being sent to the news desk only minutes after the game ends.

The press room has seen fewer confrontations between coach and writers under coaches Mike Davis, Kelvin Sampson and Tom Crean, but such conflicts weren't unusual during Bob Knight's 29-year reign. Many an interrogator had his question ridiculed, especially after a tough loss. If those concrete walls could only talk.

This is where reporter Pat Forde was told by Knight, "Some of you guys should find a new profession," as the coach quickly exited the room.

This is the place where Purdue coach Gene Keady tried to manage the news by telling reporters that the Boilermakers' win was the real news, not Knight's heaving of his chair across the court.

This is the spot where many a reporter was hit with the response, "Anyone here got an intelligent question?"

This is the room where Knight and Davis, then his assistant, tried to downplay the incident in which a student was reprimanded by calling the coach "Knight."

This is the spot where IU player Luke Recker jerked off his cap when he heard the coach coming, knowing that Knight doesn't like headgear worn indoors.

The press room is where Crean always showed up after tough losses and where Knight often didn't. It is where word processors sometimes failed and their owners screamed obscenities into the walls. It is where, in the days before wireless transmissions, six reporters on deadline would compete to use the four available telephones.

When someone's computer does fail, the victim has no closer friends than his peers from other papers. All have been in the same predicament, and all of them are quick to offer advice—and even their own computers—to help a competitor.

Reporters on the tightest deadlines (some as early as 10:15 PM) often slip into the room at halftime to write a few paragraphs about the first half. Others write from the on-court seats during intermission, adding to or deleting from the story as the second half progresses. If the game isn't close, the story may be done except for the score when play concludes.

Then, after gathering quotes and new information, reporters from multi-edition papers have to rewrite their original pieces.

Sometimes there are situations when one team takes a 10-point lead with five minutes left and the scribe writes a catchy first paragraph about the expected results. Then the trailing team may come back and regain the lead, requiring the reporter to start his story again with no assurance that the momentum won't shift a few more times.

While few changes have been made to the press room over the years, the press seating during games has changed with the times. Assembly Hall was built with three rows of press seating just above court level behind the team benches. The chairs and writing desks were affixed to the floor, but in the late 1980s two of those rows were eliminated in favor of customer seating. A moveable three-row work area was located at midcourt on the west side.

That arrangement was rued by the writers, mostly because there was barely enough desk area for their laptops, and telephones also had to sit there. The electrical outlets were in spots where the cords wouldn't connect, so a bulky extension cord was added.

However, the major glitch for reporters was that their seats were so compact that it was impossible to stand up straight for the national anthem. Getting out of the seat during play was impossible, and, in fact, one visiting reporter suffered claustrophobia while covering a game.

For a time in the 1990s the press was seated at tables alongside the court, but that was eliminated in favor of courtside chairs for fans willing to pay top dollar. The bulk of the media was relocated to the end of the court, some of them sitting directly behind students who always stood up. When Crean arrived, he instigated the "big heads" concept in which students are given large cardboard cutouts to hold up during opponents' free throws.

One press area is behind the area with the cutouts.

87 Ex-Hoosiers Flock to NBA

The NBA has always turned a favorable eye toward Indiana players, but IU's 1976 and 1981 national champions provided fertile feeding grounds for the league.

The unbeaten '76 team sent four players to the NBA, including four first-round picks. Shortly after the unbeaten season, Indiana's Scott May, Quinn Buckner, and Bob Wilkerson were selected by Chicago, Milwaukee, and Seattle, respectively, while Tom Abernethy went to the Los Angeles Lakers in the third round.

The next season Kent Benson was a first-round choice of Milwaukee, and the Indiana Pacers chose Wayne Radford in the second round of the 1978 draft.

Indiana's 1981 national champions sent three players into the NBA as first-round choices and probably would have sent a fourth had Landon Turner not been paralyzed in an auto accident. As it was, Turner was made a tenth-round pick of the Boston Celtics as a goodwill gesture by Boston general manager Red Auerbach.

Isiah Thomas was picked by Detroit and Ray Tolbert by New Jersey in the first-round of the 1981 draft. Teammate Randy Wittman was a first-round pick in the '83 draft. Other IU players drafted in '81 included Glen Grunwald, by Boston in the fifth round, and Steve Risley, by Phoenix in the eighth. The 1983 draft not only included Wittman but Jim Thomas (second

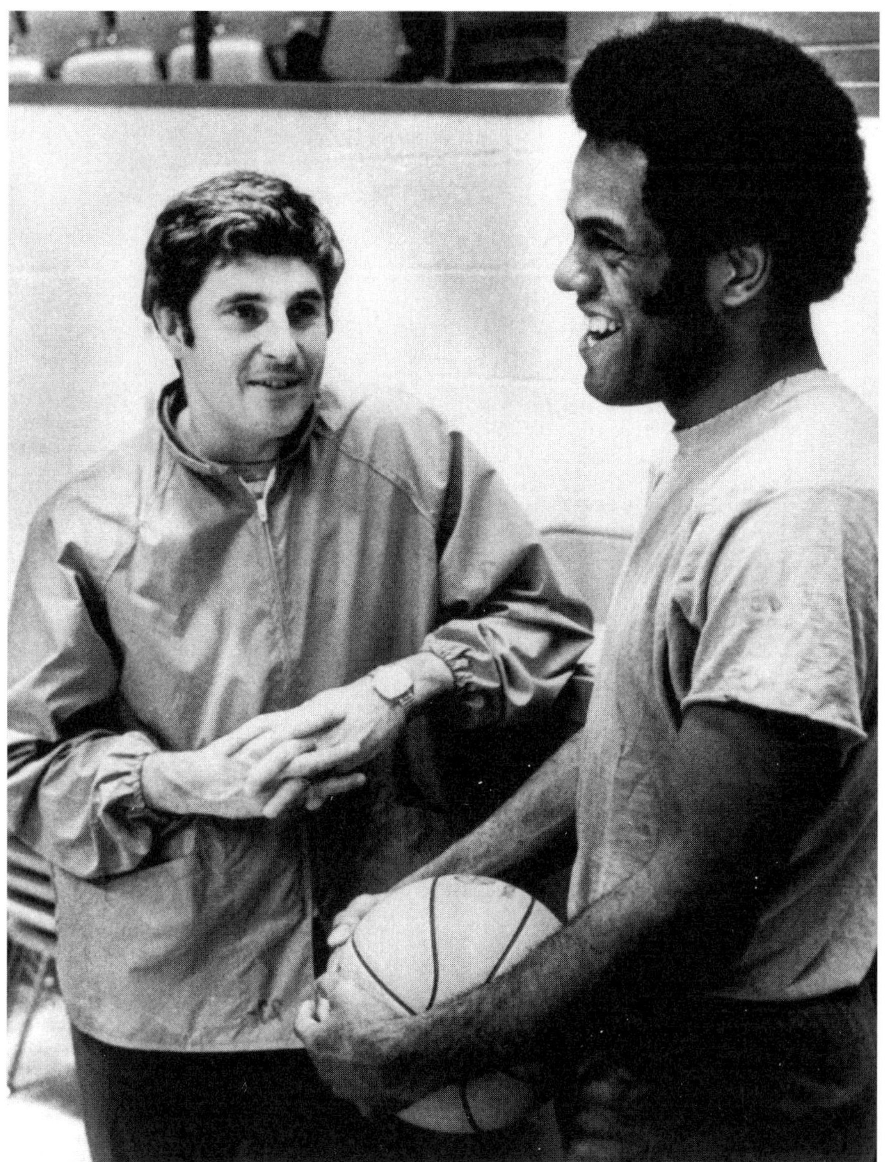

Coach Bobby Knight (left) tells All-American Scott May he was named national college basketball Player of the Year in March 1976. Knight, who guided Indiana to its second undefeated season and the top ranking in the nation, was named college basketball Coach of the Year for the second straight year. (AP Photo/RDP)

round, Indiana), Ted Kitchel (second round, Milwaukee), Steve Bouchie (fourth round, Detroit), and Tony Brown (seventh round, Indiana).

Indiana's 1987 NCAA champions had Steve Alford picked by Dallas in the second round and Daryl Thomas taken by Sacramento in the sixth. A year later Dean Garrett was a second-round choice of Phoenix and Keith Smart went to Golden State in the same round.

Other Indiana players selected by NBA teams were:

1948: Ward Williams, Fort Wayne.

1949: Duane Klueh, Boston.

1950: Jerry Stuteville, Indianapolis.

1951: Bill Garrey, Boston; Bill Tosheff, Indianapolis; Bob Swalls, Philadelphia.

1952: Sammy Miranda, Rochester.

1954: Bob Leonard, Baltimore; Charlie Kraak, Fort Wayne; Dick Farley, Syracuse.

1955: Don Schlundt, Syracuse.

1956: Wally Choice, St. Louis.

1957: Dick Neal, Boston, 11th round.

1958: Archie Dees, Cincinnati, first round.

1960: Frank Radovich, St. Louis, second round, Bob Wilkinson, St. Louis, ninth round.

1961: Walt Bellamy, Chicago, first round; Ron Horn, St. Louis, second round.

1963: Tom Bolyard, Baltimore, third round; Jimmy Rayl, Cincinnati, third round.

1965: Dick Van Arsdale, New York, second round; Tom Van Arsdale, Detroit, third round; Jon McGlocklin, Cincinnati, third round.

1968: Butch Joyner, Cincinnati, ninth round.

1969: Bill DeHeer, San Diego, eighth round.

1970: Ken Johnson, Cleveland, 10th round.

1971: Lee McCollough, San Diego, thirteeth round: James "Bubbles" Harris, Cleveland, 14th round.

1972: Joby Wright, Seattle, second round.

1973: Steve Downing, Boston, first round; George McGinnis, Philadelphia, second round; John Ritter, Cleveland, eighth round.

1975: Steve Green, Chicago, second round; John Laskowski, Chicago, second round.

1976: Scott May, Chicago, first round; Quinn Buckner, Milwaukee, first round; Bob Wilkerson, Seattle, first round; Tom Abernethy, Los Angeles, third round.

1977: Kent Benson, Milwaukee, first round.

1978: Wayne Radford, Indiana, second round.

1980: Mike Woodson, New York, first round; Butch Carter, Los Angeles, second round.

1981: Isiah Thomas, Detroit, first round; Ray Tolbert, New Jersey, first round; Glen Grunwald, Boston, fifth round; Steve Risley, Phoenix, eighth round.

1982: Landon Turner, Boston, 10th round.

1983: Randy Wittman, Washington, first round; Jim Thomas, Indiana, second round; Ted Kitchel, Milwaukee, second round; Steve Bouchie, Detroit, fourth round; Tony Brown, Indiana, seventh round.

1985: Uwe Blab, Dallas, first round.

1987: Steve Alford, Dallas, second round; Daryl Thomas, Sacramento, sixth round.

1988: Dean Garrett, Phoenix, second round; Keith Smart, Golden State, second round.

1989: Jay Edwards, Los Angeles Clippers, second round.

1993: Calbert Cheaney, Washington, first round; Greg Graham, Charlotte, first round.

1994: Damon Bailey, Indiana, second round.

1995: Alan Henderson, Atlanta, first round.

1996: Brian Evans, Orlando, first round.

1998: Andrae Patterson, Minneapolis, second round.

2000: A.J. Guyton, Chicago, second round.

2001: Kirk Haston, Charlotte, first round.

2002: Jared Jeffries, Washington, first round.

2005: Bracey Wright, Minnesota, second round.

2008: Eric Gordon, Los Angeles Clippers, first round; D.J. White, Detroit, first round.

88 Coach Was Unpredictable on the Air

Most college coaches have some type of radio or television show, and Bob Knight was no exception—except that his shows were always different than any of the others. Don Fischer, the play-by-play voice of the Hoosiers for more than 40 years, was host of *The Bob Knight Talk Show* through much of the coach's time in Bloomington.

Fischer never knew what Knight was going to do during the show, which he often did from the coaches' dressing quarters in Assembly Hall. Fischer's initial problem every week was wondering if the coach would call in on time, or on occasion wondering if he would call in at all.

The coach would always use a speaker phone, and his voice would fade out on the radio as he walked about the room doing various chores. He might leave the program to discuss something with another coach, leaving Fischer to fill the idle moments any way that he could.

For a time Knight took live questions from callers, but eventually he accepted only written questions. If a question failed to meet his standards, he would sometimes answer the question by insulting the fan. The program always had a high rating, possibly because every answer was unpredictable.

Fischer never knew what would happen next; once the coach excused himself while he took a shower. The announcer then had to fill the empty minutes with whatever came to mind.

On one occasion, Fischer was taken back by the sound of a toilet flushing.

Especially if he was airing the show from his home, the coach was heard eating on occasion, and he once asked his wife to get him a knife.

Knight's television show was often taped after Saturday games and shown by various stations on Sunday. Film clips of the previous game would be shown as Knight commented about various positives and negatives. Host Chuck Marlow would interject opinions of his own, often backing off by admitting, "You would know more about that than me."

Knight's most memorable television show occurred in 1981 following a game against Purdue in which he claimed the Boilermakers' Roosevelt Barnes reportedly threw a "sucker punch" against IU's Isiah Thomas. Knight claimed he had invited Purdue athletic director George King to appear on the show but that King had declined.

Claiming he'd rather talk to someone who was better informed, Knight brought out a donkey that he claimed represented Purdue's point of view. He introduced the donkey as Jack and said Marlow could guess his last name and then ask him any questions.

On another occasion in 1996, Knight was describing his disappointment over the lack of effort in the prior game. Suddenly, he went from a soft-spoken coach to one who kicked the floor, screamed multiple obscenities, and caused the director to yell, "Cut!"

For a time Knight did a weekly instructional program with IU golf coach Sam Carmichael. Usually Knight handed down the advice while Carmichael affirmed his thoughts. Knight would usually hit shots that often required retaking the film clip.

Somehow tapes of the show and its outtakes were leaked to the public, and the film of Knight mis-hitting shot after shot—and then cursing in all manner of language—became a hot topic over a wide area. At last look, the clip was available on YouTube.

Bob Knight the Commentator

Following his retirement as coach at Texas Tech, Bob Knight became an analyst for ESPN. In the early 1980s he reportedly considered taking a similar job with CBS but decided to remain in coaching.

During the 1979 Final Four in Salt Lake City, Utah, Knight worked as a commentator alongside Kentucky play-by-play announcer Cawood Ledford, and the pair drew high marks from listeners. During the semifinal games, Michigan State had beaten Pennsylvania, and Indiana State, with All-American Larry Bird, was en route to a victory over DePaul.

The Michigan State fans began chanting, "We want Bird!" during the second game when the observant Knight remarked, "They may want Bird, but if they get him I guarantee you there'll be a time Monday night when they'd like to give him back."

89 IU Claims 26 Mr. Basketballs

When Cody Zeller of Washington, Indiana, enrolled at IU in the fall of 2011, he became the seventh Mr. Basketball to suit up for the Hoosiers in the past 16 years. Mr. Basketball represents the best high school player in the state and enables the winner to wear No. 1 during the two-game series against the Kentucky All-Stars.

Zeller, whose oldest brother, Luke, played at Notre Dame and his other brother, Tyler, played at North Carolina, selected the Hoosiers over North Carolina and Butler. He averaged 24.6 points per game and 13 rebounds while leading the Washington Hatchets to the Class III state championship for the third straight year. He led the Indiana All-Stars to a two-game sweep over their Kentucky rivals, scoring 26 points and grabbing 15 rebounds in the second game.

Both Luke and Tyler joined Cody as Mr. Basketballs.

Cody's current teammate, Jordan Hulls of Bloomington South, was also Mr. Basketball in 2009. Other IU players who were Mr. Basketball are:

2007: Eric Gordon, North Central; 2004: A.J. Ratliff, North Central; 2000: Jared Jeffries, Bloomington North; 1998: Tom Coverdale, Noblesville; 1997: Luke Recker, DeKalb; 1990: Damon Bailey, Bedford North Lawrence; 1989: Pat Graham, Floyd Central; 1987: Lyndon Jones and Jay Edwards, Marion 1984: Delray Brooks, Michigan City; 1983: Steve Alford, New Castle; 1979: Steve Bouchie, Washington; 1977: Ray Tolbert, Anderson Madison Heights; 1973: Kent Benson, New Castle; 1970: Dave Shepherd, Carmel; 1969: George McGinnis, Indianapolis Washington; 1961: Tom and Dick Van

Arsdale, Indianapolis Manual; 1959: Jimmy Rayl, Kokomo; 1953: Hallie Bryant, Indianapolis Crispus Attucks; 1948: Bill Masters, Lafayette; 1947: Bill Garrett, Shelbyville; 1945: Tom Schwartz, Kokomo; 1940: Ed Scheinbein, Southport.

90 Felling: Did He, or Didn't He?

Bob Knight's opinion of Ron Felling was positive at one time, but that was before the former Indiana assistant responded to his firing by turning a private moment at an IU practice into the most watched 2½-second show on television.

The brief film clip, which showed Knight's hand clasping the neck of IU player Neil Reed during a practice, was sent to CNN in an unmarked manila envelope that included no letter but spoke volumes without words. The incident shown on the film led to an internal investigation by IU officials that led to Knight being fired on September 10, 2000.

Felling's friends and enemies agree on one thing—the longtime assistant coach provided the postage for the package that went to CNN. A dozen years later, Felling has never confirmed that publicly.

"I'm not saying I did, and I'm not saying I didn't," he said.

Felling said Indiana basketball secretary B.J. McElroy told him several times that Knight had called Felling the best Xs and Os coach he had on his staff.

Felling joined Knight after 16 years as a high school coach in Lawrenceville, Illinois, where his teams won four Class A state championships and had a 28-game winning streak.

Evidence of the "choking" accompanied other stories about unusual actions by Knight.

Jeanette Hargraves, an athletic department secretary, told an Indianapolis television station that Knight had thrown a vase against her office wall. Another secretary told a TV reporter Knight had physically assaulted media relations director Kit Klingelhoffer.

Neil Reed was a hero during his freshman season when he played with an injured shoulder, but by his junior season Knight apparently had soured on the smallish guard. When critics came down on Knight following the film's showing, Reed somehow became a target for Knight defenders. The hometown *Herald-Times*, which was generally supportive of Knight over his 29 years at IU, chose to avoid the term "choke." Instead, the paper said Knight's hand was "attaching" to Reed's chest.

To Knight's supporters, Felling was the real villain. Pat Knight, the coach's son and an assistant coach, accused Felling of stealing the tape.

"He's going around telling people he's got it," Pat told *The Indianapolis Star*. "Thirteen years of loyalty to someone and he's pulling that kind of stuff. It makes me sick."

Felling was a logical suspect because he had been fired by the head coach early in the 1999–2000 season. Knight listened in on a telephone conversation between Felling and Bowling Green coach Dan Dakich. Felling was the veteran on Knight's staff but was in his third season as administrative assistant. After overhearing the conversation, Knight reportedly knocked Felling into a television set, a conflict Knight said was simply a bump. Felling later sued Knight, and their lawyers settled for $25,000.

During a deposition in the lawsuit, Pat Knight was asked if his father was justified in knocking Felling into the TV. Pat's response was affirmative, and he added, "I probably would have done more.... I'd beat the shit out of Ron."

"Neil Reed was a good kid," Felling said. "He once said he would like to be buried between Assembly Hall and McDonald's. When he had an opportunity to come to Indiana it [the recruiting process] was all over.

"It's funny how he went from his freshman year playing with his arm dislocated and his shoulder harness on. I read once where Knight was quoted as saying, 'If we had more kids like Neil Reed, who were as mentally tough as he is, we wouldn't lose.' Then a year or so later he was a no-good trouble-causing player."

Felling currently lives in Bloomington part of the year and also has condominiums in Florida and Hot Springs, Arkansas.

Felling was fired before the Indiana-Kentucky game in 1999 at the RCA Dome in Indianapolis. IU's media relations office released a statement at the game saying the assistant coach had resigned in order to spend more time with his kids. Felling has three kids, all grown at that time.

Felling, who turned 72 in January of 2012, was active in basketball camps after leaving IU. His wife, Camilla, is a critical care nurse at Bloomington Hospital, but Ron spends part of the year at his condos in Benito Springs, Florida, and on Lake Hamilton in Arkansas.

"Both of them are good places to retire. I really enjoy Lake Hamilton because there are plenty of nice restaurants to pull up to by boat. I'm not much of a gambler, but they've got the Oaklawn race track," Felling said. "I've not become a great race fan, but I go and enjoy the horses. That's the track where Smarty Jones, Lawyer Ron, Afleet Alex, Kirlin, and the filly, Rachel Alexander, came out of."

91 It Really Isn't Junk, But Artifacts

Behind an unmarked steel door on the west side of Assembly Hall rests one of the building's many storage rooms. The room isn't open to the public, and the door seldom is opened, and when it is would appear to be of little use other than as a fallout shelter. The light is low-watt, all the better not to reflect the dust, and the cardboard boxes have been placed in no particular order. The room seems as useless as the Wanted posters on the bulletin board at the Mayberry jail.

Within the boxes and thick file folders rest much of the recorded history of Indiana University sports. The modern term for this place is archives, but in earlier years it would have been a cache for junk. At one time everything was located in another room off the upper hallway of the basketball arena but when IU's Media Relations Office was relocated several years ago, the boxes of newspaper clippings and news releases were hastened into whatever space was available.

When it comes to organization, this setting won't be confused with the Library of Congress.

Given a slow day, however, an intruder will find that these barren walls can talk. When he begins foraging through the papers and pictures, he finds the ultimate toyland for Hoosier fans. An attempt has been made at organization, and thick envelopes include significant information about individual athletes. One must thumb through the track and field, field hockey, and wrestling clippings to find the ones on Brian Evans, Steve Alford, and Scott May. They are there, but they present a challenge for anyone invading the rummage that might be in a hurry.

The best way to find basketball items is to check out those on football and baseball along the way. The intruder can read about Harry Gonso and the 1967 Hoosiers or about baseball star Ted Kluszewski's IU days.

Indiana basketball dates back to 1901 when the season began on February 8 and finished four games later on March 15. Information about the early years is vague but increases during the '20s and '30s and expands significantly thereafter. Some of the best early information comes from student managers' notebooks, which not only reflect the scores of the games but the cost of the team's meals.

Newspaper accounts of the early days are vague to nonexistent. Most ignore first names or game details and are filled instead with

What's In a Name, Anyway?

In more than a century of Indiana basketball, the varsity has included only three players whose last name was Smith. They were Byard Smith in 1919; Kreigh Smith, a sophomore reserve on the 1987 NCAA champions; and James Smith, who lettered in 1943.

None of the three averaged more than 2.5 points per game over their careers.

Another common name, Jones, is also hard to find among Indiana lettermen. The only ones listed are Lyndon Jones, a former Mr. Basketball who was a Hoosier from 1988–91, and Verdell Jones, who completed his eligibility in 2012.

Johnson has been a more common name among IU players. The seven Johnsons on record include Ken (1968–70), who went on to play football for the Cincinnati Bengals; Jack, a starter on IU's 1967 Big Ten champions; and Leroy, a superb all-around athlete who was on the 1960 team.

Indiana once had two Grahams (Pat and Greg) on the same team, but they are the only two players in IU history with that last name. Almost as unusual, there has been only one Green to wear an IU uniform—the sharp-shooting Steve of the 1975 team.

There have been five players named Thomas, and two of them (Isiah and Jim) made the all-Final Four team in 1981.

reporters' biased opinions and observations. One clipping from the 1950s concentrated largely on the inadequacies of the officials.

The dusty notebooks also reflect the changes in coaching styles over the years. For instance, a student manager named W.E. Keisker revealed some rules made by Coach Leslie Mann for the 1922–23 Indiana team. They included:

No eating candy.
No eating between meals.
No drinking of Coca-Cola or any soft drinks.
No smoking or use of tobacco in any form.
No drinking of coffee.
Be in bed by 10:30 PM.

There was another notable restriction set by Mann, who instigated a rule in February 1923 that his players were to refrain from any social dating until the end of the season. They weren't even permitted to socialize with women in the hallways.

"There will be no more dates, even between classes," Mann said.

Student managers served as traveling secretaries in the early days. According to Keisker's records, the IU team had a sizeable deficit after road trips during the 1922–23 season. The team had a budget of $600 for travel but spent $274.17 to go to Illinois, $70.50 for a trip to Purdue, $827.62 for a swing through Northwestern and Iowa, and $934.59 for a trip covering Wisconsin and Minnesota.

Breaking part of that down, the visit to Illinois saw $78.35 spent on meals, $20 for hotel rooms, $33.60 for Pullman train transportation, $3.50 for taxis, $3 for bandages, and $3 for street cars.

There was also $6 spent on entertainment with no further explanation given.

92 Border War Is Intense

The two schools are located about a hundred miles from the Mason-Dixon Line, Indiana to the north and Kentucky to the south.

They play in different conferences and are located in different states with different cultures. Indiana is in the Midwest, Kentucky in the South. Kentucky is big on horse racing, Indiana on auto racing. Kentucky relates to Stephen Foster's music, Indiana to Hoagy Carmichael's. Kentucky farmers raise tobacco, Indiana's raise corn.

People in both states believe "real" basketball originated on their soil.

If Indiana University and the University of Kentucky didn't both have a rich basketball tradition, there would be no rivalry. Because the two schools have combined for 13 NCAA championships, the rivalry is as hot as overcooked potatoes.

The Hoosiers and Wildcats played four times in the 1920s and didn't meet again until the early 1940s. Indiana won the first six meetings but had lost two straight when the series began a 21-year hibernation. It was during that lapse that the rivalry first began simmering, a result of similar claims of superiority.

In 1953 the Wildcats had their season suspended by NCAA violations, while Indiana posted a 23–3 record and captured the national title. The following season Kentucky returned to the NCAA's good graces and went undefeated in 25 games, while the Hoosiers went 20–4 with a lineup still intact from '53.

Top-ranked Kentucky declined a bid to the NCAA Tournament in '54 because its three best players, Cliff Hagan, Frank Ramsey, and Lou Tsioropoulos, were ineligible. No. 4 IU was upset in the tournament by Notre Dame.

Kentucky fans still like to claim they would have had the best team in 1953, a point that IU guard Bobby Leonard disputes. The Wildcats defeated '54 champion LaSalle by 13 points during the regular season and didn't win a game by fewer than six points. They had a streak of 16 games in which opponents were outscored by an average of 33.7 points.

Of course, the Southeastern Conference wasn't considered as strong in those days. As former Notre Dame coach Johnny Dee once said of the late UK coach, "Adolph Rupp has won 800 and some games. Five-hundred of them have been against Southeastern Conference teams. That's like me going down to Texas with six kids from Canada and starting a hockey league."

The series resumed in 1965 on a sporadic basis, and when Bob Knight became IU's coach, he reeled off five straight victories over the Wildcats, including a 72–65 triumph in Nashville, Tennessee, that put the Hoosiers in the 1973 Final Four.

The IU players returned to Bloomington on a Saturday afternoon and walked across the Assembly Hall court during a break in the action of a high school state finals game. Future Hoosier Kent Benson was in the stands, and said he decided to come to IU at that time.

"I think I was in the last row of Assembly Hall, and they marched across the floor diagonally with Quinn [Buckner] holding the trophy above his head. That was very impressionable. There was something about that that has stuck with me ever since," Benson said.

The Hoosiers had won their last five games against Kentucky pending the Elite Eight game in Dayton during the 1975 East Regional. The Wildcats upset the Hoosiers, who got only a cameo appearance from injured Scott May 92–90.

IU Does Well Outside Its Conference

Indiana's success against schools from major basketball conferences is a barometer of the Hoosiers' overall success over the years. At the end of the 2012 season, IU held advantages over teams from the Atlantic Coast Conference (29–20), Big East (110–59), Big Twelve (61–35), Missouri Valley (45–13), Pacific–10 (30–17), and Southeastern (53–38).

The Atlantic Coast (ACC) traditionally receives accolades as one of the strongest leagues, but Indiana has a series advantage over seven of the 12 teams currently in the ACC. IU is 7–5 over North Carolina, 4–0 against Florida State, 5–2 against Maryland, 2–0 against Georgia Tech, 5–2 against Maryland, and 2–1 against Virginia and Virginia Tech.

The Hoosiers are 3–4 against Duke.

After splitting two games in 2011–12, Kentucky continues to lead that series 32–24, but Indiana has advantages against SEC members Florida, Alabama, Auburn, Tennessee, Georgia, LSU, Mississippi State, South Carolina, and Vanderbilt.

Indiana's best records against Big East teams are Cincinnati (12–3), Notre Dame (48–21), Louisville (10–6), and Marquette (7–2).

May had broken his arm on February 22 in an 83–82 victory at Purdue and played only the first seven minutes of the Kentucky game. He sat down with the score tied at 16.

Kentucky moved ahead 24–18 before the Hoosiers rallied to go up 38–31 en route to a 44–44 halftime score, but with five and a half minutes left in the game, IU trailed by nine. Benson had 33 points, 23 rebounds, and five assists.

"Kentucky had a wonderful team, but I think the real key in our loss was us giving up 92 points," Laskowski said.

Earlier that season IU pounded Kentucky 98–74 as Knight slapped Kentucky coach Joe B. Hall on the back of the head during a mid-game conversation at midcourt.

When Mike Davis succeeded Knight as coach, he soon learned that Kentucky was the biggest headache on his schedule. Davis ran onto the court late in a game against UK in Louisville, appealing to an official that Bracey Wright had been fouled, but instead he got a technical foul. That clinched a 70–64 win for Kentucky.

Two years earlier, in his first season as IU coach, Davis stunned reporters after an 88–74 loss to the Wildcats in Freedom Hall. With midnight approaching, the Indiana coach let his emotions flow by saying, "I can't coach this team."

Expounding, he exclaimed, "Maybe the guy they bring in next year will get them to play hard. I can't do it. I'm not the guy.... What buttons do I push? No way they'll keep me for this job."

Actually, Indiana kept Davis for six seasons, but a victory over UK didn't occur until December 2007. Prior to that, Davis' preschool-aged son, A.J., had asked, "Dad, are we ever gonna beat Kentucky?"

93 Hoagy's Stardust Covers IU

Hoagy Carmichael, who spun the music to the famous "Stardust," left footprints all over Indiana University during his storied career as a music maker. Carmichael was born in Bloomington on November 22, 1899, and died in 1981 at age 82. He was named Hoagland after a circus troupe. His father was a horse-drawn taxi driver and his mother an accomplished pianist. Carmichael reportedly earned his first money ($5) playing at a fraternity party.

Hoagy received his bachelor's degree from IU in 1925 and his law degree in '26 while a member of Kappa Sigma fraternity. While on a visit to Chicago he was introduced to Louis Armstrong, with whom he would collaborate later.

In 1927 Carmichel composed his famous "Stardust," which became an American classic recorded by hundreds of artists. The song originally was named "Star Dust" but became one word after the lyrics were added in 1929, at which time it was recorded at Gennett Records studio in Richmond, Indiana, with Carmichael doing the piano solo.

During the 1930s, Carmichael composed "Georgia on My Mind," which became most famous after the Ray Charles rendition was released many years later. Hoagy wrote "Up a Lazy River" in 1930, and he became a popular singer despite a unique voice that he described as "the way a shaggy dog looks." As he put it, "I have Wabash fog and sycamore twigs in my throat."

Following his marriage in 1935, Hoagy moved to California and joined Paramount Studios for $1,000 a week writing songs for the Hollywood studio. In 1937, he appeared in the movie *Topper*, in which he serenaded Cary Grant and Contance Bennett with his song, "Old Man Moon." He went on to appear in 14 movies.

Carmichael won an Academy Award for Best Original Song with "In the Cool, Cool, Cool of the Evening," with lyrics by Johnny Mercer. Associates included Fred Astaire, Bing Crosby, Duke Ellington, Harry James, Glenn Miller, and Paul Whiteman.

The lyrics of Stardust:
And now the purple dusk of twilight time
steals across the meadows of my heart.
High up in the sky the little stars climb,
always reminding me that we're apart.
You wander down the lane and far away,
leaving me a song that will not die.
Love is now the stardust of yesterday,
the music of the years gone by.

Sometimes I wonder why I spend
the lonely night dreaming of a song.
The melody haunts my reverie
and I am once again with you.
When our love was new
and each kiss an inspiration.
But that was long ago.
Now my consolation
is in the stardust of a song.
Beside a garden wall,
when stars are bright
you are in my arms.
The nightingale tells his fairy tale,
a paradise where roses bloom.
Though I dream in vain,
In my heart it will remain:
My stardust melody,
the memory of love's refrain.

94 Jeffries, Hulls Among Few Wearing No. 1

Jared Jeffries was the first Indiana player to wear No. 1 on his jersey, and only 35 IU players have ever carried single-digit numbers. Almost all of those have been in the past 25 years.

The No. 1 uniform has been worn by five players, including current guard Jordan Hulls. Three men who played under Kelvin Sampson wore No. 1—Armond Bassett, Evan White and Michael Santa. The latter three played only one year, and White and Santa participated in only three games in 2009.

All-American Isiah Thomas looks for an opening in the St. Joseph defense during the NCAA Mideast Regional in Bloomington, Indiana, on March 23, 1981. (AP Photo)

Only A.J. Moye, James Hardy, DeAndre Thomas, Christian Watford, and Matt Roth have carried the No. 2 shirt, and Roth has since switched to No. 30.

Bob Knight broke his own precedent when he allowed Jay Edwards to wear No. 3 and Lyndon Jones to carry No. 4 in the late 1980s. The first to wear No. 3 was Jerry Stuteville in 1948 and Edwards was followed by Charlie Miller, Tom Coverdale, D.J. White, Maurice Creek, and Daniel Moore, who has also switched to No. 11.

The early single-digit players were All-American Bill Garrett (No. 8) and Gene Ring (No. 7), both from 1949–51. Karl Satter wore No. 6 in 1951, and Satter, Ring, and Garrett are the only Indiana players to carry their respective numbers.

The most popular number has been 23, which was worn by 23 different Hoosiers. They were Jerry Bass, Delray Brooks, Bobby Capobianco, Don Cox, Chuck Franz, Larry Gipson, Eric Gordon, Al Harden, Steve Hart, Steve Heiniger, Bode Hill, Charles Hodson, Sean Kline, Kevin Lemme, Jamal Meeks, Craig Morris, Vernon Payne, Jim Phipps, Kipp Schutz, Keith Smart, Ronald Taylor, Rob Turner, and Jim Wisman.

Twenty Hoosiers have worn No. 24: Steve Ahlfeld, Ray Pavy, Steven Gambles, Jeff Howard, Robert Kent, Herbie Lee, Michael Lewis, Sherrill Marginet, Brandon McGee, Kenny Morgan, Matt Nover, Ray Pavy, Vernon Pfaff, Tyrie Robbins, Dave Shepherd, Daryl Thomas, Robert Vaden, Randy Wittman, John Wood, and Jack Wright.

The next most popular numeral is 20, worn by Jim Barley, Mike Bedree, Rick Calloway, Jack Campbell, Goethe Chambers, Bill Cunningham, Greg Graham, Dave Granger, Mike Niles, Andre Owens, A.J. Ratliff, Allen Schlegelmilch, Jerry Schofeld, Jim Thomas, Gary Tofil, Bobby Wilkerson, Sherron Wilkerson, Nick Williams, and Frank Wilson.

Some McDonald's Stars Left Early

The McDonald's All-American team has been the earmark of high school greatness and the measuring stick for colleges who recruit them. The McDonald's All-Stars play an exhibition game once a year at rotating sites.

Indiana University has attracted 25 McDonald All-Americans since 1977 when Jeffersonville's Tommy Baker and Anderson Madison Heights' Ray Tolbert enrolled. Others have been:

> 1978: Landon Turner; 1979: Isiah Thomas; 1981: John Flowers; 1983: Daryl Thomas; 1984: Delray Brooks; 1985: Rick Calloway; 1987: Jay Edwards; 1988: Eric Anderson; 1989: Greg Graham, Pat Graham; 1991: Damon Bailey, Alan Henderson; 1993: Sherron Wilkerson; 1994: Andrae Patterson, Neil Reed; 1996: Jason Collier; 1997: Luke Recker; 1998: Dane Fife; 2000: Jared Jeffries; 2002: Bracey Wright; 2004: D.J. White; 2007: Eric Gordon; 2011: Cody Zeller.

For a variety of reasons, only 10 have finished their four years at IU. Those who didn't were Baker, Turner (injuries), Thomas, Flowers, Brooks, Callaway, Edwards, Wilkerson, Reed, Collier, Recker, Jeffries, Wright, and Gordon.

Most numbers higher than 50 were assigned to big men, including Kent Benson, Steve Bouchie, Chris Lawson, Jon McGlocklin, and Mike Szymanczyk at No. 54. Todd Lindeman and Jeff Newton were among those with No. 50.

Numbers worn by other IU stars included Calbert Cheaney (40); Don Schlundt (34); Isiah Thomas (11); Quinn Buckner and Bobby Leonard (21); Walt Bellamy and George McGinnis (35); and Scott May and Mike Woodson (42).

The only Hoosier to wear No. 0 is current player Kory Barnett.

95 Wilkerson, Knight Had Eye-to-Eye Meeting

When Sherron Wilkerson enrolled at Indiana University in the fall of 1993, everyone said he and Coach Bob Knight would butt heads.

They meant that figuratively, but it turned out to have a literal interpretation when coach and player went forehead to forehead during a game at Michigan State in 1994.

Wilkerson led Jeffersonville to the Indiana high school championship yet had the reputation of being a free spirit who might not fit in the strict mold of a disciplinarian coach. He had been named Mr. Basketball for the two-game series against Kentucky, but after scoring a team-high 14 points in the first game, he refused to play in the second game at Indianapolis. He reportedly was miffed at playing only 19 minutes in the game at Louisville and turned in his No.1 jersey.

Wilkerson, a 6'4" guard, was stripped of the Mr. Basketball title after saying he "could care less" about the honor. Indiana fans compared Wilkerson with Lawrence Funderburke, who four years earlier had arrived at IU with a similar reputation and left school after six games.

As was the case during much of Knight's 29-year career at Indiana, he was constantly focused upon by television cameras. The networks knew the coach could do something unique at any moment, and they wanted to make sure it was on film.

The game at Michigan State was held on March 9, 1994, and the Hoosiers were about to lose for the third time in four outings 94–78. Wilkerson was called to the bench after missing a three-point shot and motioning to officials that he had been hit in the shooting hand by a Spartan defender. Wilkerson took his seat, and the coach rushed in to discipline him. Jerking forward, Knight slammed his head into Wilkerson's, and Sherron looked away with a puzzled gaze.

The head-butting was caught on ESPN's film and shown repeatedly over the next 24 hours. It was the perfect opportunity for Knight's critics to claim the volatile coach had head-butted his player intentionally. Knight said otherwise, adding that he had had back trouble that contributed to the bumping. Wilkerson later said he was angered at first but later concluded that it was accidental.

"The whole thing was totally blown out of proportion," Wilkerson said.

During his sophomore season Wilkerson was averaging 7.5 points per game when he was dismissed from the team on January 23 after being arrested for domestic battery. Bloomington police were called to an apartment where a 20-year-old woman said Sherron had struck her in the face.

Wilkerson was given a 180-day suspended sentence and a year's probation after pleading guilty to a misdemeanor charge. He was also ordered to undergo anger-control counseling.

"I wasn't a bad person, but I needed to be reprogrammed. I was headed down the wrong path," he told *The Indianapolis Star*.

After his sophomore season Wilkerson enrolled at Rio Grande, a college with about 2,400 students in Ohio. From there Wilkerson played overseas with teams from Brazil, Turkey, Sweden, and Israel. After a 10-year professional career, he returned to the United States and took a variety of coaching positions, including head coach at Herron in Indianapolis in 2009–10. He was recently hired as an assistant to Pat Knight at Lamar University.

Sherron earned a degree at Indiana-Southeast where he was an assistant coach under former Louisville forward Wiley Brown, and he was also a coaching aide at Jennings County High School in North Vernon.

96 Trip to IU Game Offers Food Choices

Unless you want to settle for hot dogs and nachos from the Assembly Hall concession stands, you'll probably want to find an eating place in the Bloomington area that meets your needs. Following are a few suggestions:

If you're in the mood for a juicy steak, a good choice is Janko's Little Zagreb, located a block west of the Monroe County Courthouse at 223 West Sixth Street. The steaks are a little pricey, and the atmosphere is red-and-white checkered table cloths with a high noise level. However, the meat is regarded by many as the best in town.

The out-of-the way restaurant is located in what was once a feed store, and the old Monon trains used to stop across the street. The business was founded in 1979.

Another favorite for steaks is the Longhorn Steakhouse at 721 South College Mall Road. It's a chain restaurant that offers a clean, western ambience.

The Texas Road House, located off State Road 37 on the west side of town, has been the most visited restaurant in Bloomington over the past several years. It's a budget-minded, western-themed eatery where service is quick and a meal with a small steak, potato, and salad hits the spot. The spare ribs have won awards.

If you're looking for a popular spot where students and fans hang out, then Nick's English Hut, 423 East Kirkwood Avenue, is one of the most popular spots in the Big Ten. *Playboy* magazine named it one of America's 10 best sports bars.

Nick's was founded in 1927 by Nick Hrisomalos who served such items as egg sandwiches and fried bologna. When prohibition ended in 1933, he began serving beer and Nick's remains one of the city's favorite watering holes. Guests at Nick's over the years have included Roberta Peters, Truman Capote, Henry Mancini, Kurt Vonnegut, Art Buchwald, Ernie Pyle, and the entire 1984 Olympic basketball team.

Another popular gathering place is Yogi's Grill and Bar, which was opened in 1992 near the campus at 519 East Tenth Street. Popular downtown spots include the Scholars Inn, Trojan Horse, Uptown Café, Scotty's Brewhouse, and Kilroy's, which has three locations near downtown.

Opie Taylor's, a downtown sandwich place, is a favorite of many.

If you like pizza, Bloomington is the place to be. Graduates from decades back often stop at Café Pizzeria, 405 East Kirkwood Avenue. The atmosphere (more red-and-white table cloths) hasn't changed, and eating pizza there is like reliving your first kiss.

Mother Bear's, 1428 East Third Street, was called the best pizza in Indiana by *USA Today* and was listed among the nation's top nine pizzerias by *People* Magazine. Many former students visit Pizza-X, which has five locations in the area, to get their breadsticks.

Fans who want to eat before arriving in Bloomington might consider Gray Brothers Cafeteria located on State Road 67 in Mooresville. Lines there can be long, but it's worth the wait simply for the pies. Visitors from the east might enjoy a stop in Brown County where the Nashville House was holding court even before IU won its second national championship.

97 School Song Erupts From Hallway

There are many reasons Indiana fans fall in love with their school's basketball traditions. One of the most unusual involves Martha the cleaning lady.

Martha is the centerpiece of a commercial for Farm Bureau Insurance, but mostly she promotes IU basketball. She was first seen during the 1970s and was recently returned to circulation in Assembly Hall.

The commercial begins with an empty hallway in Assembly Hall. Soon Martha is heard whistling before she comes into sight softly singing, "Indiana, Our Indiana," the school's fight song. Dressed in a white work dress and red apron, Martha increases both her volume and passion as she approaches the camera, extolling the Hoosiers' virtues with an operatic voice. When the song ends, she continues mopping as if no one had heard her.

The short film clip was used in the 1970s to open telecasts of IU games on WTTV, Channel 4. It is now shown on the giant scoreboard above the court minutes before the tipoff. As it was in its earlier years, the commercial has proved to be extremely popular.

98 Johnson Found Niche in Football

Ken Johnson's goal in life was to play in the NBA, and his success at Indiana might have indicated that dream could have come true. Johnson averaged 18.2 points and 12 rebounds per game in 1969, his senior year at IU.

However, his 6'6", 240-pound frame sent his destiny in another direction, one that would lead to him playing seven seasons in the NFL.

A native of Anderson, Indiana, where he starred in both sports, Johnson first tried out with the Dallas Cowboys, who tried to make him an offensive tackle. Released by Dallas, Johnson was claimed by the Cincinnati Bengals, who tried him in the defensive line.

Milan, Muncie Players Became Teammates

Two players from opposite sides in the famous 1954 Indiana state high school championship game became teammates at Indiana. Gene Flowers, a starting forward for Muncie Central, was a Hoosier from 1957–59, playing in 45 games and averaging almost five points per game.

Glenn Butte, who was a sophomore reserve for Milan High in 1954, played from 1958–60 for the Hoosiers and averaged about a point a game over 18 appearances.

Tiny Milan upset Muncie Central 32–30 on a late basket by Bobby Plump and the game was the foundation for the popular movie *Hoosiers.*

Johnson not only had found his sport but his position. Between 1971 and '77 the former basketball player starred as a defensive end in Cincinnati.

Ken retired after the 1977 season at the age of 30, his decision prompted by a knee injury. His retirement years were not without tragedy because his sister was killed in a traffic accident involving a drunk driver. Ken was involved in a near tragedy when his van was struck by a train and dragged the length of a football field.

Johnson now speaks weekly to various youth groups.

99 Basketball's Greatest Timeout

A first-time visitor would be startled by what appears to be a cavalry charge erupting in Assembly Hall. As the IU band strikes up the "William Tell Overture," the Hoosier cheerleaders and pom pon girls run onto the court, each carrying a flag that spells out I-N-D-I-A-N-A H-O-O-S-I-E-R-S.

The ceremony occurs with about eight minutes left in every Indiana home game, as regularly as the eruptions of Old Faithful. The cheerleaders and poms run loops around the playing floor, culminating with an on-your-knees salute to a larger IU flag held aloft by a male cheerleader mounted on his mates' shoulders.

Former television analyst Billy Packer once called it college basketball's greatest timeout.

Each game one or two fans are pulled out of the stands and allowed to carry a flag and run patterns with the cheerleaders. It is a worthwhile goal for any Hoosiers fan.

100 It's Not Just Basketball

Indiana University has won five NCAA championships, but IU isn't simply a basketball school. The men's soccer program claims seven NCAA titles, and the men's swimming and diving team has six national championships.

Indiana was the nation's best swimming and diving program under James "Doc" Counsilman and Hobie Billingsley and won 140 successive dual meets and 20 consecutive Big Ten titles. IU's six national swimming titles came from 1968–73.

In the early 1970s a writer for *Sports Illustrated* wrote, "A good case can be made for the 1971 Indiana swimming team being the best college team ever—in any sport."

The swimming team's most famous alum is Mark Spitz, who won seven gold medals in the 1972 Olympics in Munich, Germany.

The men's soccer team won the NCAA in 1982, '83, '88, '98, '99, 2003, and 2004 with the first six coming under Coach Jerry Yeagley and the last under his successor, Mike Freitag.

Six Hoosiers have won the Hermann Trophy, which is awarded to the nation's top collegiate player. IU players have been named All-Americans on 52 occasions.

When Yeagley, a Pennsylvania native, first came to IU, his attempts to form a varsity soccer team were rebuffed by the university. As a club team, IU beat many of the nation's top varsity programs and eventually gained varsity status.

Sources

1.

Douchant, Mike. *Inside Sports College Basketball* (Canton, MI: Visible Ink, 1997), p. 223.

Laskowski, John, and Stan Sutton. *John Laskowski's Tales from the Hoosier Locker Room: A Collection of the Greatest Stories Ever Told* (Champaign, IL: Sports Publishing LLC, 2003), p. 10.

3.

Meunier, John, *The Herald-Times*, September 11, 2000, p. A–1.

Johnson, Marda, and Beth Moellers, *The Herald-Times*, September 11, 2000, p. A–1.

Houser, Lynn, *The Herald-Times*, September 11, 2000, p. B–1.

Meunier, John, *The Herald-Times*, September 14, 2000, p. A–1.

4.

Sutton, Stan, *The Courier-Journal*, March 10, 1991, p. B–1.

Turner, Landon, and Stan Sutton. *Landon Turner's Tales from the 1980–81 Indiana Hoosiers* (Champaign, IL: Sports Publishing LLC, 2005), pp. 21–22, 108–116, 127–28.

5.

Delsohn, Steve, and Mark Heisler. *Bob Knight: The Unauthorized Biography* (New York: Simon & Schuster, 2006).

Los Angeles Times, February 24, 1985.

7.

Delsohn, Steve, and Mark Heisler. *Bob Knight: The Unauthorized Biography* (New York: Simon & Schuster, 2006), pp. 78–79.

8.

Kindred, Dave, *The Sporting News*, January 5, 1998.

White Jr., Gordon S., *The New York Times*, March 23, 1975.

Delsohn, Steve, and Mark Heisler. *Bob Knight: The Unauthorized Biography* (New York: Simon & Schuster, 2006), p. 95.

9.

Laskowski, John, and Stan Sutton. *John Laskowski's Tales from the Hoosier Locker Room: A Collection of the Greatest Stories Ever Told* (Champaign, IL: Sports Publishing LLC, 2003), p. 88.

10.

Dakich, Dan, Personal interview, July 25, 2007.

11.

Turner, Landon, and Stan Sutton. *Landon Turner's Tales from the 1980–81 Indiana Hoosiers* (Champaign, IL: Sports Publishing LLC, 2005), pp. 144–47.

15.

Douchant, Mike. *Inside Sports College Basketball* (Canton, MI: Visible Ink, 1997), pp. 117–22.

17.

Laskowski, John, and Stan Sutton. *John Laskowski's Tales from the Hoosier Locker Room: A Collection of the Greatest Stories Ever Told* (Champaign, IL: Sports Publishing LLC, 2003), pp. 32–33.

Graham, Tom, and Rachel Graham Cody. *Getting Open: The Unknown Story of Bill Garrett and the Integration of College Basketball* (New York: Atria Books, 2006).

Gray, Hetty. *Net Prophet: The Bill Garrett Story* (Indiana: Sugar Creek Publishing. 2001).

18.

Douchant, Mike, and Jim Nantz. *Inside Sports College Basketball* (Canton, MI: Visible Ink, 1997), pp. 25, 32–35.

Laskowski, John, and Stan Sutton. *John Laskowski's Tales from the Hoosier Locker Room: A Collection of the Greatest Stories Ever Told* (Champaign, IL: Sports Publishing LLC, 2003).

19.

Byrd, Cecil K., and Ward W. Moore. *Varsity Sports at Indiana University: A Pictorial History* (Bloomington, IN: Indiana University Press, 1999).

21.

Douchant, Mike. *Inside Sports College Basketball* (Canton, MI: Visible Ink, 1997), pp. 38–49.

Laskowski, John, and Stan Sutton. *John Laskowski's Tales from the Hoosier Locker Room: A Collection of the Greatest Stories Ever Told* (Champaign, IL: Sports Publishing LLC, 2003), p. 79.

22.

Sutton, Stan, *The Courier-Journal*, March 6, 1993, p. B–1.

23.

Wikipedia Foundation, the free encyclopedia.

24.

Sutton, Stan, *The Herald-Times*, September 14, 2000.

26.

Laskowski, John, and Stan Sutton. *John Laskowski's Tales from the Hoosier Locker Room: A Collection of the Greatest Stories Ever Told* (Champaign, IL: Sports Publishing LLC, 2003), pp. 30–31.

27.

Delsohn, Steve, and Mark Heisler. *Bob Knight: The Unauthorized Biography* (New York: Simon & Schuster, 2006), p. 194.

Graham, Andrew, *The Herald-Times,* March 18, 1995.

Delsohn, Steve, and Mark Heisler. *Bob Knight: The Unauthorized Biography* (New York: Simon & Schuster, 2006), p. 252.

McCann, Gary, *The Herald-Times,* March 18, 1995.

28.

Laskowski, John, and Stan Sutton. *John Laskowski's Tales from the Hoosier Locker Room: A Collection of the Greatest Stories Ever Told* (Champaign, IL: Sports Publishing LLC, 2003), pp. 96–98.

30.

Hammel, Bob, and Kit Klingelhoffer. *Glory of Old IU: 100 Years of Indiana Athletics* (Champaign, IL: Sports Publishing LLC), p. 158.

Douchant, Mike. *Inside Sports College Basketball* (Canton, MI: Visible Ink, 1997), p. 204.

34.

Houser, Lynn, *The Herald-Times,* March 22, 2002.

Sutton, Stan, *The Herald-Times,* March 22, 2002.

35.

Kitchel, Ted, Personal interview, August 20, 1997.

36.

Bikoff, Ken, *Inside Indiana,* February 14, 2010.

37.

Hammel, Bob, and Kit Klingelhoffer. *Glory of Old IU: 100 Years of Indiana Athletics* (Champaign, IL: Sports Publishing LLC, 1999), p. 93.

Laskowski, John, and Stan Sutton. *John Laskowski's Tales from the Hoosier Locker Room: A Collection of the Greatest Stories Ever Told* (Champaign, IL: Sports Publishing LLC, 2003), pp. 83–84.

38.

Houser, Lynn, *The Herald-Times*, January 8, 2001.

Sutton, Stan, *The Herald-Times*, January 8, 2001.

Personal interview, August 24, 2007.

40.

Wertheim, L. Jon, *Sports Illustrated*, November 3, 2008.

Korman, Chris, *The Herald-Times*, November 5, 2006.

USA Today, October 13, 2006.

41.

Hoopedia, NBA, 2011.

42.

Sutton, Stan, *Inside Indiana*, November 20, 2011.

Buckeye Planet, November 2003.

Wikipedia Foundation, the free encyclopedia, November 21, 1911.

43.

Houser, Lynn, *The Herald-Times*, November 27, 2006.

44.

Richards, Phil, *The Indianpolis Star*, March 21, 1992.

Hammel, Bob, *The Herald-Times*, March 16–21, 1992.

Sutton, Stan, *The Courier-Journal*, March 21, 1992.

Klassen, Teri, *The Herald-Times*, March 16, 1992.

45.

Hammel, Bob, and Kit Klingelhoffer. *Glory of Old IU: 100 Years of Indiana Athletics* (Champaign, IL: Sports Publishing LLC), p. 158.

Douchant, Mike. *Inside Sports College Basketball* (Canton, MI: Visible Ink, 1997), p. 204.

46.

Locke Tates, and B. Iback, *Caught in the Net,* Leisure Press, 1982.

Rhoden, William C., *The New York Times*. November 8, 1989.

Locke, Tates, personal interview, December 1987.

Locke, Tates, Wikipedia Foundation, the free encyclopedia.

48.

Wikipedia Encyclopedia, 1994.

49.

Sutton, Stan, *The Courier-Journal*, March 23, 1992.

Hammel, Bob, *The Herald-Times*, March 23, 1992

Delsohn, Steve, and Mark Heisler. *Bob Knight: The Unauthorized Biography* (New York: Simon & Schuster, 2006).

50.

Delsohn, Steve, and Mark Heisler. *Bob Knight: The Unauthorized Biography* (New York: Simon & Schuster, 2006).

Wikipedia Foundation, the free encyclopedia.

52.

Van Arsdale, Tom, Personal interview, October 19, 2007.

54.

Hammel, Bob, *The Herald-Times*, March 13, 1994.

Klassen, Teri, *The Herald-Times*, March 26, 1992.

55.

Sutton, Stan, *The Herald-Times*, June 1, 2005. p. B–1.

56.

Wertheim, L. Jon. *Transition Game: How Hoosiers Went Hip-Hop* (New York: G.P. Putnam's Sons, 2005), p. 169.

57.

O'Rourke, John, *Albuquerque Tribune*, March 28, 1992.

62.

Turner, Dorie, Associated Press, August 2, 2010.
USA Today, Gannett Company, Inc., August 2002.

63.

Breaking Away, Wikipedia Foundation, the free encyclopedia.

64.

Woodson, Mike, Personal interview, September 5, 2007.

65.

Wikipedia Foundation, the free encyclopedia.
Forbes.com, April 2011.
ESPN The Magazine, July 14, 2013.

66.

Hollis, John, *Atlanta Journal-Constitution*, April 6, 2009.
Weidie, Kyle, *Bullets Forever*, August 12, 2008.
Wikipedia Foundation, the free encyclopedia.

67.

The Daily Herald-Telephone, February 3, 1959.
The Indianapolis Star, February 3, 1959.

69.

Brown, Russ, multiple personal interviews.
Wolfe, Rich, *Oh, What a Knight?/Nightmare*. pp. 10–15.

70.

Dakich, Dan, Personal interview, April 20, 2009.

71.

Woodley, David, Personal interview, February 9, 2012.

72.

Crabb, Chuck, Personal interview, March 7, 2012.

73.

Crabb, Chuck, Personal interview, March 7, 2012.

74.

Terhune, Jim, *The Courier-Journal*, November 23, 1987.
Sports Illustrated, November 30, 1987.

75.

Crabb, Chuck, Personal interview, March 7, 2012.

76.

Sutton, Stan, *The Courier-Journal*, March 6, 1989.
Hammel, Bob, *The Herald-Times*, March 6, 1989.
Sullivan, Paul, *Chicago Tribune*, March 30, 1989.
Wikipedia Foundation, the free encyclopedia.

77.

Sutton, Stan, *The Herald-Times*, March 5, 2002.
Patrick, Dick, *USA Today*, March 7, 2002.

79.

Wikipedia Foundation, the free encyclopedia.

Forbes, J.T., *Home Pages*, Indiana University, 2000.

82.

Laskowski, John, and Stan Sutton. *John Laskowski's Tales from the Hoosier Locker Room: A Collection of the Greatest Stories Ever Told* (Champaign, IL: Sports Publishing LLC, 2003), pp. 56–58.

85.

Wilson, Doug, *The Herald-Times*, March 15, 2008.

86.

Sutton, Stan, *Inside Indiana*, January 9, 2010, p. 12.

88.

Laskowski, John, and Stan Sutton. *John Laskowski's Tales from the Hoosier Locker Room: A Collection of the Greatest Stories Ever Told* (Champaign, IL: Sports Publishing LLC, 2003), pp. 131–32.

90.

Delsohn, Steve, and Mark Heisler. *Bob Knight: The Unauthorized Biography* (New York: Simon & Schuster, 2006).

Personal interview, October 4, 2011.

Sutton, Stan, *Inside Indiana*, November 2011, p. 64.

91.

Laskowski, John, and Stan Sutton. *John Laskowski's Tales from the Hoosier Locker Room: A Collection of the Greatest Stories Ever Told* (Champaign, IL: Sports Publishing LLC, 2003).

92.

Douchant, Mike. *Inside Sports College Basketball* (Canton, MI: Visible Ink, 1997), p. 83.

Laskowski, John, and Stan Sutton. *John Laskowski's Tales from the Hoosier Locker Room: A Collection of the Greatest Stories Ever Told* (Champaign, IL: Sports Publishing LLC, 2003), pp. 25, 30.

93.

Wikipedia Foundation, the free encyclopedia.

www.Stlyrics.com

94.

2012 Indiana Media Guide, pp. 131–71.

95.

The Plain Dealer, North Vernon, Indiana, July 22, 2009.

Hammel, Bob, *The Herald-Times*, March 13, 1994.

Bozich, Alex, *Inside the Hall.com*, September 1, 2009.

Chicago Tribune, June 27, 1993.

100.

Wikipedia Foundation, the free encyclopedia.

About the Author

Stan Sutton is a retired sportswriter who spent 25 years with *The Courier-Journal* in Louisville, Kentucky, before becoming sports editor of *The Herald-Times* in Bloomington, Indiana, in 2000. He has covered Indiana University athletics since 1984, serving most recently as a columnist for *Inside Indiana* magazine.

Sutton was inducted into the Indiana Sportswriters and Sportscasters Hall of Fame in 2004 and has co-authored previous books about IU basketball with former players John Laskowski and Landon Turner. He is a native of Mays, Indiana, who moved to Shelbyville, Indiana, while in high school. He and his wife, Judy, have lived in Bloomington for 25 years.